NARCOTICS AND THE LAW

American Bar Foundation
1967

NARCOTICS
AND THE LAW

A Critique

of the American Experiment

in Narcotic Drug Control

by William Butler Eldridge

Second Edition, Revised

The University of Chicago Press
Chicago and London

Library of Congress Catalog Card Number: 67-25528

THE UNIVERSITY OF CHICAGO PRESS, CHICAGO & LONDON
THE UNIVERSITY OF TORONTO PRESS, TORONTO 5, CANADA

Second Edition published 1967

Printed in the United States of America

PREFACE

TO THE FIRST EDITION

THE PREPARATION OF THIS STUDY was, in no small measure, facilitated by the cooperation and assistance of many individuals and agencies. The author was afforded, particularly by the Federal Bureau of Narcotics and the Federal Bureau of Prisons, interviews and unpublished data, the lack of which would have rendered an already difficult task nearly impossible. Talks with members of the United States Public Health Service, and a visit to the treatment facility at Lexington, Kentucky, were of invaluable aid in reaching a better understanding of the problems of the physicians, psychiatrists, and sociologists who work with narcotic addicts. State and local police departments in New Jersey, New York, Ohio, Michigan, and Illinois, as well as the Metropolitan Police Department of Washington, D.C., afforded the author interviews and information, the results of which are reflected in this study. State commissions in Illinois and New Jersey graciously complied with frequent requests for information, discussions, and explanations. Though it was not possible to visit California, the cooperation of agencies in that state made it possible to obtain a clear picture of their anti-narcotics effort.

In addition to the many individuals connected with agencies mentioned above, the author wishes to express sincere appreciation to the members of the Joint Committee of the American Bar Association and the American Medical Association on Narcotic Drugs, to Mr. Malachi Harney, former Superintendent of Narcotic Control in Illinois, and to Professor Alfred R. Lindesmith of Indiana University.

Except in certain specific considerations which are clearly indicated in the text, this study is limited to the opiates and their synthetics. This limitation in no way suggests that there are not

v

serious problems connected with the non-opiate narcotics and with barbiturates, tranquilizers, and similar compounds. It is the opiates, however, which constitute the big problem in the United States. Other drugs present questions requiring a totally different approach on the part of the researcher, whether he be lawyer, physician, psychiatrist, or sociologist.

Also, no attempt has been made to describe and analyze the operations of the intricate system of international control by which the United States and other countries seek to control the production and flow of narcotics from nation to nation. Again, this omission should not suggest that the author considers this aspect of the problem either insignificant or resolved. Rather, the omission is made because the yardstick by which domestic control can be measured is completely inapplicable to the international scene.

This study is not an attempt to proselyte a social judgment on narcotic addiction. The initial chapters, however, present some of the social questions involved in narcotics use and traffic so that the reader can obtain some feel for the social complexities involved before reaching the empirical evaluation of the American system of narcotics control. It is hoped that the chapters dealing with the development of the problem and the misconceptions surrounding addiction will provide a background for the discussion which follows. These chapters also support the final recommendations enumerating certain areas where additional information must be obtained.

CONTENTS

TABLES

Canst thou not minister to a mind diseas'd,
Pluck from the memory a rooted sorrow,
Raze out the written troubles of the brain,
And with some sweet oblivious antidote
Cleanse the stuff'd bosom of that perilous stuff
Which weighs upon the heart?

SHAKESPEARE, *Macbeth, Act V, scene iii*

O just, subtle, and all-conquering opium! that, to the hearts of rich and poor alike, for the wounds that will never heal, and for the pangs of grief that "tempt the spirit to rebel" bringest an assuaging balm; ... and through one night's heavenly sleep callest back to the guilty man the visions of his infancy, and hands washed pure from blood.... Thou only givest these gifts to man; and thou hast the keys of Paradise.

DE QUINCEY, *Confessions of an English Opium Eater*

That humanity at large will ever be able to dispense with Artificial Paradises seems very unlikely.

ALDOUS HUXLEY, *The Doors of Perception*

Chapter One

DEVELOPMENT OF THE PROBLEM

R AISING THE QUESTIONS involved in the use or misuse of narcotics generally evokes one of two impressions in the mind
of the public. On the one hand, there is a mystic scene of
oriental opulence where languid mandarins gently puff ivory-
inlaid pipes, filling the air with a sinister blue haze. The other
view embraces a slovenly, emaciated youth with a glassy stare,
jerky muscles, and a demoniacal leer huddled in a shabby loft
where he furtively prepares a makeshift hypodermic with
illegally gotten heroin. Both views have their counterparts in
reality, but neither truly portrays narcotics use in the mid-
twentieth century. These images are rooted in the history of
narcotics use and in misconceptions about the effect of the
drugs. The goal of an objective evaluation of current narcotics
problems must begin with an examination of the drugs themselves and an understanding of the role they have played in
the past.

"Narcotics" is a term of convenience used to designate opium,
cocaine, marijuana, and their derivatives, and the many synthetic compounds which produce physiological results similar to those of the natural drugs. All drugs derived from the
opium poppy are termed opiates, and all are depressants. The
most important derivatives from the standpoint of present narcotics problems are heroin, morphine, and dilaudid. All of these

1

drugs are highly addicting within all definitions of addiction.[1] The users develop a compulsion to take the drug and to secure it by any means. Psychological or physiological dependence upon the drug ensues as the body chemistry becomes adjusted to a regular intake; discontinuing its use generally causes the familiar symptoms of the withdrawal syndrome in varying degrees of intensity. As the body continues to adjust, it is necessary to increase intake to achieve the effect accompanying the initial dose. Withdrawal can be accomplished fairly easily under present medical methods, but a tendency to relapse is implicit in addiction.

Cocaine is derived from the coca leaf which is grown principally in South America. It is a powerful stimulant, but is not physically addicting.[2] The use of cocaine in this country, once a problem, has diminished to the point of near extinction, except for use in conjunction with heroin or morphine to heighten the effect of the depressant drugs.[3]

Marijuana, while it has the initial effect of a stimulant, is actually a depressant. Like cocaine, it is not physically addicting.[4] Marijuana is almost exclusively smoked in the form of cigarettes in the United States,[5] though, from time to time, it has been used extensively in the East as hashish.[6] While the use of cocaine has diminished as a problem drug, many writers believe that marijuana still presents a subject of serious concern. Marijuana smoking is held up as a vicious practice, pro-

1. An authoritative definition, widely accepted, is that promulgated by the World Health Organization, quoted in INTERDEPARTMENTAL COMMITTEE ON NARCOTICS, REPORT TO PRESIDENT OF THE UNITED STATES 3–4 (1961): "Drug addiction is a state of periodic or chronic intoxication, detrimental to the individual and to society, produced by the repeated consumption of a drug (natural or synthetic). Its characteristics include: (1) An overpowering desire or need (compulsion) to continue taking the drug and to obtain it by any means; (2) A tendency to increase the dose; (3) A psychic (psychological) and sometimes a physical dependence on the effects of the drug."

2. Pescor, *The Problem of Narcotic Drug Addiction,* 43 J. CRIM. L., C.&P.S. 473–74 (Nov.-Dec. 1952).

3. Winick, *Narcotics Addiction and Its Treatment,* 22 LAW & CONTEMP. PROB. 12 (Winter 1957).

4. Pescor, *supra* note 2.

5. ANSLINGER & TOMPKINS, THE TRAFFIC IN NARCOTICS 19–20 (1953).

6. *Ibid.*

ductive of brutal depravity, and a stepping-stone to the use of opiates,[7] although this view is not uniformly held.[8] Cocaine and marijuana figure prominently in the total story of narcotics use in the United States, and will be discussed from time to time in this work, but it is unquestionably the opiates which constitute our chief concern in this country today,[9] and it is with them that this study will predominantly deal.

The origin of the use of opiates is lost in antiquity. The earliest known references to their medicinal use predate the seventh century B.C.[10] Literary and scientific writings have extolled the therapeutic and pleasure-giving attributes of the poppy from the earliest times to the present.[11] The opium poppy probably was first grown in Asia Minor, from whence its cultivation spread to India. It is believed that the drug was first carried to China by Arab traders, perhaps as early as the ninth century, A.D. Not until the latter half of the eighteenth century, however, did its importation into China become heavy through the trading of the Portuguese and the British East India Company.[12] By the early 1800's the flow of opium into China had reached proportions sufficient to alarm the Emperor. The ineffectiveness of controls and the lack of cooperation from the British touched off the Opium Wars of 1840–42.

The strong identification of opium with China in the public eye can probably be ascribed to the appeal of the romantic, mysterious, and esoteric. The Opium Wars doubtless served to focus attention on the opium habits of the Chinese, but it was the occultation which whetted the interest and invited flamboyant conjecture as to what went on in panoplied opium dens.

---

7. *Id.* at 18–26.
8. Pescor, *supra* note 2.
9. CITIZENS' ADVISORY COMMITTEE TO THE ATTORNEY GENERAL ON CRIME PREVENTION, NARCOTIC ADDICTION—REPORT TO ATTORNEY GENERAL EDMUND G. BROWN 22 (California, 1954).
10. TERRY & PELLENS, THE OPIUM PROBLEM 54 (1928).
11. Virgil, *Georgics*, I, 78; Virgil, *Aeneid*, IV, 486. For a concise review of the history of opium see Macht, *The History of Opium and Some of Its Preparations and Alkaloids*, 64 J.A.M.A. 477 (Feb. 6, 1915).
12. Macht, *supra* note 11.

Chinese use of opium was restricted almost exclusively to smoking. Around the practice grew up a highly stylized ritual requiring elaborate paraphernalia, a specialized argot, professional attendants, and the disposition to enjoy both the drug and the pageantry associated with it.[13] The association with narcotics of western literati, such as Coleridge [14] and De Quincey,[15] served only to intensify the picture of the opium user as a mystic, and every opium den as a pleasure dome fit for Kublai Khan.

The United States, like the other countries of the Western world, fell heir in due course to this dubious legacy of the East. Opium smoking found its way into the United States through San Francisco soon after Civil War.[16] It was virtually uncontrolled in this country until the passage of the Harrison Anti-Narcotic Act in 1914, though some effort had been made to limit its importation through taxation measures. Conjecture as to the extent of the use before 1914 varies greatly, but the figures on the annual opium importation show that the practice spread widely.[17] While opium smoking by Americans followed the oriental practices for a time, it soon changed when it found its way into the underworld. It then began to lose its mystical appeal and assumed, in popular opinion, the dimensions of a menace.[18]

Several other important factors contributed to the growth of narcotics use in the United States in the last half of the nineteenth century. The discovery of the hypodermic needle in the 1840's, and its subsequent extensive use for injecting narcotics during the American Civil War, resulted in such widespread use of opiates that the addiction became known as the "army

13. MAURER & VOGEL, NARCOTICS AND NARCOTIC ADDICTION 36–43 (1954).
14. See LOWES, THE ROAD TO XANADU —A STUDY IN THE WAYS OF THE IMAGINATION (1927).
15. DE QUINCEY, CONFESSIONS OF AN ENGLISH OPIUM EATER (1821) is particularly interesting in view of recent psychiatric theories of the character and personality features which favor addiction.
16. TERRY & PELLENS, *op. cit. supra* note 10, at 72.
17. *Id.* Table IV, at 44.
18. LINDESMITH, OPIATE ADDICTION 188 (1947).

disease." [19] This practice, which continued after the war and created many unfortunate addicts, had the beneficial result of awakening some medical writers to the dangers of indiscriminate use of the needle in administering opiates.[20] But it was not until 1900 that the majority of medical textbooks began to warn the practitioner of the need for caution.[21]

Perhaps the most significant aggravation of the problem in the United States came from the vicious practices of the patent medicine business. The general curatives usually contained a potent dose of some narcotic which relieved the symptoms for which the medicine was taken and from which physical dependence often developed. As the populace became concerned over their "drug habits," the patent medicine manufacturers quickly responded with more nostrums offered as cures for addiction. The viciousness of the practice lay in the fact that most of these "cures" were in reality preparations containing another opium derivative, so that the patient merely substituted one drug for another, often at a considerably increased price, with the added result that his addiction habit frequently was intensified.[22]

The lack of, or at best diffident, concern of American medicine contributed to the exacerbation of the drug problem in the late nineteenth and early twentieth centuries. The failure of medical teachers and textbook writers to appreciate the insidious danger of narcotics abuse sent many physicians out to minister to the sick and suffering without warning as to the even greater anguish which might flow from ill-advised administration of opiates.

By 1900 the medical schools and textbook writers had begun to remedy their earlier deficiency in narcotics instruction. But another effort to combat narcotic addiction was brewing a situation which ironically would aggravate the problem still

19. MAURER & VOGEL, op. cit. supra note 13, at 6.
20. TERRY & PELLENS, op. cit. supra note 10, at 69–71.
21. Id. at 72.
22. See ADAMS, THE GREAT AMERICAN FRAUD 111–21 (1912).

further. In 1898 diacetylmorphin, in due time to become famous or infamous as heroin, was first produced in Germany.[23] The properties of the drug were completely misunderstood during this early period. Many writers extolled its pain-relieving qualities while assuring readers that heroin was free of addiction liability; it was a panacea.

> The prominent place held by opium derivatives in therapeutics, the constant calls on every physician to relieve pain and induce sleep with drugs, and the relative inadequacy of all substitutes for opium combined from the outset to stimulate the use of heroin. It was apparently the ideal preparation—potent analgesic and sedative—at the same time possessing other qualities highly desirable in certain ailments, above all, freedom from the dreaded so-called "habit-forming" qualities of the parent drug.[24]

Before the physical action of heroin was clearly understood, its use had added more fuel to the already flaming opium problem. The awakening of physicians to the addiction liability of the drug was slow, and the curtailment of its use still slower. In 1906 the Council on Pharmacy and Chemistry of the American Medical Association tentatively accepted heroin for inclusion in a list of new drugs, but with the following warning:

> In large doses it may produce dizziness, nausea, and occasionally constipation, and in poisonous amounts, twitching of the extremities, great exhaustion, and dimness of vision. . . . The habit is readily formed and leads to deplorable results.[25]

After the properties of the drug were fully appreciated, many physicians recommended that the use of heroin be banned completely in this country, arguing that it had no peculiar advantage sufficient to outweigh the immense danger from its highly addictive nature. Others felt that there were uses to which heroin could be put that no other drug could satisfy,

23. For an interesting discussion of the early hopes for heroin and its uses by the medical profession, see TERRY & PELLENS, *op. cit. supra* note 10, at 75–84.
24. *Id.* at 77–78.
25. 47 J.A.M.A. 1303 (Oct. 20, 1906).

and argued against prohibiting its availability to physicians for use in treatment and pain relief. The public, due to common knowledge of the properties of heroin and inflammatory articles from many quarters, became alarmed about the burgeoning use of heroin. As a result, production of the drug was banned in the United States.[26]

The extent of the use of narcotics in the United States before the passage of the Harrison Act in 1914, both through legitimate medical channels and through illicit traffic, remains unknown, though writers can, and do, find figures to support almost any view of the magnitude of use.[27] All of the studies which produced these figures have imponderable unknown quantities which cast doubt upon their accuracy and applicability. It is safe to say, however, that the problem was large—large enough to promote the concern which resulted in governmental intervention in 1914 with the passage of the Harrison Act.

Several factors contributed to the enactment of the Harrison Act. The adherence of the United States to the Hague Convention of 1912 [28] obligated this country to control the domestic sale, use, and transfer of opium and coca products.

26. 21 U.S.C. § 173 (1958) prohibits the importation of opium for manufacture of heroin. This same controversy over the value of heroin arose in England, but the disagreement was viewed as a reason for the government's not entering a ban on the drug, and heroin is still prescribed in the United Kingdom.

27. Hynson, Report of the Committee on Acquirement of the Drug Habit, 74 A.J. PHARM. 547 (Nov. 1902) estimating at least 2,000,-000; Eberle & Gordon, Report of the Committee on Acquirement of the Drug Habit, 75 A.J. PHARM. 474 (Oct. 1903) estimating 1,000,-000 opium smokers in addition to other users of opiates; TRAFFIC IN NARCOTIC DRUGS—REPORT OF SPECIAL COMMITTEE OF INVESTIGATION APPOINTED MARCH 25, 1918, BY SECRETARY OF TREASURY (June, 1919) estimating over 1,000,000 addicts; KOLB & DUMEZ, THE PREVALENCE AND TREND OF DRUG ADDICTION IN THE UNITED STATES AND FACTORS INFLUENCING IT (Public Health Reports, May 23, 1924), stating that the addict population never exceeded 246,-000. For an examination and critical analysis of the studies reporting the extent of narcotics addiction in the United States see TERRY & PELLENS, THE OPIUM PROBLEM 1–52 (1928).

28. Suppression of the Abuse of Opium and Other Drugs, Convention and Final Protocol Between the United States and Other Powers, Jan. 23, 1912, and July 9, 1913, 38 Stat. 1912, T.S. No. 612.

The original object of the United States Government in initiating the international movement for the suppression of the opium traffic was to bring to an end the deplorable habit of opium smoking, which had taken a deep hold in the Philippine Islands, and was widespread throughout the Far East, especially in China.[29]

It soon came home to the American authorities, however, that the opium problem was not restricted to the Far East.

Immediately on the appointment of the American Opium Commission, under the authority of an act of Congress, it was discovered that the United States, in calling upon the other nations of the world to join with it in suppressing this traffic, had itself since 1860 permitted the importation of opium prepared for smoking and had collected thereon an aggregate revenue of over $27,000,000.[30]

It was recognized that the ban on importation of opium into this country was creating the threat that certain areas of the nation, particularly "the Pacific slopes," might become opium producers.[31] Representative Harrison wished to clean the hands of the American reformers who sought to establish world controls on opium production by establishing revenue control in this country that would virtually prohibit the domestic cultivation of the opium poppy,[32] and by strengthening the control over importation of crude opium from other countries.[33]

It was also recognized that the states had not been successful in their efforts to limit the sale of narcotics to legitimate channels.[34] Mr. Harrison reported the unanimous view of "State, Territorial and municipal officials" that state laws could never be effective until they were buttressed by federal legislation.[35] For the first time, the Congress looked upon opium as a signifi-

29. H.R. REP. No. 24, 63d Cong., 1st Sess. 1 (1913).
30. *Ibid.*
31. H.R. REP. No. 22, 63d Cong., 1st Sess. 1–2 (1913).
32. *Id.* at 2.
33. H.R. REP. No. 24, 63d Cong., 1st Sess. 1 (1913).
34. H.R. REP. No. 23, 63d Cong., 1st Sess. 3 (1913); S. REP. 258, 63d Cong., 2d Sess. 4 (1914).
35. *Ibid.*

cant domestic problem which, if not dealt with effectively and immediately, would precipitate widespread social destruction. Addressing himself to the nearly tripled use of opium between 1870 and 1909, Mr. Harrison reported for his Committee:

> This enormous increase in the importation of and consumption of opium in the United States is startling and is directly due to the facility with which opium may be imported, manufactured into its various derivatives and preparations, and placed within the reach of the individual. There has been in this country an almost shameless traffic in these drugs. Criminal classes have been created, and the use of the drugs with much accompanying moral and economic degradation is widespread among the upper classes of society. We are an opium-consuming nation today.[36]

The enactment of the Harrison Act marked an embarkation upon a totally new approach to the narcotics problem. That approach can best be described as an effort which set out to control the non-medical use of narcotics and evolved into the prohibition of non-medical uses and the control of medical uses. Popular support for governmental policies was strong, though not always grounded upon accurate information or intelligent appraisals. During the period of widespread narcotics use with virtually no control, the public's phantasmagoria had shifted rapidly. The problem was no longer restricted to an insulated Chinese cabal. Former mild concern changed into genuine alarm as the populace was informed that "dope fiends" threatened to permeate our entire society. This change occurred in the early 1900's and shaped the course of future happenings in the United States.[37] It is probable that the shift in attitude was due largely to the tremendous increase in opium smoking in the last years of the nineteenth century and the increased association of that habit with the underworld. Considerable notoriety attached to the adoption of opium smoking by the underworld,

36. H.R. REP. No. 23, 63d Cong., 1st Sess. 2 (1913).
37. Kolb, *Let's Stop This Narcotics Hysteria*, Saturday Evening Post, July 28, 1956, p. 19; LINDESMITH, OPIATE ADDICTION 183 (1947).

gradually leading the public to view all addicts as criminals, and their criminality as the manifestation of their addiction.[38] The alarm generated by the exaggerated reports of teen-age addiction in the early 1950's [39] completed the shift. The dope fiend image of the early twentieth century was modified as to age and responsibility. The drug user emerges from this last metamorphosis as a young teen-ager who may be the victim of his own immaturity and the vicious predatory greed of organized crime, but who bears the seed of degrading contagion.

Whatever the reason for the change in the public attitude, the change cannot be questioned. The exemplification of the attitude is present in a large body of federal and state legislation aimed at ostracizing the narcotic addict on the ground that he presents a threat to the well-being of society.[40] Legislation, treatment policies, and public attitude reflect a judgment that narcotic addiction is an evil to be stamped out at any cost. Dissatisfaction with this judgment has been manifested in recent years by an increasing number of responsible individuals and organizations who are questioning the approach which has prevailed in this country for the past forty years [41]—namely, the application of increasingly severe penalties in an effort to stamp out the use of narcotics except by patients suffering serious pain

38. Lindesmith, *op. cit. supra* note 37, at 188.
39. Deutsch, What We Can Do about the Drug Menace 5 (Public Affairs Pamphlet No. 186, 1952).
40. The United Nations Narcotics Commission has added to its definition of narcotic addiction a clause specifying that drug addiction is "detrimental to the individual or society." See Anslinger & Tompkins, *op. cit. supra* note 5, at 67, 242.
41. Joint Committee of the American Bar Association and the American Medical Association on Narcotic Drugs, Drug Addiction: Crime or Disease? (Interim and Final Reports, 1961); New York Academy of Medicine, Subcommittee on Drug Addiction, *Report on Drug Addiction,* 31 Bull. N.Y. Acad. Med. 592 (1955); Howe, *A Physician's Blueprint for the Management and Prevention of Narcotics Addiction,* 55 N.Y. State J. Med. 341 (1955); Eggston and Berger, *Should We Legalize Narcotics,* Coronet, June 1955, p. 30; Stevens, *Make Dope Legal,* Harper's Magazine, Nov. 1952, p. 40; Kolb, *Let's Stop This Narcotics Hysteria,* Saturday Evening Post, July 28, 1956, p. 19; Berger, *Richmond County Medical Society's Plan for the Control of Narcotics Addiction,* 56 N.Y. State J. Med. 888 (1956); Lindesmith, *Traffic in Dope: Medical Problem,* The Nation, April 21, 1956, pp. 337–39.

from illness other than that which is the result of addiction.

Assuming that the articulated criticisms of the present approach represent a potential awareness on the part of the informed public that it is time for a change, it is imperative that efforts be made to provide the information upon which a valid social judgment can be made. There must be a recognition of the factors involved, determination of the facts, an intelligent appraisal of opinion, and an appreciation of the considerable body of knowledge acquired by medicine and psychiatry since 1914.

The picture of narcotics traffic and use in the United States is comprised of myriad interacting forces and interests. It will be readily seen that it is impossible to approach any aspect of the problem from the point of view of a single discipline, and that any effort, if it is to be realistic, must be a concerted action of all the people whose professional and public interests bear on the problem. But before such concerted action is commenced there must come a social judgment as to the nature and effect of narcotic addiction—the extent of the problem and the actual danger presented by it. Such a judgment must be made independently of the present legal status of the narcotic addict and the artificial environment in which he operates.

Despite the considerable writings in this area, practically none examines this problem without a preconceived, and usually unstated, starting point that drug addiction is an intrinsically depredating evil. The degree of that evil will vary from "sad and unfortunate" to "heinous," depending, not upon an examination of the effects of narcotics use, but generally upon the approach the writer intends to espouse thereafter. Even the advocates of so-called more progressive approaches, such as free distribution of drugs or medical dispensation as in the British system, advance their views in an apologetic tone, arguing the impossibility of control as evidenced by the continued prevalence of illegal addiction.

The critical view of addicts and addiction grew out of a great many misconceptions. Those misconceptions have been kept viable by a succession of inaccurate information, sometimes innocent and sometimes artful, which has in time created a whole body of dope mythology effectively blocking public support for a dispassionate inquiry. The social questions are not so clearly defined as many would have us believe. The following chapter will examine some of the more common pronouncements concerning the social dangers of narcotic addiction.

Chapter Two

SOCIAL ATTITUDES AS A FACTOR
IN CONTROL POLICIES

SOCIETY HAS MADE a judgment that indulgence in narcotics is wrong. Perhaps the most significant basis for the judgment lies in the ethical and philosophical foundations of our religious and moral culture. It is a culture which values the rational process, which distrusts rule of the senses, and which views the appetite for physical gratification as insatiable—so insatiable, in fact, that it can destroy the ability of the individual to make reasoned choices in the pursuit of the ultimate goals of man.[1] Religion, as well as the ancient philosophers, conceived those goals to be bound up with wisdom, perception of truth, and the harmonious relationship of Man, the Deity, and the Universe.

> Steadiness, inward calm, and harmony have been extolled by all the great religious systems—Christian, Buddhist, Taoist, Vedantist; nor need one be a saint or a philosopher to hunger after this inner tranquility. It is natural to desire such a state, for without it no real happiness is possible.[2]

These qualities are best developed by the exercise of philosophy, by inner discipline, by the practice of virtue. It is wrong

1. Aristotle, *Ethica Nichomachea*, III, 11–12, °1117 b 22–1119 b 20.

2. DE ROPP, DRUGS AND THE MIND 3 (1960).

13

to expect from a drug those gifts which saints and sages have
sought to achieve through the most dedicated spiritual efforts.[3]

Narcotics have also been condemned by philosophers because they destroy the reality of natural relationships. The drug
user is in a world of unreality, untouched by the natural pangs
of pleasure and pain which dictate the exercise of free will.

> The possibility of pain is necessary to the discipline of habit. . . .
> The possibility of mental suffering is also necessary to elementary
> self-preservation and perhaps to mature psychic health as well.
> Fear is intense suffering, but it is very useful at times. Nothing is
> more certain to result in physical, mental, social and moral dis-
> integration than the habitual use of narcotics for the relief of pain,
> especially of mental pain.[4]

It must be recognized that ultimate philosophical and religious tenets play a large part in the social judgment concerning narcotics. This is as it should be. There are grave moral
questions involved in the use of narcotics for pleasure or for
the attainment of artificial tranquility. It is not the purpose of
this discussion to raise or treat these moral questions. It is its
purpose, however, to examine the more frequently described
effects of narcotics use, so that moral questions may be considered free of misconception.

What is myth and what is fact in the voluminous literature
on the nature of narcotic addiction and the character of the
narcotic addict? Very few of the frequently announced cate-
goricals can be supported or refuted by the kind of conclusive,
concrete evidence which eliminates the possibility of divergence
of opinion. When subjected to careful scrutiny, however, most
of these over-simplified generalizations will fall in the face of
evidence that narcotic addiction is as individual in its etiology,
psychology, and result as are the personalities involved. Some
charges against the evils allegedly embodied in narcotic addiction, while true, are in reality charges against the iniquity of

3. *Id.* at 3–4.   4. KING, THE PROBLEM OF EVIL 180 (1952).

criminals who prey upon the need of the addict. Such considerations are important, but they should be dealt with as problems in the larger context of organized crime rather than as problems peculiar to, and intrinsic in, the use of narcotics. It is important to evaluate all of these charges dispassionately in order to appreciate the actual and total social challenge presented by narcotic addiction in the United States today.

The discussion which follows attempts to deal with the accuracy of widely disseminated categorical statements concerning drug addiction. It is recognized that case histories or incomplete data may be found to support almost any statement, but it is not recognized that non-typical occurrences, even when very serious, warrant making such occurrences the basis of statements apparently describing characteristic results of drug addiction. Such practice, always intellectually dishonest, is particularly reprehensible where it provides the basis for unreasoned persecution of individuals.

The use of certain drugs, notably cocaine, under certain circumstances may produce some of the results dealt with below, but cocaine use is no longer of great significance in the United States. It is the opiates and their synthetics which constitute the prime problem in this country.[5] In the following discussion

5. Excluding marijuana, more than 90% of the narcotics seized at ports and borders and within the United States in 1959 were opiates. U.S. TREASURY DEPARTMENT, BUREAU OF NARCOTICS, TRAFFIC IN OPIUM AND OTHER DANGEROUS DRUGS, Table 6 (1960). The total weight of marijuana seized was much larger than the weight of the other narcotics, but the comparative weights are not significant. The importance of marijuana in the general narcotics problem is a subject of considerable controversy, but the potency of the drug and the manner of its use in the United States indicate that probably its most serious aspect is in leading the user toward addiction to the more potent opiates. See Pescor, *The Problem of Narcotic Drug Addiction*, 43 J. CRIM. L., C. & P.S. 471, 473–74 (Nov.-Dec., 1952); NYSWANDER, THE DRUG ADDICT AS A PATIENT 29–31 (1956). Some writers consider that even this aspect of marijuana use is exaggerated and that marijuana is relatively unimportant. Bowman, *Some Problems in Addiction*, in HOCH & ZUBIN (eds.), PROBLEMS OF ADDICTION AND HABITUATION 164 (1958); *contra*, MURTAGH & HARRIS, WHO WALK IN SHADOW 71–72 (1959); ANSLINGER & TOMPKINS, THE TRAFFIC IN NARCOTICS 18–26 (1953). While marijuana is supposed to be the narcotic most widely used by young people, an extensive study among young drug

of the alleged effects of narcotics use, if the effect is not one attributable to the opiates, the implication that such effects are the general results of the use of narcotics is considered unwarranted.

Narcotics ravage the human body

ONE OF THE most popular and understandable images of the narcotic addict is the physical wreckage of a human body debilitated by opiate misuse. The following description from a police journal is illustrative of the source of such an image:

> To be a confirmed drug addict is to be one of the walking dead. . . . The teeth have rotted out; the appetite is lost and the stomach and intestines don't function properly. The gall bladder becomes inflamed; eyes and skin turn a bilious yellow. In some cases the membranes of the nose turn a flaming red; the partition separating the nostrils is eaten away—breathing is difficult. Oxygen in the blood decreases; bronchitis and tuberculosis develop. Good traits of character disappear and bad ones emerge. Sex organs become affected. Veins collapse and livid purplish scars remain. Boils and abscesses plague the skin; gnawing pain racks the body. Nerves snap; vicious twitching develops. Imaginary and fantastic fears blight the mind and sometimes complete insanity results. Often times, too, death comes—much too early in life. . . . Such is the torment of being a drug addict; such is the plague of being one of the walking dead.[6]

The medical profession, however, has found little cause for alarm in the physiological symptoms of narcotic addition. In fact, the difficulty often arises that cases go unrecognized except

---

users in Chicago showed that 90% used heroin. ILLINOIS INSTITUTE FOR JUVENILE RESEARCH AND THE CHICAGO AREA PROJECT, DRUG ADDICTION AMONG YOUNG PERSONS IN CHICAGO 5 (1953).

6. *The Scourge of Narcotics,* Spring 3100 at 7 (Dec. 1958) quoted by Richard Kuh, *Dealing with Narcotics Addiction,* Part One, The New York Law Journal, June 8, 1960, p. 4, col. 1, in which Mr. Kuh, who is Administrative Assistant to the New York County District Attorney, urges a program of compulsory hospitalization for drug addicts.

by doctors trained in treatment of drug addiction and alerted
to the necessity of careful examination to detect them.[7] Even
then it may not be an easy task without sophisticated testing
methods.

There are few pathognomonic physical characteristics by which
the opiate addict can be recognized as such. Scars and abscesses
which result from intravenous injections of opiates are among the
few helpful overt diagnostic characteristics. The cocaine or benze-
drine addict may show pupil dilation, tachycardia, and tremulous-
ness. It is difficult to recognize a marijuana smoker, although he
sometimes has a characteristic facial flush. Opiates may be de-
tected by analysis of an addict's urine for as much as ten days
after the drug was last used. There may be emaciation from lack
of food, both because opiates often diminish the appetite and
because the addict's money is being used to buy drugs. *Little or
no evidence exists to show that the continued use of any opiates
causes permanent changes in the brain or central nervous system,
or that it causes any changes except the body's greater tolerance
of the drug. There is no conclusive evidence on opiates' effect on
life-span, although they have been said to shorten life.*[8] (Emphasis
added.)

Despite the palpable disagreement of the two preceding
statements, the terms of the first cannot be labeled absolutely
false, and therein lies its treacherous nature. Most of the symptoms attributed to the "confirmed drug addict" may be found
singly in cases of abuse of various drugs. Some of the symptoms
may result from *withdrawing the drug,* but not from the drug
itself. Prolonged cocaine sniffing may produce inflamed nostrils
or a perforated nasal septum. Veins may collapse and abscesses
appear, but these are the results of unsterile equipment, impure

7. Bobbitt, *The Drug Addiction
   Problem,* 14 Am. J. Med. 538
   (May 5, 1953).
8. Winick, *Narcotics Addiction and
   Its Treatment,* 22 Law & Con-
   temp. Prob. 9, 13 (Winter 1957).
   For a readable discussion of the
   physiological results of addiction
   see Nyswander, *op. cit. supra*
   note 5, at 29–30. See also Joint
   Committee of the American
   Bar Association and the Amer-
   ican Medical Association on
   Narcotic Drugs, Drug Addic-
   tion: Crime or Disease? 45–50
   (Interim and Final Reports, 1961).

drugs, and improper methods of injection, not of the drug itself. There may be a diminution of sexual drive or activity, but no permanent organic damage. Each symptom described probably has as its basis cases where such a result was attributed to prolonged narcotics use, but to make a composite of all those symptoms and offer it as the prototype of the confirmed drug addict is, to put it most charitably, misleading. The latter evaluation of the physiological effect of drug addiction is so universally held by experts in this field [9] that any serious inquirer could not fail to appreciate the inaccuracy of the lurid picture painted by the material first quoted.

Narcotics destroy morality

IT IS OFTEN asserted that addiction to narcotics destroys the moral fiber of the addict, that his character deteriorates and his habits become evil.[10] This is a particularly difficult indictment to assay because it seldom has a point of reference. It may well be that many drug addicts display a morality which alarms the law enforcement officer or the social worker, but in assessing the role of drug addiction as a contributor to that morality, other factors are often overlooked which appear to be far more important determinants.

The addict in the United States usually comes from the area characterized by the lowest incomes, the lowest educational level, and the lowest social status.[11]

9. See INTERDEPARTMENTAL COMMITTEE ON NARCOTICS, REPORT TO THE PRESIDENT OF THE UNITED STATES 4 (January 1961).
10. See quoted material accompanying note 6 *supra*.
11. See Clausen, *Social and Psychological Factors in Narcotic Addiction*, 22 LAW & CONTEMP. PROB. 34 (Winter 1957) and sources cited therein. See also HOCH & ZUBIN, *op. cit. supra* note 5, at 2–3. Recent statistical compilations show a marked over-representation of Negro and Puerto Rican minorities in metropolitan areas. *Hearings Before the Subcommittee of the Committee on Appropriations of the House of Representatives,* 86th Cong., 2d Sess. 140 (Jan. 26, 1960). It is interesting to note, however, that studies made twenty years ago showed an entirely different ethnic representation. DAI, OPIUM ADDICTION IN CHICAGO (1937). Yet recent studies indicate that the same geographic parts of the city are producing the addicts who happen at present to be largely Negroes and Puerto Ricans. ILLINOIS INSTITUTE FOR JUVENILE

The picture of the delinquent subculture found within the urban slum has been drawn many times. Perhaps less familiar is the fact that the law-abiding and morally responsible citizens of such areas also tend to share many beliefs and attitudes which are different from those held in the larger middle-class society. Middle-class Americans often find it difficult to realize that the goals to which they aspire and the values which they take for granted do not entirely pervade the population. Socio-economic status is significant not merely in terms of the physical style of life that can be maintained and the security from want that is offered by a stable and adequate income; it is also reflected in the approach one takes to pleasure and to pain. The lower-class pattern of life, for example, puts a high premium on immediate physical gratification, on free expression of aggression, on spending, and sharing. Cleanliness, respect for property, sexual control, educational achievement—all highly valued by middle-class Americans—are of less importance to the lower-class family or are phrased differently.

The child growing up amid the disorganization of an urban slum has available neither the models upon which to pattern himself nor the assurance that being "good" will pay off. Indeed, he is likely to hear and see that "everybody has his racket" and to learn early in life that this applies to the representatives of law and order as well as to underworld groups.[12]

Excluding the participation in crimes to produce money for drugs, which will be discussed later, little evidence has been adduced to show that the morality of the drug addict undergoes a significant modification as a result of his drug use. It would appear, rather, that the addict, in arousing middle-class

---

RESEARCH AND THE CHICAGO AREA PROJECT, REPORT OF THE CHICAGO NARCOTICS SURVEY 44 (1953). The implication of the effect of environmental factors on the use of narcotics seems inescapable. For comparable statistics relating to treated juvenile addicts in New York City see COLUMBIA UNIVER-SITY SCHOOL OF PUBLIC HEALTH AND ADMINISTRATIVE MEDICINE, A FOLLOW-UP STUDY OF TREATED ADOLESCENT NARCOTICS USERS (Ray E. Trussell, M.D., ed.), Chapter 11 (1959). [Hereinafter referred to as TRUSSELL REPORT.]

12. Clausen, *supra* note 11, at 42.

emotion by his drug use, brings the mores of his subculture into question. Rather than deal with the question of the morality of lower-class patterns, the middle-class arbiters of the moral ethic label them a result of degenerate narcotics use.

Narcotic addicts are a sexual menace

ANY ASSERTION that sexual violence is a general or predictable result of narcotic addiction is untrue. This myth developed during the time when cocaine addiction was more extensive than at present. Cocaine can produce such a relief from inhibition, coupled with exhilaration, that the user may commit some violent act, possibly sexual, that he would not commit while free of the influence.[13] Despite the fact that cocaine has ceased to be a problem in the United States,[14] the myth of the sexual menace from the "dope fiend" has been kept alive by suggestive references to "dope parties" and "vicious crimes" which are readily translated by popular imagination into orgiastic sprees following use of drugs. The truth of the matter is that the opiates depress the sexual appetite, thus actually diminishing the probability of sexual crimes being committed by addicts.[15]

Statistics, medical and psychiatric observation, and police experience all demonstrate that there is a great deal of anti-social activity on the part of narcotic addicts. This does not answer the question, however, as to how much of this activity may be attributed to the drug use alone. The historical evidence just as clearly demonstrates that in the era before the advent of repressive laws, anti-social conduct was not a characteristic of the opium addict.[16] In fact, the very nature of the opiates would

13. TERRY & PELLENS, THE OPIUM PROBLEM 271, 505 (1928).
14. ANSLINGER & TOMPKINS, *op. cit. supra* note 5, at 281.
15. Pescor, *The Problem of Narcotic Drug Addiction*, 43 J. CRIM. L., C. & P.S. 471, 476; TRUSSELL REPORT 117–21; Wikler and Rasor, *Psychiatric Aspects of Drug Ad-*

diction, 14 AM. J. MED. 567–68 (May 1953).
16. Kolb, *Let's Stop This Narcotics Hysteria*, Saturday Evening Post, July 28, 1956, p. 19. For an extensive digest of the material relating to the characteristics of the addict population before 1925, see TERRY & PELLENS, *op. cit. supra* note 13, at 1–53.

seem to give the lie to arguments that the drug produces aggressive anti-social behavior. Opiates are depressants which lull the user into a state of euphoria where everything is "right."

> The euphoria of the addict is a feeling of temporary well-being, induced by the drug's suppression of discomfort or pain. The addict's "high" is a feeling of aloofness from current situations and a postponement of decisions or urgencies. The drug *is* the decision. It provides a feeling of security and self-sufficiency. It temporarily helps to establish self-confidence and quell any disturbing aggressiveness. The drug itself is so fulfilling that it becomes the center of the user's life.[17]

Still leaving aside the question of the addict's crimes to secure money, nothing has been shown to demonstrate that the use of opiates generally produces, in and of itself, serious dangers to the physical well-being of the addict or the social well-being of the community. There is assuredly cause for concern in the euphoric effect of opiates which cause the addict to experience a false sense of security, self-sufficiency, and the rightness of things, when the very opposite may be the actuality. The question is not, however, peculiar to opiate use. Alcohol presents a similar problem of greater magnitude,[18] as do the barbiturates and tranquilizers.[19] It is not intended to suggest that we should ignore the social problems implicit in narcotics use because we ignore them elsewhere, but only that the problem should be recognized for what it is, free of unfounded hysteria.

Drug use makes weak, ineffective members of society

AGAIN THE shortcomings of the majority of addicts are singled out for criticism in a context which suggests that drug use is the responsible factor. The problem is not so simple. The potential strength and effectiveness of the addict should be measured against his own capabilities or those of the subculture from

17. Winick, *Narcotics Addiction and Its Treatment*, 22 LAW & CONTEMP. PROB. 9, 14 (Winter 1957).

18. Kolb, *supra* note 16.

19. Winick, *supra* note 17, at 9, 11.

which he comes, rather than against society's ideal. It appears far more likely that the addict responds to his weakness and ineffectiveness by using drugs rather than the reverse.

> The cause of addiction is not drugs but human weakness. Addiction usually is a symptom of a personality maladjustment rather than a disease in its own right. The psychiatric conditions which underlie drug addiction are chiefly the neuroses and the character disorders.... They (neurotic patients) include nervous, tense individuals with a great deal of anxiety and many somatic complaints; compulsive neurotics; persons with conversion hysteria—strange paralyses, anesthesias, etc. Individuals with character disorders were formerly termed psychopaths. Usually they are irresponsible, selfish, immature, thrill-seeking individuals who are constantly in trouble—the type of person who acts first and thinks afterwards. The majority of addicts do not fall clearly into either the neurotic or character disorder groups but have characteristics of both classes.[20]

Thus it appears that addiction merely represents a way in which some people suffering from neuroses and character disorders react to their problems. Many people who are not addicts experience these psychiatric difficulties from time to time in their lives. The fact that some choose to resolve their difficulties by resorting to drugs is probably due to a great many circumstances,[21] not the least of which is the social attitude in their own respective communities.

> The types (of personalities) most commonly found included the passive dependent individuals with weak ego strength who have never made a satisfactory adjustment to the exigencies of everyday living.... Drugs simplify their struggle and appear to aid their adjustment.

20. ISBELL, WHAT TO KNOW ABOUT DRUG ADDICTION 2 (Public Health Service Publication No. 94, 1951).
21. WIKLER, OPIATE ADDICTION 5 (1953). Whether or not an individual will use drugs "appears to depend on other factors—the availability of the drugs, suggestion by associates, legal restrictions, painful illnesses, attitude of social groups, etc., as well as the state of the individual's own internalized controls."

Certain social factors appear influential in determining addiction. The addict with a dependent personality structure may come from a social group in which addiction is acceptable and differs only in terms of his use of narcotics from the dependent personality who comes from a cultural subgroup in which addiction is taboo but "neurotic" complaints in one guise or another are commonplace and allowed. The ill-defined back aches and "liver and stomach troubles" are but verbal adaptations to basic neurotic problems for which drugs also provide unfortunate solutions.[22]

The generalization that addicts are the weak, ineffective members of society has a dual vice. First, there is a suggestion implicit in the statement that there is something unique about the weakness or ineffectiveness when these qualities are demonstrated by an addict. Such a suggestion is highly misleading. Second, there is an inference that the use of drugs is the causal factor of the infirmities observed. Actually the reverse would appear to be true, namely, that the addict uses drugs as an attempted method of adjustment. What the actual effect of the drug will be again depends upon the individuality of the user.

The effects of opiate use on the individual as a member of society are determined in part by the strength of competing motivations. The gratification of "primary" needs by the simple expedient of using opiate drugs may have disastrous social consequences if the individual's productivity has been determined largely through necessity of satisfying his own hunger and sexual urges. Such individuals will give up such responsibilities for others as they have assumed and find, in opiates, the means of pursuing a hedonistic and narcissistic existence of no value to society. While this result is very commonly observed, there are credible reports of some individuals who are unable to function effectively in their work without the use of opiates because of "emotional" problems which appear to be satisfied by the drugs.

22. Chapman, *Management and Treatment of Drug Addiction* 9 J. CHRONIC DISEASES 315, 319 (March 1959).

Usually such persons are highly skilled professional people whose strongest motivations appear to spring from needs for high social esteem. They readily admit that opiates depress their sexual urges, but point out that these have been handled ineffectively by them in the past, and the absence of sexual relations is welcomed by both the husband and wife. However, the social stigma which the use of opiates entails, and the necessity for increasing the dose progressively soon raise serious problems.[23]

What would our hypothetical maladjusted individual do if he did not turn to drug use? He would find some other means of coping with his problem which might be either more or less alarming to society than his addiction. He might turn to the barbiturates or alcohol as a substitute for drugs. He might seek gratification by "acting out" his maladjustment through open expressions of hostility, sexual aggressiveness, exhibitionism. The significant point is that many of the ills attributed to narcotics use would exist with or without illegal addiction. Drug use simply represents the attempt of certain persons to deal with the problems confronting them because of their individual personality structure or the social structure of their communities. It may well be that drugs are a socially undesirable solution to the individual's problems, but, if so, our effort should be directed toward finding a solution that is acceptable.

Narcotic addicts are criminals

Except for the medical addict who receives a licit supply of drugs to relieve severe pain, it is inescapably true that narcotic addicts are criminals, since possession of narcotics is uniformly prohibited [24] and addiction itself made a crime in some jurisdictions.[25] The allegation of criminality of addicts is usually presented, however, as a characteristic of all drug users apart from such offenses as addiction, possession, or even stealing to

23. WIKLER, *op. cit. supra* note 21, at 57.

24. See Appendix B, p. 149 *infra*.
25. *Ibid.*

get money for drugs.[26] Depending upon the approach of the person making the statements, it may be alleged that the criminal record precedes the addiction [27] or that it comes as a result of the addiction.[28] The experience of police [29] as well as the admissions of drug addicts [30] leaves little doubt that addicts indulge in a wide variety of predatory crime to produce money with which to support their addiction. Evidence obtained in governmental investigations indicates that the range of cost may vary considerably,[31] but considering the educational and income status of the group from which most addicts are drawn, it is always a cost clearly beyond the earning power of most of them.[32] Again we are presented with a subject which should be the concern of the community, namely, the danger inherent in the use of a substance which produces such a desire that crimes are committed to secure it. However, the consideration of this problem should be made in an appropriate context. The addict is drawn from a subculture which does not have the same respect for property as a larger middle-class segment of American society.[33] Thus, in trying to appreciate the intensity of the compulsion which drives addicts to crime to secure money, one must first appreciate that in less compulsive situations, the addict or non-addict from a lower-class subculture will probably not exercise the personal restraint expected by the majority of society.

A great deal of evidence has been marshaled to demonstrate

26. "The ranks of both addicted and non-addicted drug peddlers are filled with persons dedicated to a life of lawlessness, and the arrest and incarceration of these people on narcotics charges has incidentally protected the public from the depredations of thieves, robbers, and other vicious criminals engaged in organized crime." ANSLINGER & TOMPKINS, op. cit. supra note 5, at 272.

27. ANSLINGER & TOMPKINS, op. cit. supra note 5, at 267–78.

28. LINDESMITH, OPIATE ADDICTION 172 (1947).

29. Finestone, Narcotics and Criminality, 22 LAW & CONTEMP. PROB. 69, Table II, at 71 (Winter 1957).

30. Hearings Before the Special Senate Committee to Investigate Organized Crime in Interstate Commerce, 82d Cong., 1st Sess., pt. 14 passim (1951). [Hereinafter referred to as Crime Committee Hearings.]

31. Ibid. The price ranged from $3 to $80 per day. Id. at 81, 296.

32. TRUSSELL REPORT, 51–79.

33. See quoted material accompanying note 12, supra.

the extensive non-narcotic criminal activity of the addicts before their first arrest on a narcotics charge.[34] From this it is often claimed that the persons who become involved in the "evil" of narcotics are simple manifesting another facet of their anti-social character and behavior and are antipathetic to socially acceptable ideas of law and morality long before addiction.[35]

There arises immediately the question of the validity of the data on which these assertions are based. It is obvious that the first narcotics arrest is not coincidental in time with the first narcotics use. Criminal activity before this time may well have been in support of a yet-undetected habit. In determining the extent to which prior criminal activity is truly unrelated to narcotics use, the starting point must be the time when the offender *first used* narcotics. That information must, in most cases, be obtained from the addict. If the addict believes that more sympathy for his present difficulty will be engendered if he indicates a recent acquaintance with narcotics, that is probably the information he will supply. If his judgment indicates the reverse, it is reasonable to assume that long use will be stated.

Assuming for the moment that all the studies have been successful in determining accurately the point at which addiction occurred, and that a number of narcotic addicts have had a record of criminal activity before becoming addicted, the significance of that fact must still be determined. The fact that addicts have criminal records proves no more about the causal

34. STATE DEP'T OF JUSTICE, BUREAU OF CRIMINAL STATISTICS, NARCOTICS ARRESTS IN CALIFORNIA, July 1, 1959–June 30, 1960 at 9, Table 8, Chart IV (Dec. 5, 1960); TRUSSELL REPORT 28–29, 43–50.

35. U.S. TREASURY DEP'T, BUREAU OF NARCOTICS, TRAFFIC IN OPIUM AND OTHER DANGEROUS DRUGS 6–7 (1960). *But see* U.S. TREASURY DEPT., BUREAU OF NARCOTICS, MEMORANDUM REGARDING NARCOTIC CLINICS, THEIR HISTORY AND HAZARDS 6 (1938) quoted by King, *The Narcotics Bureau and the Harrison Act: Jailing the Healers and the Sick*, 62 YALE L. J. 736, 738, at note 13 (1953): "Under these conditions [legalized opium smoking in Formosa] the only attributable cause for greater criminality among narcotic addicts than non-addicts is the direct effect of the use of narcotics upon the character of the user. . . . It is because drug addiction causes a relentless destruction of character and releases criminal tendencies."

role of drug addiction than the fact that underprivileged persons have criminal records proves about the causal role of poverty and deprivation. The factors discussed in the previous section must be understood and weighed carefully in either situation.

Any appreciation of the relationship between addiction and crime must also take into account the legal structure in this country which has forced narcotics traffic into the underworld. There is a considerable body of expert opinion to the effect that there are psychological factors which create "proneness toward addiction," and that this proneness is present in all classes of people in all walks of life.[36] In the United States, the law and public opinion have labeled the narcotic addict a criminal, and have forced all transactions in narcotics into a criminal setting. Therefore, many of the people who by virtue of personality and character disorders would be prime targets for addiction are deterred because they are not identified with the world of crime. Without such an identity, it is extremely difficult to obtain drugs in this country. An unknown, respectable-looking, white-collared clerk does not just walk into the drug-selling area of New York's East Harlem or Chicago's Southside and pick up a "deck" of heroin because he heard that it might relieve the anxieties he is experiencing. It is quite possible that the only real relation between prior criminal activity and drug addiction in this country is that only those who are known in criminal circles can readily obtain drugs. There is one exception: persons in the medical and paramedical professions also have ready access to narcotics. The logic of the argument that access determines the class of the user is borne out by the fact that, as compared with the general population, the rate of addiction is thirty times higher for people in these professions.[37]

36. DEUTSCH, WHAT WE CAN DO ABOUT THE DRUG MENACE 12–13 (Public Affairs Pamphlet No. 186, 1952).

37. NEW YORK CITY YOUTH BOARD, IN-SERVICE DEPARTMENT, REPORT OF THREE-DAY CONFERENCE ON NARCOTIC ADDICTION AND THE TEENAGER 16–17 (October 1959).

Under the British system, where drug addiction is not regarded as a correlative of criminal activity, there is practically no evidence of any relationship between addiction and crime.[38] Further, before the legal suppression of narcotics sales in the United States, addiction was commonly found among the higher social strata.[39] Only after the traffic became illegal did addiction become allied with crime.

These observations are not intended to militate against control of narcotic drugs, since the controls, under the conditions hypothesized, are keeping many people from beginning narcotics use. It is, however, important to realize the significance of the criminal records of narcotic addicts for what it is. When that significance has been clearly understood and appreciated, it will be possible to make a social judgment as to the justifiability of ostracizing narcotics users by criminal sanction in order to dissuade a portion of the populace from indulging in narcotic drugs.

Addiction is contagious

THE CHARGE that addiction is contagious is perhaps one of the most effective weapons of those who wish to perpetuate the social anathema of drug use. The evidence is overwhelming that addiction has the spreading character of a contagious disease. Most addicts state that they began using drugs by associating with others who used drugs.[40] Such initiation is similar to the way most people learn to smoke or drink, but unfortunately the public is led to believe that there is a deliberate effort on the part of addicts and peddlers to recruit new users.

It is also widely believed that addicts have a positive mania for making new addicts on the assumption that "misery loves company." It is true that addiction is spread by addicts—that's what makes it a highly dangerous contagion—but the manner of spread

38. Schur, *British Narcotics Policies,* 51 J. CRIM. L., C. & P.S. 619, 622–24 (Mar.-Apr. 1961).

39. TERRY & PELLENS, *op. cit. supra* note 13, at 1–53.

40. *Crime Committee Hearings.*

is usually a casual one. Often an addict shows great reluctance in "breaking in" a neophyte.[41]

The testimony of addicts before a Senate investigating committee also indicated that very few addicts are introduced to drugs by peddlers who offer initial doses free in order to trap the adventurous and unwary into addiction. Some of the addicts adverted to known cases where persons were introduced to drugs by peddlers, but the common method was through associates.[42]

Again the true situation presents a grim problem. The contagious character of addiction is an aspect of the problem which must be kept in the forefront of awareness when any attempt at solution is considered or undertaken. It is equally important, however, to remove the impression that the narcotic addict is gleefully seducing the flower of American youth into drug use as a fiendish vengeance against a society which refuses to permit his own indulgences. The problems apparent in the true nature of the spread of addiction are not less serious than those which would be presented by a diligently proselyting addict population. Indeed, the actual mechanics of addiction spread are probably more dangerous since the cause lies not within the relatively small body of addicts but in the much larger cultural subgroup from which addicts come. The efforts of a concerned public should be directed toward erasing the class values which applaud anti-social behavior in certain strata of the social structure. Considering the demonstrated effect of social acceptance on the likelihood of addiction, it would appear that therein lies the fertile soil favoring spread of addiction through association.

Once an addict, always an addict

IT IS ALMOST unavoidable that we should find a very confused public when the statements of professional people concerned

41. DEUTSCH, op. cit. supra note 36, 42. Crime Committee Hearings.
    at 12.

with drug addiction are completely beyond reconciliation. Almost all drug addicts, we are told, want to get off and remain off drugs.[43] Any opiate addict can be treated successfully except those with an incurable malady or the infirm, says a government agent.[44] Still, the rate of relapse is 90 percent or better, argues a critic of intramural treatment.[45] The sad and unfortunate truth is that there is not enough known about what happens to drug addicts after treatment to evaluate accurately either the treatment procedures being followed or the true nature of addiction. It is known that many addicts are curable, but figures on the rate of success are almost totally lacking.

Of the more than seventeen thousand patients admitted to the United States Public Health Service Hospital at Lexington, Kentucky, from 1935 to 1955, 64 percent never returned, 22 percent returned once, 6 percent returned twice, and the remaining 8 percent returned three or more times.[46] It is not claimed, however, that anything like 64 percent of the patients have abstained from the use of narcotics after release from Lexington; the more frequently quoted figure being about 25 percent.[47] Results in the treatment of adolescent addicts at Riverside Hospital in New York City have been less encouraging,[48] probably due to difficulties in the treatment of adolescents which do not apply to the treatment of more mature addicts.[49]

Pescor's study of patients released from Lexington is interesting but far from conclusive or all-revealing. Four methods were utilized in following the progress of dischargees: (1) in-

43. MAURER & VOGEL, NARCOTICS AND NARCOTIC ADDICTION 163 (1954).
44. Treas. Reg. 35, Art. 117 (1919).
45. Berger, *Dealing With Drug Addiction, A Reply to Mr. Kuh,* in U.S. TREASURY DEP'T, BUREAU OF NARCOTICS, CONTROL AND REHABILITATION OF THE NARCOTIC ADDICT 13 (1961).
46. Lowry, *Hospital Treatment of the Narcotic Addict,* 20 FEDERAL PROBATION 42, 50 (December 1956).
47. PESCOR, FOLLOW-UP STUDY OF TREATED NARCOTIC DRUG ADDICTS (Supplement No. 170 to Public Health Reports, 1943).
48. TRUSSELL REPORT.
49. Ausubel, *Dealing With Drug Addiction, A Defense of the Kuh Plan,* in U.S. TREASURY DEP'T, BUREAU OF NARCOTICS, CONTROL AND REHABILITATION OF THE NARCOTIC ADDICT 25 (1961).

formation secured from patients who returned to the hospital; (2) information secured from the Federal Bureau of Investigation when any former patient is arrested and the arresting agency requests a fingerprint identification; (3) information secured from probation officers on prisoner patients who are still under supervision; and (4) information secured from replies to letters of inquiry addressed to patients or their relatives, such letters assuring absolute confidence. Of the patients on whom information was secured, 74.7 percent had relapsed and 25.3 percent had abstained. Of the total patients discharged, 39.9 percent were *known* to have relapsed and 13.5 percent were *known* to have abstained.

The methods were admittedly crude. The danger in the first two methods is that they are heavily weighted toward identifying the relapsed addict. Information from probation officers reveals relapses and abstentions, but only those occurring during the somewhat coercive period of probation. The fourth method depends solely upon the voluntary cooperation of former patients. The study did not attempt to project the percentages of known relapse and abstention to cover the remaining patients on whom no information was received. Such a projection would be unwarranted considering the methods used in securing the information. In view of the illegal status of drug addiction, it is likely that a large percentage of the relapsed patients were discovered.[50] Conversely, it is likely that the abstention percentage of the patients whose subsequent history was unknown would be relatively high.

Unfortunately, the study has become the basis for statements about the success of Lexington by critics and defenders who accept the figures as a total picture. Critics, if they cite any authority, will say that the hospital succeeds in only 13 percent of its cases. In less formal discussion or writing, critics will inch

50. Interviews with federal and local enforcement officials indicated a consistent conviction that habitual use of illicit narcotics over a period of two years would bring almost all such users to the attention of the police.

up the relapse figures without stating a source.[51] Even the
defenders of Lexington utilize the 25 percent known abstentions as the measure of success.[52] Neither is accurate. Both are
misleading unless qualified by the technique of investigation.
The same criticism is true of references to the studies made of
Riverside Hospital.[53]

It is almost incredible that legislatures and administrative
agencies, willing to appropriate huge sums of money for enforcement and hospital activities connected with the drug problem, have not seen the necessity for full and complete study of
the progress of treated addicts.[54] It is strongly asserted by the
Federal Bureau of Narcotics that institutional treatment is the
only proper method of treating drug addicts.[55] This pronounce-
ment, while originally based upon qualified medical consensus,
and still supported by many addiction specialists,[56] has never
been subjected to the searching evaluation which could result

51. "The relapse rate at the federal hospitals is known to be in excess of 90%, and if complete figures could be obtained, is probably even higher. 95% is a conservative estimate." Berger, *supra* note 45, at 14.
52. Ausubel, *supra* note 49.
53. The TRUSSELL REPORT made use of most of the same sources of information in following up patients treated at Riverside. Only a small percentage remained unknown in this study. It should be noted, however, that the "two per cent success" figure often attributed to the TRUSSELL REPORT findings really relates to the number of patients who had no further difficulty with their communities. Dr. Trussell and his associates were concerned with the overall rehabilitation of Riverside patients. Consequently, any instance indicating that the patient was not adjusting to society was regarded as a "failure" whether or not narcotics were involved.
54. Financial support has recently been received by the personnel at Lexington for a detailed follow-up study on the approximately 1,000 former patients living in Kentucky. When it is completed, considerable caution should be exercised in applying the findings to the national scene. The study should, however, be very valuable in developing follow-up techniques.
55. U.S. TREASURY DEP'T, BUREAU OF NARCOTICS, CONTROL AND REHABILITATION OF THE NARCOTIC ADDICT, *Foreword* (1961).
56. The present policies of the Federal Bureau of Narcotics appear to have been inherited from its predecessor, the Federal Narcotics Control Board. The stand of the American Medical Association in 1924, that ambulatory treatment was inadvisable, is most frequently cited in support of this view. However, the medical profession has shown some dissatisfaction of late with the 1924 statement. See American Medical Association, Council on Mental Health, *Report on Narcotic Addiction*, 165 J.A.M.A. 1707 (Nov. 30, 1957).

from a thorough follow-up study of treated addicts. Such a study is imperative in the light of present knowledge.

Relapse should be recognized as a predictable symptom of addiction. The nature of relapse is not so thoroughly understood as to permit its characterization as definitely psychological, sociological, or pharmacological,[57] but whatever its nature, it should be accepted in the same way in which relapse is accepted in many chronic diseases. Success should not depend upon whether a former drug user goes to his grave abstaining from drugs, but upon the length of time and the conditions under which treatment has enabled him to function successfully without drugs. It is not enough to remove the patient from drug use if thereafter he suffers intensely from emotional disturbance, maladjustment, and disorientation from his social community. Substitution of one illness for another hardly seems to merit the term "cure." Similarly, a physician who treats an addict who subsequently remains abstinent for ten, five, or even three years, hardly deserves to have his efforts labeled a "failure."

———————————

Unfortunately, among those who have become interested [in the opium problem] from a professional, legislative, administrative, sociologic, commercial, or other point of view, there has been an almost continuous controversy as to practically every phase of the narcotic situation, with the result that all the way from the causes on through development, course, and treatment of the condition, to say nothing of its underlying nature and methods of control, there has been a lack of unanimity of opinion. These differences have been expressed in reports of scientific research, textbooks on medicine, legislative acts, judicial opinions, and administrative procedures—in general, in the opinions and efforts of all who, from one motive or another, have appeared to seek a solution.

57. NYSWANDER, THE DRUG ADDICT AS A PATIENT 54–55 (1956).

In view of the importance of the problem it is astonishing that little specific information on even the main features of this condition is available in any one place. In general, students and writers appear to have approached the subject from only a limited experience—with too meagre a basis of fact—and to have emphasized unduly one or another feature to the total exclusion of related data. This tendency quite naturally may have led the more or less casual reader as well as possibly legislators, administrators, and others officially or professionally connected with the individuals involved, to prejudicial attitudes and unwarranted generalizations.[58]

The words are those of Dr. Charles Terry in 1928. Despite his, and other dedicated efforts, there has been little change.

58. TERRY & PELLENS, THE OPIUM PROBLEM, Intro. at xiii-xiv (1928).

Chapter Three

THE LEGAL PROFESSION CALLS
FOR RESEARCH

THE EARLIEST significant consideration given by the American legal profession to the problems inherent in governmental control of narcotic drugs in the United States occurred in 1932 when the American Bar Association approved the Uniform Narcotic Drug Act.[1] Amendments offered by the Commissioners on Uniform State Laws in 1942 and 1948 also were approved. Narcotic drug laws again became a concern of the American Bar Association in 1951 in another context, when its Commission on Organized Crime considered, but disapproved,[2] the mandatory minimum sentences and minimum penalties of the first Boggs Act.[3] The consideration of the provisions of the Boggs Act generated enough interest in the narcotics problem to move the American Bar Association Section of Criminal Law to create a Standing Committee on Narcotics and Alcohol in 1953. After surveying the federal and state legislation on the subject, the Committee proposed the following resolution which was passed by the American Bar Association House of Delegates in February 1955: [4]

1. 9B UNIFORM LAWS ANNOTATED 274.
2. 76 A.B.A. REP. 387, 411 (1951).
3. Act of Nov. 2, 1951, 65 Stat. 767, 21 U.S.C. § 174 (1952). Cf. 68A Stat. 860, 26 U.S.C. § 7237 (Supp. III, 1956).
4. 80 A.B.A. REP. 408 (1955). Because of procedural requirements, sections 1 and 2 of the resolution were referred by the House of Delegates to the Research and Library Committee of the American Bar Foundation without prejudice to the right of the Section of Criminal Law to investigate and explore with the American Medical Association the possibilities of a joint study.

35

RESOLVED, that the Section of Criminal Law through its Chairman or other appropriate representatives he may appoint, be and hereby is authorized:

1. To explore with the American Medical Association on the possibilities of a jointly conducted study of the narcotic drug traffic and related problems, by and on behalf of the organizations through their own research facilities or in collaboration with other interested persons or organizations.

2. To investigate through the American Bar Foundation the availability of funds from sources outside the Association in aid of the study described in the preceding paragraph, and with the approval of the American Bar Foundation to utilize such funds as may be found to be available for that purpose.

3. To urge the Congress of the United States to undertake a reexamination of the Harrison Act, its amendments, and related enforcement and treatment policies and problems.

Pursuant to the resolution, negotiations were opened with the American Medical Association which responded favorably to the suggestion of cooperation between the organizations. A Joint Committee was established consisting of Rufus King, Chairman, Judge Edward J. Dimock, and Abe Fortas for the American Bar Association, and Dr. Robert H. Felix, Dr. Isaac Starr, and C. Joseph Stetler for the American Medical Association.

Considerable study and effort were devoted to the determination of particular areas and problems which should be dealt with by the Joint Committee. The Russell Sage Foundation provided the Committee with financial and personnel assistance to be used in the examination of existing data and the formulation of one or more specific research proposals. By December of 1956 the areas to be studied had been reviewed, and Judge Morris Ploscowe, Director of the study, announced the following aims:

1. To survey existing sources to find out how much already existing material was available and could be relied on;

2. To determine what experiments and research projects ought to be sponsored by the Joint Committee to remedy the deficiencies in present knowledge of the field; and

3. To draw conclusions where possible from existing sources as to any areas which appear capable of accurate analysis without further study.

With the above aims in view, Judge Ploscowe and the Russell Sage staff prepared a report entitled *Some Basic Problems in Drug Addiction and Suggestions for Research*. The Joint Committee approved the Ploscowe study "without formally adopting the language or specific appraisals,"[5] and included it as an appendix to the Committee's Interim Report. Chairman King made a comparative study of the drug laws of Great Britain and other European countries which was included as Appendix B. The Committee commended "the thoughtful, realistic appraisal of the problem of drug addiction and the critical analysis of present policies toward drug addicts contained in Judge Ploscowe's report. He has clearly spelled out the need for a revision of present attitudes toward and present approaches to drug addicts and drug addiction."[6]

The Joint Committee agreed to go forward with the preparation of plans for research projects in five of the specific areas suggested by Judge Ploscowe's report.[7]

An out-patient experimental clinic for the treatment of drug addicts

IT IS NOT readily apparent what the exact scope of this activity would be as it is described by the Joint Committee. The final report recommends "an experimental facility for the out-patient

5. JOINT COMMITTEE OF THE AMERICAN BAR ASSOCIATION AND THE AMERICAN MEDICAL ASSOCIATION ON NARCOTIC DRUGS, DRUG ADDICTION: CRIME OR DISEASE? 10 (Interim and Final Reports, 1961). [Hereinafter referred to as JOINT COMMITTEE REPORT.] The JOINT COMMITTEE REPORT has been published under the above title by the Indiana University Press. Because of the general unavailability of the original report, all page references will be to this volume.
6. *Ibid.*
7. *Id.* at 11–13, 103–15.

treatment of drug addicts, to explore the possibilities of dealing with at least some types of addicted persons in the community rather than in institutions." [8] Considering the Committee's approval of the Ploscowe report without formal adoption of its specific appraisals, it is difficult to determine how much of the activity envisioned by Judge Ploscowe is contemplated by the Committee. Judge Ploscowe recommends that "if the clinic does not succeed in taking and keeping the addict patient off drugs after a period of intensive treatment, its personnel should then consider supplying the addict with sufficient drugs for his needs, so that he does not have to patronize the illicit peddler." [9] The Report of the American Medical Association Council on Mental Health, completed shortly before the Ploscowe study, considered this question carefully. The Council found that the establishment of drug-dispensing clinics was not feasible, though this opinion should be subject to frequent review in the light of new scientific knowledge that may become available.[10] Of course, the proposed experimental clinic might provide some of this knowledge, which possibility was adverted to by the Council on Mental Health [11] and by Judge Ploscowe.[12] However, the wording of the Joint Committee recommendation, together with the reservations of the Council, leaves in doubt the Committee's intention as to the scope of the experimental clinic. Nowhere in either of the reports is the dispensing of drugs considered as treatment, but rather as a weapon against the

8. *Id.* at 161 (emphasis added).
9. *Id.* at 105.
10. American Medical Association, Council on Mental Health, *Report on Narcotic Addiction,* 165 J.A.M.A. 1968, 1973 (Dec. 14, 1957).
11. *Id.* at 1970. The Ploscowe report intimates that the Council disapproved the establishment of dispensing clinics, but favored the establishment of an experiment designed to test the hypothesis that clinics would eliminate the illicit traffic. This picture is not accurate. The material following Judge Ploscowe's quotation from the Council (JOINT COMMITTEE REPORT 102) indicates that the Council considered the possibility of such an experiment, but felt that ethical questions presented an objection as well as legal and experimental difficulties. Nowhere in the A.M.A. Council Report did this writer find support for the establishment of even an experimental dispensing clinic at the present time.
12. JOINT COMMITTEE REPORT 103.

illegal traffic. The specification of an experimental clinic for the out-patient treatment of addicts suggests that the Joint Committee chose to leave the dispensing experiments for a later date.[13]

The clinic proposal was by far the most controversial aspect of the *Joint Committee Report*. Reaction seemed to ignore completely the carefully worded proposal in the Ploscowe report calling for a limited number of addict subjects in a wholly experimental atmosphere. The object of the experiment would be to test some of the hypotheses about addiction treatment and rehabilitation in hopes of adding to the meager data on which present policies are based. Critics of the *Joint Committee Report* seem to believe that the recommendations are for the immediate establishment of "dope cafeterias" for any and all who care to sample the wares. The most cursory examination of the research proposal would dispel such a notion.

The Federal Narcotics Bureau quickly published an impassioned reply to the Interim Report, consisting of comments from the Bureau's Advisory Committee.[14] The document, nearly twice as long as the *Joint Committee Report*, is replete with vituperative attacks on the Committee, its individual members, Judge Ploscowe, the two Associations, and even the writers cited in the footnotes. Many of the attacks on the research pro-

13. In the Final Report, the Joint Committee states: "We need much more information than is presently available about the best means of handling addicts who, despite the best professional efforts, continue to be dependent on drugs. An experiment conducted by experts (as proposed above in this report) should be charged with getting information on this point." JOINT COMMITTEE REPORT 164. Again, it is unclear whether the suggested experiment relates to dispensing drugs to unresponding patients or whether the experiment should be directed toward discovering new methods of treatment which might be effective when applied to presently unresponsive patients.

14. U.S. TREASURY DEP'T, BUREAU OF NARCOTICS ADVISORY COMMITTEE, COMMENTS ON NARCOTIC DRUGS: INTERIM REPORT OF THE JOINT COMMITTEE OF THE AMERICAN BAR ASSOCIATION AND THE AMERICAN MEDICAL ASSOCIATION ON NARCOTIC DRUGS (1959). It is worth noting that every member of this committee had well-publicized views on narcotics control before his selection. Of the 14 authors, 5 are or have been narcotics agents. The Advisory Committee was formed to answer the Joint Committee Report.

posals are typical expressions of those who defend the status quo by ridiculing any suggested change.[15]

A remarkable document, cluttered with capital letters, bold-face type, italics and exclamation points, the Advisory Committee report uses every argument conceivable, even when they are contradictory, to belittle the ABA-AMA report. It is filled with repetitions, misquotations and scorn, and resembles a screech more than an argument. On several issues, Anslinger's group makes intelligent, critical points, but these are made so loudly they are hard to hear. The whole tenor of the document indicates Anslinger does not want to win the discussion as much as he wants to eliminate it.[16]

The decision as to the merit of the proposal for an out-patient treatment and dispensing clinic involves complex medico-legal questions. The American Medical Association has also recognized the ethical problems.[17] As argued by Judge Ploscowe, the present laws and treaties which govern United States policy should not be an impediment to an experimental clinic. It would

15. UNITED STATES TREASURY DE-PARTMENT, *op. cit. supra* note 14. "You asked me to comment on this report. This is difficult to do. One wonders if the effort is worth-while." (*Id.* at 51). "Had only the Committee and Judge Ploscowe ... [considered past history] such a report would never, in good conscience, have been written." (*Id.* at 71). "The ABA-AMA Interim Report is so utterly bereft of basic principles of logic, that I have spent many days in what seems to be a futile effort to piece together its several segments, to the end that it become recognized as an intelligent approach to one of the world's most challenging problems." (*Id.* at 72). "It is incredible that one so obviously biased and uninformed should attempt to speak for the American Bar Association and the American Medical Association." (*Id.* at 120). Despite the allega-tions that the Committee Report "is replete with mis-statements, ambiguities, contradictions and as-sumptions of fact not in evidence," the critics seem less than certain of what the prevailing conditions are. One Narcotics Bureau supervisor agrees with the report that "domestic controls on registered dealers are so effective that the traffic has been fed almost exclusively on smuggling activities." (*Id.* at 109). Another supervisor says: "The practitioners representing the American Medical Association show either frightening ignorance or callous disregard of the abuse and diversion of legitimately produced narcotic drugs and the addiction to such drugs intended for the care of the sick and injured." (*Id.* at 120).

16. Meisler, *Federal Narcotics Czar*, The Nation, February 20, 1960, p. 159, at 161.

17. See note 11 *supra*.

appear, however, that the establishment of an experimental *dispensing* clinic should await the findings in the remaining research proposals. A better understanding of the etiological and relapse factors in addiction will doubtless improve the administration of a clinic program. It is essential that the experiment, if it proves desirable, commence under the most favorable circumstances possible. After experience with an out-patient *treatment* clinic; after causative and relapse factors are better understood; after an educational program has had time to prepare the addict and the public for a change in the social view of addiction—then, perhaps, an experimental dispensing clinic can answer some of the remaining questions.

A *study of relapse and causative factors in addiction and rehabilitation*

THE JOINT COMMITTEE and Judge Ploscowe recommend elaborate follow-up studies of drug addicts treated in the presently existing facilities. It is anticipated that a great deal about the nature of relapse as well as the original factors causing addiction can be learned from the successes and failures of current treatment methods. The study is palpably indispensable to any effort at evaluating present treatment policies. This proposal appears to be the logical jumping-off point for the entire research program recommended by the Joint Committee. Its results could conceivably shape the course of other research efforts. Conversely, its results could render the other efforts unnecessary or of limited value. If the study shows that the present methods are more satisfactory than is generally believed, or that the causative factors are not amenable to practical measures for removal or control, then large areas of the remaining research proposals would need to be redirected.

Educational and preventive research

IT IS REASONABLY argued that a program should be undertaken to educate the public to the nature and dangers of narcotics use. It is also suggested that other preventive measures should be developed, though nothing appears in either the *Joint Committee Report* or the Ploscowe report to suggest what these other measures might be.

As for the educational objective, Judge Ploscowe suggests that the measures would be similar to those taken against venereal disease. The measures would certainly be similar, but the result probably would be less spectacular. The spreading use of penicillin during the venereal disease campaign was of immeasurable assistance. Without the synergistic combination of education and a powerful new weapon against addiction, the campaign should not be expected to have so widespread an effect. However, despite the arguments of some authorities,[18] such an effort is well worth the undertaking even if only a few are deterred from experimenting with drugs.[19]

Legal research

THE COMMITTEE suggests a critical study directed at the "uncertainty at present both in the ambiguous provisions of some of our narcotic drug statutes and in the court decisions through which they have been applied," and expresses its doubt as to the soundness and validity of the premises on which the laws are based.[20] Judge Ploscowe's recommendation for legal research is based upon two convictions: first, that the whole approach to addiction as a matter of criminality is wrong, and, second, that the study of the administration of the laws govern-

18. See ANSLINGER & TOMPKINS, THE TRAFFIC IN NARCOTICS 219–22 (1953).
19. Many of the addicts interviewed by a Senate Committee, especially the young ones, indicated that they would never have started using narcotics if they had known the consequences. Some indicated that they knew narcotics were addicting, but felt they could avoid becoming "hooked." They say that had they understood how powerful the qualities of the drug were, they would never have tried it. *Hearings Before the Special Senate Committee to Investigate Organized Crime in Interstate Commerce*, 82d Cong., 1st Sess., pt. 14 *passim* (1951).
20. JOINT COMMITTEE REPORT 12.

ing narcotics, discussed below, will demonstrate that it is also ineffective.[21]

The Joint Committee and Judge Ploscowe do not seem to be addressing the same problem. While the tenor of the *Joint Committee Report* clearly indicates that it is out of sympathy with the present approach to addiction problems, the legal research recommendation is directed toward clearing up ambiguities and doubts as to the validity of some of its facets. Judge Ploscowe, on the other hand, considers the system wrong. Assuming that the medical research is satisfactory, and assuming a new social judgment is forthcoming, he suggests research to prepare a new uniform or model narcotic drug act. The new legislation would attempt two things: (1) to create a new method of dealing with addicts, consisting of the substitution of treatment for incarceration and the providing of legal supplies of drugs to non-rehabilitate cases; and (2) to provide the most effective controls and sanctions against peddlers and illicit traffic.

Research in the administration of present laws

THE JOINT COMMITTEE's recommendation is directed toward learning how the present legislation is operating. Judge Ploscowe also is concerned with this aspect of the administrative study, but more specifically he would direct the effort toward discovering what has been the actual effect of the more recent severe penalty legislation on the whole narcotics problem. The two suggestions are not really discrete, their difference resting largely on the extent of the research recommended.

In addition to the five projects proposed by Judge Ploscowe and adopted by the Joint Committee, Judge Ploscowe's report contains a recommendation that there be collected and published a volume of selected readings on narcotic addiction. This volume would be of considerable value in determining the increase in scientific knowledge and changes in attitude and

21. *Id.* at 113–14.

approach since the publication nearly forty years ago of the pioneer work by Terry and Pellens.[22]

The Interim Report states the intention of the Joint Committee to develop specific project designs for the research proposed. In its Final Report, however, the Committee recommends its own dissolution without offering such programs. It is suggested, rather, that further development be carried on by research facilities available to the two Associations.[23] The House of Delegates of the American Bar Association approved the Final Report and adopted resolutions commending the Joint Committee and recognizing the need for inquiry into the whole area of narcotic drug traffic and related problems.[24] Similar action was taken by the American Medical Association.[25]

The American Bar Foundation had, since the creation of the Joint Committee, consulted with the Committee and the Section of Criminal Law on the research planning project. After the dissolution of the Joint Committee the Foundation began taking an active part in the study of narcotics control laws. A careful study of the Committee's reports was made with a view toward developing research project designs. Considerable difficulty emerged.

The two separate recommendations for legal research appear to overlap and coalesce into one project requiring a tremendous expenditure of time and money with only dubious possibility of producing a meaningful result. It would require a compilation and analysis of the statutes and case law of the federal government and all the states wherever the subject of narcotic drugs is touched upon. After completion of this task, a field study of police departments, public prosecutors, courts, penal institutions, treatment facilities, and probation programs would

22. TERRY & PELLENS, THE OPIUM PROBLEM (1928).
23. 84 A.B.A. REP. 540 (1959).
24. *Ibid.*
25. AMERICAN MEDICAL ASSOCIATION —AMERICAN BAR ASSOCIATION NARCOTIC DRUG COMMITTEE REPORT in PROCEEDINGS OF THE HOUSE OF DELEGATES OF THE THE AMERICAN MEDICAL ASSOCIATION 38–40 (107th Annual Session, June 8–12, 1959).

be required if the administrative study is to answer the questions posed by Judge Ploscowe.

The advisability of seeking support for and embarking upon the entire suggested legal research program was subjected to serious examination. Several important factors militated against such a step. First, it appeared that forty-nine jurisdictions [26] have adopted the Uniform Narcotic Drug Act or substantially similar legislation, resulting in a fairly single-minded approach to drug problems at the state level. Also, federal legislation has already been examined and discussed in numerous careful studies.[27] The ambiguity referred to by the Joint Committee occurs chiefly in the regulation of medical practice, a matter which is discussed fully and competently by Judge Ploscowe.[28] Apart from the role of physicians in treating addiction, the legislation does not present a problem of ambiguity. Certainly, grave questions as to the validity of the present control approach may be and have been raised, but such questions are not resolved by statutory analysis.

Second, an assessment and evaluation of the correctness of the present legal approaches to narcotics problems would be very difficult until a substantial portion of the suggested medical research has been completed. The significant thrust of the proposed legal research is toward the drafting of a new act to implement the findings of the medical research. Without the data which the medical studies would reveal, it seemed both presumptive and unpropitious to undertake research having new legislation as its goal. Any proposal for sweeping revision of legislation in this field should reflect the most careful consideration of all possible factors and be supported by the most complete evidence of the need for change.

26. All states except California, New Hampshire, and Pennsylvania. For statutory citations see Appendix B, p. 149 *infra*.
27. Comment, *Narcotics Regulation*, 62 YALE L.J. 751–87 (April 1953); King, *The Narcotics Bureau and the Harrison Act: Jailing the Healers and the Sick*, 62 YALE L.J. 736–49 (April 1953); Note, *Narcotics Regulation: A Study in Irresolution*, 34 TEMPLE L.Q. 310–22 (Spring 1961).
28. JOINT COMMITTEE REPORT 68–82.

Third, consideration was given to the possibility of duplication in research effort. A cursory search indicated that extensive study had been given to narcotics problems by many agencies, though not in the scope and depth deemed necessary by the Joint Committee. However, from an examination of other studies, it was clear that much of the information desired was not available. An accurate determination of the lacunae in discoverable data seemed highly desirable.

Fourth, Judge Ploscowe's report starts with an unproved assumption that the current approach to narcotics problems in this country is wrong and inefficacious. The assumption is based upon the assertion that the United States has a greater proportion of addicts than any other country of the Western world despite a half century of strict governmental control. Initially expressed in terms of doubt, the report moves toward the statement that "strict law enforcement and severe penalties are therefore not the easy answers to the problems of drug addiction. We must look elsewhere for a rational drug control program for this country." [29] Granting that no solution will be easy, the evidence has not been marshaled to demonstrate that severe penalties are or are not the answer to the narcotics problems of the United States. Many factors contribute to make the situation in the United States different from that of most countries of "the Western World." The non-homogeneous population of the United States, composed of many unintegrated racial, ethnic, and nationality groups, is a distinguishing factor. The wealth of the citizens of this country makes it a prime target for illicit trafficking. The pressures of a highly competitive society create an atmosphere ripe for the peace-giving effect of the drugs. On the other hand, the pace creates in some the never-ending desire for new thrills. All of these and more factors contribute to the creation of a problem in the United States distinct from those of other countries. This is not to suggest that these conditions necessarily justify the criminal sanction ap-

29. JOINT COMMITTEE REPORT 22.

proach to addiction,[30] but only that a numerical comparison of drug users is not an accurate or complete measure of the effectiveness of the "American system."

Since the adoption of the Harrison Act [31] there has been but one approach in the United States,[32] namely, that of criminal sanction applied to all offenders against the narcotics laws. In recent years the federal government and many of the states have increased markedly the severity of penalties imposed upon such offenders. The law enforcement authorities have claimed that such changes in the penal statutes have significantly reduced the narcotics problem throughout the country.[33] They are joined in this claim by numerous lawmakers,[34] medical authorities,[35] and others concerned with the social and moral implications of narcotics traffic and addiction.[36]

There has been a recent surge of objection to the prevailing system by competent, sincere, and conscientious people as evidenced by the *Joint Committee Report,* the plan of the New York Academy of Medicine,[37] and articles by distinguished

30. Canada, which has long followed a system similar to that of the United States, appears to have found it unsatisfactory. On June 12, 1961, the Canadian Parliament passed Bill C–100 providing for a new approach to the control of narcotic drugs. This bill places complete discretion in the judiciary to determine appropriate measures against criminal addicts. It contemplates treatment instead of imprisonment for all addicts, criminal and non-criminal, peddlers and non-peddlers. See remarks of E. D. Fulton, Minister of Justice, in 105 CANADIAN H. C. DEB. (No. 126) 5982–88 (4th Sess., 24th Parliament, June 7, 1961).

31. Act of Dec. 17, 1914, 38 Stat. 785, 26 U.S.C. §§ 4701–36 (Supp. III, 1956).

32. Excluding the brief experience with narcotics clinics which was not designed as a control measure, but as a temporary effort to deal with problems brought about by the abrupt cessation of legal sale.

33. See testimony of Commissioner Anslinger in *Hearings Before the Subcommittee of the House Committee on Appropriations,* 86th Cong., 2d Sess. 133–83 (Jan. 26, 1960).

34. Committee on the Judiciary, *Narcotic Control Act of 1956,* S. REP. No. 1997, 84th Cong., 2d Sess. 6–7 (1956).

35. TERRY, SANTA RITA REHABILITATION CLINIC TEN-YEAR REPORT 1949–1959, at 10. "Law enforcement, not the practice of medicine, is the chief weapon." (n.b., The Santa Rita Rehabilitation Clinic is operated under the Alameda County Sheriff's Department.)

36. INTERDEPARTMENTAL COMMITTEE ON NARCOTICS, REPORT TO THE PRESIDENT OF THE UNITED STATES (February 1956).

37. New York Academy of Medicine, Subcommittee on Drug Addiction, *Report on Drug Addiction,* 31 BULL. N.Y. ACAD. MED. 592 (1955).

scholars in fields concerned with aspects of the narcotics problem.[38] The supporters of the status quo, however, have succeeded in entrenching in popular and legislative opinion the view that severe penalties are not only effective against narcotics problems, but also the *only* approach which can be considered by intelligent and informed people.[39]

From this controversy emerged the nucleus of the present project. Present policies are attacked by critics on two grounds: (1) the policies are inhumane, and (2) the policies are ineffective. Humanity is a matter of subjective opinion; effectiveness is a question of fact. The American Bar Foundation decided to attempt a resolution of the question as to the effectiveness of present narcotics policies, the results of the study to determine, perhaps, the course of further and larger efforts.

38. Howe, *A Physician's Blueprint for the Management and Prevention of Narcotics Addiction*, 55 N.Y. STATE J. MED. 341 (1955); Eggston and Berger, *Should We Legalize Narcotics*, Coronet, June 1955, p. 30; Stevens, *Make Dope Legal*, Harper's Magazine, November 1952, p. 40; Kolb, *Let's Stop This Narcotics Hysteria*, Saturday Evening Post, July 28, 1956, p. 19; Berger, *Richmond County Medical Society's Plan for the Control of Narcotics Addiction*, 56 N.Y. STATE J. MED. 888 (1956).

39. "Thus there is general agreement among medical, enforcement, and legislative authorities that narcotic traffickers, addicts and nonaddicts alike, must be removed from society for a long period of time as a deterrent to bring about possible rehabilitation and to prevent the contamination of others. At this time in the twentieth century, it is only the uninformed and publicity seekers who would attack this problem otherwise." Speer, *Documentation of the Narcotics Addiction Problem in the United States* in HOCH & ZUBIN (eds.), PROBLEMS OF ADDICTION AND HABITUATION 149 (1958). Mr. Speer is Assistant to the Commissioner of the Federal Narcotics Bureau.

Chapter Four

AN EMPIRICAL EVALUATION
OF THE AMERICAN SYSTEM

T_HE_ R_ESEARCH_ C_OMMITTEE_ of the American Bar Foundation recommended in early 1960 that the initial effort of the Foundation should be limited to a "study of the statutes and court decisions concerning narcotics of six to ten states, together with the Uniform Narcotic 'Law and federal laws, describing their respective provisions, comparing them, and affording a preliminary evaluation of their effectiveness." [1] The Board of Directors subsequently approved the recommendation.

A project plan was accordingly designed aimed at evaluating the effectiveness of the legislation by correlating statutory enactments with changes in the complexion of the narcotics problem. It was anticipated that the study would be conducted through library searches; correspondence with officials, agencies, and other authorities throughout the country; limited interviews; and examination of reports, treatises, statistics, and any other data revealing the actual experiences of the states. Field studies of the administration of the narcotic drug laws were not planned for this initial effort.

The decade 1951–1960 produced many important changes in the statutory law and many claimed salutary changes in the

---

1. A_MERICAN_ B_AR_ F_OUNDATION_, R_E-_ M_EETING_ 2 (ABF Research Docu-
   SEARCH C_OMMITTEE_, R_EPORT OF_ ment No. 10, Feb. 19, 1960).

narcotic addiction and traffic picture in the United States. It is also a period rich with information supplied by writers, investigative committees, and law enforcement officials. A study of the changes in statutory regulation during this period was settled upon as the best initial approach to the objectives of this project.

Seven states and the District of Columbia were selected for the study. New York, Illinois, California, and Michigan were chosen because they represent the areas of the United States with the most severe narcotics problems. These four states account for more than three-quarters of the known addicts.[2] Three other states, New Jersey, Ohio, and Missouri, were chosen because they represent states where it is claimed that increased penalties have dramatically reduced the narcotics problem.[3] These three states are also considered a valid selection for other reasons. They are all contiguous to one or more of the states with a severe situation, and would presumably have ready access to sources of supply. Each of them, like their more severely affected neighbors, has a large proportion of its population concentrated in one or two metropolitan areas, the usual fecund culture for illicit traffic and use. Further, each of the states has in its metropolitan areas large population segments of low-income, low-education, unintegrated minority groups which provide the bulk of known narcotic addicts.[4] The District of Columbia was added to the study since it represents an area of essentially federal administration.

I

Obtaining the information called for in the statutory search presented no serious difficulty, chiefly because all of the states

2. *Hearings Before the Subcommittee of the Committee on Appropriations of the House of Representatives,* 86th Cong., 2d Sess. 139 (Jan. 26, 1960).

3. U.S. TREASURY DEP'T, BUREAU OF NARCOTICS, GRAPHIC RESULTS OF MANDATORY PENALTIES AGAINST PEDDLERS (1958).

4. *Hearings, supra* note 2, at 139.

selected for this study [5] except California [6] have adopted the Uniform Narcotic Drug Act.[7] As is so frequently the case, the Uniform Act has been changed considerably by all of the states enacting it, but the changes are for the most part minor variations in terminology and structure. All of the states, including California, prohibit the same types of activity, prescribe essentially the same types of safeguards for the public, and regulate the medical and paramedical professions in essentially the same way.

The Uniform Narcotic Drug Act was first adopted by the National Conference of Commissioners on Uniform State Laws in 1932 after an effort of five years. The Act was adopted in response to extensive demand for uniform legislation to reach those areas of narcotics activities which could not be reached by the taxing power of Congress through the Harrison Act.[8]

The Uniform Act is drafted with unusual clarity, conciseness, and flexibility. Provision is made for bringing newly discovered drugs with addiction-forming or addiction-sustaining liability within the control of the Act by incorporation of federal law and by rule of state officers.[9] Recognizing the incalculable value of narcotic preparations to everyday health and comfort, the Act provides for the exemption of many household remedies

5. D.C. CODE ANN. §§ 33–401 through 33–425 (1951, Supp. 1960); ILL. REV. STAT. ch. 38, §§ 192.28–1 through 192.28–44, 192.33 through 192.37 (1959); MICH. COMP. LAWS §§ 335.5–335.78, 335.151–335.157, 335.201 –335.214 (1948, Supp. 1956); Mo. ANN. STAT. §§ 195.010–195.210 (Vernon 1952, Supp. 1960); N.J. STAT. ANN. §§ 24:19–1 through 24:18–49 (1940, Supp. 1960); N.Y. PUB. HEALTH LAW §§ 3300–3366; N.Y. PEN. LAW §§ 1747, 1751–1752; OHIO REV. CODE ANN. §§ 3719.01–3719.22, 3719.99 (Baldwin 1958, Supp. 1960).

6. CAL. HEALTH & SAFETY CODE §§ 11000–11797.

7. 9B UNIFORM LAWS ANNOTATED 279.

8. National Conference of Commissioners on Uniform State Laws, Prefatory Comment to Uniform Narcotic Drug Act, 9B U. L. A. 275 (1932).

9. UNIFORM NARCOTIC DRUG ACT § 1(14). This provision was incorporated in 1952 at the suggestion of the Federal Bureau of Narcotics because of the development of synthetic drugs. No state has enacted the precise language of this statute, but many have made provision for the easy inclusion of synthetic drugs legislation.

which contain narcotics in such small quantities as to create little danger.[10]

Who may sell and possess narcotics and under what conditions, is explicitly defined. The Act prescribes certain methods for transactions involving narcotics and prohibits all others. To facilitate control, provision has been made for the maintenance and preservation of documents and records reflecting all legitimate transactions in narcotics. Prohibitions clearly outlaw every contact with narcotic drugs except those expressly permitted by the Act, including activities indirectly facilitating illicit traffic such as maintaining a place where narcotics are used.

A section is set aside for penalties, but, of course, no penalties are prescribed or suggested. Much of the supposed variation in the state laws actually stems from the different treatment given to the penalty clause by the state legislatures.[11] The offenses created, together with their variations and degrees, are multiplex. However, comparative examination shows that despite the profusion of distinction in offenses based on such matters as the age of the parties or the drug involved, the application of control is fairly uniform in most jurisdictions.

Possession

THE POSSESSION of narcotic drugs, except as provided by the statutes, is uniformly prohibited. The prohibition is generally extended to cover actual as well as constructive possession.[12] Possession by one defendant is chargeable to a co-defendant where the circumstances show their complicity.[13] The control, care, or management of the drug must be real, not passing, fleeting, or shadowy.[14]

10. *Id.* § 8.
11. The penalty provisions of all the states and the District of Columbia appear in chart form in Appendix B, p. 149 *infra.*
12. State v. Campisi, 42 N.J. Super. A.D. 138, 126 A.2d 17 (1956), *reversed in part on other grounds,*
23 N.J. 513, 129 A.2d 880 (1957); People v. Matthews, 18 Ill.2d 164, 163 N.E.2d 469 (1960).
13. People v. Potter, 4 Misc.2d 796, 162 N.Y.S.2d 439 (1957).
14. United States v. Landry, 257 F.2d 425 (7th Cir., 1958).

The general proscription as to possession has been elaborated upon by statute and court decision. In New York, the quantity of illegal narcotics possessed may determine the charge and punishment. Possession of large amounts of drugs [15] creates a rebuttable presumption of intent to sell. The offense is a felony, and the penalties are the same as those for sale. Possession of a moderate amount of drugs [16] does not create the presumption, but is nevertheless a felony carrying a three- to ten-year sentence for the first offense. Possession of quantities less than that necessary for a felony is a misdemeanor, punishable by not more than a year in prison or a fine not in excess of $500.

Law enforcement officials interviewed in New York stated that the provisions of the statute hamstring the entire enforcement operation. Peddlers and addicts carry a grain or so less than the felony minimum, thus avoiding the risk of imprisonment. This practice impedes efforts to control the traffic and creates a morale problem. The statutory distinction based on amount possessed is criticized as being unrealistic. While it is designed to provide a more lenient and sympathetic treatment for the user, it results only in shielding the very peddlers who are victimizing the user.

The objections to the New York statute can readily be seen and appreciated. The statute nevertheless represents the first significant step by a legislature to reach the peddler and at the same time recognize that the addict should not be gathered up in the same net. While the problems inherent in the statute are apparent, it cannot be determined how extensive these

15. An aggregate of one or more ounces of a preparation containing 1% or more of either heroin, morphine, or cocaine or any marijuana, 100 or more marijuana cigarettes, two or more ounces of a preparation containing raw or prepared opium, two or more ounces of a preparation containing one or more of any of the prohibited drugs. N.Y. PEN. LAW § 1751(2).

16. An aggregate weight of one-eighth ounce of a preparation containing 1% or more of heroin, morphine, or cocaine, or one-quarter ounce of a preparation containing any marijuana, 25 or more marijuana cigarettes, one-half ounce of a preparation containing raw or prepared opium, or one-half ounce of a preparation containing one or more of any of the prohibited drugs. N.Y. PEN. LAW § 1751(3).

problems are. Figures on both arrests and convictions for narcotics offenses in New York show no decline since the statute was enacted in 1956.[17] In fact, there has been a fairly consistent rise. In the course of this research it was not possible to obtain from New York figures on arrests and convictions broken down by offense charged. A comparison of figures on a charge-by-charge basis before and after the enactment of the weight-test provisions might support some interesting conclusions as to its effect.

California and Ohio also create a separate offense of possession with intent to sell, but do not provide a presumptive evidence rule for the determination of intent, presumably leaving the determination to the attendant circumstances. Unlike New York, the penalties imposed, though still very heavy, are lighter than those for sale.[18] If the statutes are really aimed at reaching the drug peddler and protecting the addict from the harsher penalties, the New York practice of punishing possession with intent to sell as severely as sale would appear more valid. Why should the seller who has not found an opportunity to sell be treated more lightly than the seller who has made a sale? The peddler is regarded as a parasitic menace to society. If his incarceration is a social boon, the length of his sentence should not depend upon his success as a salesman, but rather upon the threat he poses to society.

The New York statute has the capacity to satisfy one coterie of critics of the present system of narcotics control. In its amount-of-drugs-possessed classification lies the possibility of discriminating between the small-time addict peddler who sells only a small amount of drugs to support his own habit, and the big-time operator. How realistic the permitted amounts are when considered from this point is another question. The amounts were cut drastically by the 1956 legislation.

---

17. Statistics provided by the Federal Bureau of Narcotics.
18. A first offense of possession for sale in California carries a five- to fifteen-year sentence; in Ohio, ten to twenty years.

The New Jersey statutes do not make a distinction between possession and possession for sale. A similar result was attempted, however, by interpretation of the Appellate Division of the New Jersey Superior Court.[19] Since addiction is made an offense under the Disorderly Conduct Act [20] and is not mentioned in the Uniform Narcotic Drug Act, the Court rationalized that both acts were intended by the Legislature to co-exist. Recognizing that some possession is inevitable in the use of drugs, the Court decided that such possession as was for imminent personal use was not the type of possession punishable under the narcotics law.

> Upon full study of the legislative history of the statutes referred to and of the evolving public policy relating to punishment of offenders in narcotics cases, the conclusion is inescapable that the enactment of the Disorderly Conduct Act provisions was intended to constrict the scope of the possession punishable under the Uniform Act. The over-all legislative purpose is (1) to impose severe, long-term penalties ... [under the Uniform Narcotic Drug Act] upon traffickers and those whose dealings with or possession of narcotics conduces to illegal distribution and use, and (2) to impose short-term rehabilitation-oriented sentences ... [under the Disorderly Conduct Act] upon those who do not deal in or otherwise handle narcotics illegally.[21]

The Supreme Court of New Jersey managed to escape the conclusion.[22] The high court stated that every possessor of narcotics has the power to dispense and, therefore, constitutes a potential source of illegal traffic. The main thrust of the opinion is a reflection of the arguments offered by law enforcement officials, namely, that any distinction between offenders based on addiction or non-addiction makes the task of law enforcement more difficult. Absent an express declaration by the

19. State v. Reid, 62 N.J. Super. A.D. 303, 162 A.2d 873 (1960).
20. N.J. STAT. ANN. §2A:170–8 (1940, Supp. 1960).
21. State v. Reid, *supra* note 19, at 878.
22. State v. Reid, 170 A.2d 419 (N.J. Sup. Ct., 1961).

Legislature, the Court refuses to recognize the distinction. Accordingly, the situation in New Jersey remains unchanged and typical of the interpretation placed upon the possession clauses of the statutes.[23] An addict may be, and frequently is, punished for his addiction and for possession of drugs.

Sale

THE PROHIBITION against sales of narcotics by unauthorized persons is generally construed to include almost every transaction between individuals in which illegal drugs are involved.

> The "sale" of narcotics prohibited by criminal statutes is much broader in scope than the concept of a sale which obtains in other branches of the law. It may include a transfer by gift as well as one for consideration in money.[24]
>
> ... A mere gift, a simple offer or agreement to sell, or the delivery to one who has agreed to purchase, constitutes a sale of narcotics, notwithstanding the fact that no consideration is paid or that the sale is not fully completed by payment of the agreed price.[25]

The interpretations made by the courts are in accord with the apparent intention of the legislatures to reach all transactions and to score with great severity the transfer of illicit drugs. In one area, however, the intent of the legislature is not so clear and the interpretations are predictably muddled. The federal statutes make no reference to prescriptions in the list of prohibited transactions. In order to reach the activities of physicians, the federal courts considered the writing of a prescription as a part of the transaction which results in sale by the druggist.[26] The early decisions indicated that a physician who

23. Despite the fact that possession is necessarily an element in sale or use, the United States Supreme Court has held, in a five-to-four decision, that each act may be punished by a separate sentence and the sentences may run consecutively. Gore v. United States, 357 U.S. 386, 78 Sup. Ct. 1280 (1958). See also 6 UTAH L. REV. 274 (Fall 1958); 67 YALE L.J. 916 (1958).

24. People v. Glass, 16 Ill.2d 595, 158 N.E.2d 639, 640 (1959).

25. People v. Robinson, 14 Ill.2d 325, 153 N.E.2d 65, 69 (1958).

26. See Annot., 13 A.L.R. 853 (1920).

acts in concert with a druggist by prescribing drugs for those not having a legitimate need for them is guilty of "sale." In *Doremus* v. *United States* [27] no concerted action was charged, but the court found that the facts left no doubt that in some instances the druggists filling the prescriptions knew of their illegal nature. The conviction of the physician for illegal sale was upheld on those counts where the facts supported such a conclusion. The intimation of the court was that such a finding would not be upheld on other counts where the facts did not so clearly indicate that the druggist knew that the prescriptions were unlawful.[28]

That the reservations of the court in *Doremus* were not long shared, is clearly demonstrated by the course of events in a 1946 New York case.[29] A physician pleaded guilty in a federal district court to a charge of "unlawful sale of narcotics." The sale charge was based on the doctor's prescribing drugs for an addict apart from the normal course of his professional practice. Sale being a felony, the Board of Regents of the University of the State of New York found that the physician's license to practice medicine was automatically revoked. State statutes provide for such automatic revocation upon conviction of any felony. There was no concert between the physician and the druggists who filled his prescriptions, and no evidence to suggest that the druggists knew or had reasons to suspect that the prescriptions were anything but legitimate. The physician-defendant asked the District Court for an amendment to the certificate of conviction showing the actual facts of the case. The District Court Judge wrote:

> I feel in the interest of justice that the application should be granted. The true fact is that what we actually call a sale was not made. It is a sale by reason of a legal conclusion. In other

27. 262 Fed. 849, 851 (5th Cir., 1920).
28. *Id.* at 853.
29. Tonis v. Board of Regents, 295 N.Y. 286, 67 N.E.2d 245 (1946).

words the defendant took part in an act which was part of a whole transaction which eventually resulted in a sale.[30]

The New York Court of Appeals held that the prescribing of a drug under the circumstances described is not a sale within the meaning of the state narcotic statute. The word "prescribe" is included among the prohibited activities in the state law, along with sale, barter, exchange, etc.; but the penalty section which establishes certain offenses as felonies does not include prescribing. The court held that the federal conviction for "sale" was not a felony conviction under the New York law, and that the physician's license could not be revoked automatically.

The problem confronting the New York court is not likely to occur frequently. The majority of states list all of the ways in which drugs may be transferred, including prescription and administration, in one section of the act. The penalty clause will provide one penalty for all violations of that entire section. Thus, in most of the states, the prescribing of drugs other than in the course of professional practice would be equated with sale. The question which confronted New York as to whether or not a legal sale actually occurred would not arise.

Professional practice

IN THE ATTEMPT to curb by legislation the illicit flow of narcotics, it was unavoidable that the legitimate flow would also have to be controlled. This meant that there must be regulation of the handling of drugs by the professional practitioner. The law permits the prescribing of drugs in the course of professional practice and in good faith. The obvious problems inherent in this language have been thoroughly discussed by competent writers,[31] and will not be belabored here. Certain

30. *Id.* at 287, 67 N.E.2d at 246 (1946).
31. JOINT COMMITTEE OF THE AMERICAN BAR ASSOCIATION AND THE AMERICAN MEDICAL ASSOCIATION ON NARCOTIC DRUGS, DRUG ADDICTION: CRIME OR DISEASE? (Interim and Final Reports, 1961);

AN EMPIRICAL EVALUATION OF THE AMERICAN SYSTEM

other direct and indirect regulations of professional practice do require comment.

California and Illinois [32] require all prescriptions for narcotics to be written on triplicate forms provided for that purpose by the state. Unauthorized possession of the blanks is a misdemeanor.[33] Enforcement authorities interviewed in Illinois stated that the official prescription blanks were a very significant weapon, since they almost completely removed the problem of forged prescriptions. Stolen prescription books were more easily traced because of the serial numbering. One copy of the form is retained by the physician; the second copy is filed by the physician with the state; and the third copy is given to the patient to present to the druggist who retains it in his file. This procedure makes state inspection of records much simpler.

Another aspect of the official forms, though praised by enforcement people, raises questions as to its desirability. The prescribing of narcotics for legitimate purposes has declined considerably since the adoption of the new forms. It is argued that the physicians are merely exercising more discretion than formerly in the doling out of narcotic preparations. While this may be true, it is inevitable that the necessity to file one copy of every narcotics prescription with the state interferes with the unrestricted exercise of discretion in prescribing. The constant superintendence of the physician's decision in the prescription of drugs cannot help but affect his selection of medication when the choice between narcotics and non-narcotics is close. Some of the people interviewed think this is as it should be. It would appear, however, that even the most indirect influence upon the doctor's choice of treatment "in good faith and in the

---

King, *The Narcotics Bureau and the Harrison Act: Jailing the Healers and the Sick,* 62 YALE L.J. 736 (1953); King, *Narcotic Drug Laws and Enforcement Policies,* 22 LAW & CONTEMP. PROB. 113 (Winter 1957); Note, *Narcotics Regula-*

tion: A Study in Irresolution, 34 TEMP. L.Q. 310 (Spring 1961).
32. CAL. HEALTH & SAFETY CODE §§ 11162, 11166.05; ILL. REV. STAT. ch. 38, §§ 192.28–13 through 192.28–16 (1959).
33. *Ibid.*

course of his professional practice only" should be weighed very carefully and utilized only as a last resort in the battle against drug use and traffic.

Narcotics agents in New Jersey and Ohio indicated that the triplicate prescription form is not necessary in their states. Close cooperation between the police, doctors, and druggists' associations has been effective in combating prescription forgery. Any lost or stolen prescription pad is reported to the police and the druggists' association, who in turn inform all druggists in the area of the theft and of the necessity to check carefully any prescriptions reported to have been written by the physician-victim. Enforcement agents in these states believe that their system is as effective against forgery as the official forms' method. If this be the case, the convenience of inspection is certainly not worth the dangers of inhibiting medical practice.

California reaches the furthest extreme in direct regulation with its statutory prescription for a course of treatment to be given by individual doctors to their addicted patients.[34] The statute permits a maximum dosage of narcotics which may be administered during withdrawal for the first fifteen days, a lower maximum for the second fifteen days, and prohibits administration thereafter. Institutional treatment of drug addicts is prescribed by law, and the acceptable institutions are specified. The requirement that all doctors treating patients for addiction register them with the state is designed to prevent addicts from taking "cures" from successive doctors or more than one doctor at a time and thereby obtaining a supply of drugs.

The wisdom of such a course is open to serious question. An immediate and obvious danger is the establishment of a precedent which permits the legislature under even the most competent advice to determine a proper course of medical treatment. Even if the authority to legislate such procedures is limited to

34. CAL. HEALTH & SAFETY CODE §§ 11390–11395, 11425–11426.

medical problems of great social significance, the danger is not greatly diminished. What is to prevent similar legislative determination of the proper course of treatment for alcoholism, venereal disease, or even mental illness? Further, the individuality of addiction problems discussed in Chapter Two clearly indicates that treatment must be fitted to the individual. The statutory drug allowances seem adequate for withdrawal, but the objections to a non-flexible statutory treatment program are not met by a showing that the treatment ordered is generally adequate.

Addiction

CALIFORNIA, the District of Columbia, Illinois, Michigan, and New Jersey make addiction an offense. Addiction is defined in these states in varying terms but includes occasional users as well as persons who may be physically addicted to narcotics. California and Illinois provide a mandatory sentence of not less than ninety days and up to one year. As much as five years probation may be imposed upon convicted addicts, conditioned upon their application for, and undergoing of, treatment for addiction. In any case, however, the ninety-day confinement must be served in a penal or medical institution. The legislation is a reflection of the strong feeling that rehabilitation must be undertaken only after the addict has been withdrawn from drugs, and that such withdrawal can be accomplished only in a drug-free environment. Michigan law provides a fine of not more than $2,000 and confinement for not more than one year. The statute also provides that any person sent to any institution under this section shall receive psychiatric and medical care aimed at curing his addiction. Separate provisions are made for civil commitment of persons not under charges for any crime. New Jersey, as discussed above, treats addicts as disorderly persons.

The District of Columbia has a unique approach, enacted in 1956. An addition to the Uniform Narcotic Drug Act provides for the punishment of vagrant narcotic drug users. The prosecution must show that the accused person is a drug user or a convicted narcotics law violator. In addition, it must be shown that he is a vagrant. In this act the latter requirement may be satisfied by showing the usual indicia of vagrancy, or that the accused is in any place where narcotic drugs are kept, found, used, or dispensed. The vagrancy requirement may also be satisfied by showing that the accused wandered about at late or unusual hours, either alone or in company of other drug users or drug law violators, and was unable to give a good account of himself. Only two cases dealing with the statute have been reported.[35] These cases rule that it is not necessary to show that the defendant knew that his associates were users or drug law violators, nor is it necessary to show that the defendant knew the place he was visiting was a place where drugs were kept or used. The result is that a narcotics user or drug law violator is held absolutely accountable for his associations and whereabouts. Punishment may be a fine of not more than $500 or imprisonment for not more than one year. In the discretion of the judge, conditions may be attached to the sentence, including medical examination and treatment.

The writer discussed the statutory classification of addiction as a crime with law enforcement officers in most of the states under study. Much opinion was given freely about the deterrent effect of the statutes, as well as their effectiveness against the "contagion" of addiction, their importance as a protection for society, and their function in persuading addicts to obtain treatment. Such arguments do not hold up under scrutiny since compulsory civil commitment could accomplish all of the same objectives. The real value to law enforcement officials is that such statutes provide an effective bargaining point in the search for further information. Addicts turn informer much more readily with the threat of imprisonment facing them. Under the

35. Jenkins v. United States, 146 A.2d   Harris v. United States, 162 A.2d
    444 (D.C. Munic. Ct. App., 1958);   503 (D.C. Munic. Ct. App., 1960).

terms of the vagrant-drug-user statute, every convicted narcotics offender would be subject to a new sentence for "vagrancy" for the slightest misstep. The justification for such an approach is not readily apparent. The infirmity created by the statute is enduring. Fifty years of exemplary behavior do not erase it. Successful treatment and subsequent abstinence from narcotics use do not remove it. The prospects for rehabilitation are dimmed considerably when the subject knows that no amount of effort on his part will eradicate a former error.

This latter objection is also applicable to the registration statute passed by the federal government [36] and the State of New Jersey.[37] Under the federal act, any narcotics user or person convicted of a violation of any narcotics law must register with customs officials on departure from and return to the United States. Failure to comply can bring a three-year sentence. Customs officials say that as a matter of practice, any person who has not been in trouble with the police for five years or more will not be bothered. Nevertheless, no such provision is made in the statute. Again, the courts have said that the public welfare nature of the statute removes any requirement of a criminal intent on the part of the violator. In short, if a person falls in the class of those required to register, there is no defense.

Similar is the New Jersey requirement that all persons convicted of narcotics offenses must register with the police in any place where they remain more than twenty-four hours. The penalty for failure may be a year in prison.

All of the arguments which are posed against the application of criminal sanctions to addiction are even more strongly applicable against the registration requirements. The only practical value in such requirements is that it gives the police notice of the identity and activities of narcotics violators. When one remembers that the narcotics enforcement officers insist that they

36. 18 U.S.C.A. § 1407 (Supp. 1961). 37. N.J. Stat. Ann. § 2A:169A (1940, Supp. 1960).

know virtually every addict in the country, it is difficult to justify this burden upon addicts and violators except as thinly disguised additional punishment.

Miscellaneous provisions

STATUTES in all the states under consideration include maintaining a place where narcotic drugs are kept or used within the definition of common nuisances and prohibit such nuisances. All have added hypodermic needles and paraphernalia for the administration of narcotics to the list of items, the possession and sale of which are regulated. The state statutes also provide for the forfeiture of vehicles used for the transportation of illicit drugs.

California and Illinois prohibit the sale of a non-narcotic substance under the misrepresentation that the substance is a narcotic. Both states provide a maximum of ten years imprisonment for the offense; Illinois adds a minimum of one year. The reason for the statutes is not clear. It strains credulity to believe that they were designed to protect the drug buyer from fraud. In view of the psychological aspects of drug addiction, it may have been felt that these bogus preparations served to continue the addiction habits during periods of drug scarcity. If this be the case, the penalty should be the same as that for sale, which it is not. Whatever be the reason, one result is apparent. It is not necessary to prove that a suspect sold an actual narcotic in order to prosecute him. If the substance proves to be other than a narcotic, or if the evidence is lost, or if the chain of custody breaks down, a possible ten-year sentence is still available on the more subjective evidence that the defendant furnished a substance alleged to be narcotic.

Illinois, Michigan, New Jersey, and New York require physicians to report all addicts who come to their attention. Several law enforcement officers interviewed in these states indicated that the requirement is not of great value. The police usually know about the addicts anyway. If the addict is seeking treatment voluntarily, the police don't want to bother him. This attitude further supports the view that the real purpose of the laws making addiction a crime is to facilitate the detection of larger crimes.

Sentences

THE VARIATION in the penal structure is charted in Appendix B *infra*. It will be noted that some states provide a minimum penalty for any violation of the provisions of the act. By its terms, this would include a failure to keep records as required by the statute, improper labeling, failure to return unused portions of narcotic drugs, and similar minor nonfeasance. Where there is a minimum penalty of not less than two years imprisonment for the first offense, it is difficult to believe that the penalty was intended to, or does, apply to minor infractions. Field research in these states would be necessary to determine what the actual practice is.

The chart and notes show the almost unanimous trend toward increasing the severity of penalties in all the states.[38] Maximum sentences of forty or more years as well as an increasing number of life sentences are liberally sprinkled through the provisions. Death penalties have been added for sales to minors. Nearly half of the states have some limitation on suspension, probation, or parole which applies specifically to narcotics violations. Occasionally there will be a backing off. Illinois repealed its provision requiring registration of all addicts. Missouri repealed its provision denying suspension, probation, and parole to all narcotics offenders. Such occasions are rare. Despite the dearth of really conclusive evidence of the effect of severe repressive laws, which will be discussed next, the statutes consistently

---

38. Since the preparation of the charts, California has passed Assembly Bill No. 9, May 4, 1961, which increased the penalties on all offenses, prohibited probation on second offenders and all offenses of adults selling any narcotic other than marijuana to a minor.

appear to reflect the idea that severity and severity only can cope with the problem.

II

The lack of accurate, complete, and fully-revealing statistics and data on the administration and effect of drug control policies in the United States is at one time understandable and astonishing. It is understandable because only recently has there been an appreciation of the complexity of the problem. Further, it is only recently that the policies have faced any serious challenge. The need for supporting information had not arisen previously. Yet it is astonishing that those charged with the administration of the laws did not, for their own edification, make adequate studies to determine how effectively the laws were meeting the drug problem. The paucity of data is even more astonishing in the light of the many unqualified claims made in the name of severe mandatory sentences. It is recognized that statistical compilations are not all-revealing. The opinions and experience of people who devote their lives to law enforcement are also valid and valuable sources of information. There are aspects of any clandestine activity which cannot be revealed in the reports of arrests, convictions, and sentences. There can be a detectable change in the attitude of "the street," reflecting changes in police or legislative policies. Such experience must be weighed carefully, but it is not a total answer for the inquirer who seeks to understand the workings of criminal laws, any more than the arrest rate is the total answer. Unfortunately, there is available much more opinion than fact.

The reasons for the lack of reliable information are many. Such system as exists for the collection of data relies on a pyramidal structure. Small areas report to large areas which report to districts which report to the federal agency. Obviously, the opportunity for omissions and duplications is multiplied. Rarely is there a clearly understood standard procedure for reporting, or for determining what is reportable. Where consistent established procedures exist, they vary considerably from place to place. In many areas, no special body is charged with the responsibility of accumulating information. The danger of lifting statistics compiled for a specific purpose and using them for another purpose is obvious, yet many narcotics reports are simply extracts from other reports. Many of the supposed reports showing narcotics activity are in reality compiled from statistical records showing *police* activity. A report showing the number of arrests made by a narcotics squad is a necessary and helpful document to a police commissioner, but 1,000 arrests may represent 200 offenders or even fewer.[39] To add to the confusion, terminology may vary greatly. Arrest may mean the act of bringing an individual to the police station, or it may mean placing charges against a suspect. Comparison requires extensive background study if *any* valid conclusions are to be drawn.

It is imperative to recognize the inadequacies of the "documentation" so freely supplied in the area of narcotics control. Some of it is valid; some is significant but questionable; some is so incomplete as to be useless. In every case it is necessary to discover the sources from which the information came, compare the purposes for which it was compiled with the proposition for which it is offered, evaluate consistency, discover the lacunae in coverage, and, where possible, reconcile differences in terms of reference. Following is a discussion of the data available from the areas which are the subject of this report. It is not intended that the matter presented here be taken as exhaustive of all sources, nor as an evaluation of all the information which can be secured. The critical analysis is offered as support for the conclusions and recommendations which will be offered later.

39. For example, the Chicago Police Narcotic Bureau has more than 85,000 files on narcotic offenders, but a new file is made each time a person is arrested. It cannot be ascertained how many offenders are involved, but during 1960, 96% of the arrests were of persons who had been arrested previously by the Chicago police on a narcotics charge.

Federal

THE BEST potential source of information on the activities of addicts, peddlers, and enforcement officials is the Bureau of Narcotics in the United States Treasury Department. This agency keeps records reflecting its own activity in the enforcement of federal narcotics laws. It also receives reports from state and local agencies throughout the country showing arrests, convictions, and juvenile violations of the narcotics and marijuana laws. Since 1953 the Bureau has maintained a running census of the addict population. From this central accumulation of reported activity one should be able to secure a fairly complete picture of narcotics activity across the nation. Unfortunately, the accuracy, completeness, and validity of the sources are so questionable that heavy reliance upon Bureau publications is dangerous.

The first big weakness in the compiled national figures is the lack of uniform standards to guide the reporting agencies. No state or local law enforcement agency interviewed had ever received from the Bureau of Narcotics a set of instructions for standardized reporting. In many cases the local federal agent assists in the preparation of state and city police reports, but obviously this cannot be done in every case. When asked about this deficiency, a spokesman for the Bureau indicated that such instructions were not necessary since "everybody knows what we want in the reports." Investigation revealed otherwise. One metropolitan narcotics agent in charge of preparing the reports stated that he had first provided the Bureau with a report showing the total number of arrests made by the Narcotics Squad of the city police. The report brought federal agents immediately, who revised the report to bring it into accord with the reporting practices of other cities. The Bureau did not want the report to show any offenses except those in which actual narcotics were a part of the evidence. Therefore, arrests for possession of hypodermic needles, addiction, maintaining a common nuisance, etc., were not included as "reportable" arrests.

Considering the responsibility of the Bureau to enforce the federal laws, which are tax measures on narcotic preparations, it is understandable that its officers should concern themselves chiefly with those cases in which possible violations of those laws are involved. Granting the propriety of their interest and system, it is still misleading to label such compilations "total narcotics and marijuana arrests and convictions." [40] Once the scope of the federal data is understood, it should still be possible to utilize them effectively for comparison of activity in different states and for comparison of chronological fluctuations, but again the lack of standard reporting methods casts doubt upon the reliability of the information compiled. Interviews with enforcement agents indicate that the confidence of the Washington office in the reporting system is not well-founded. The report form [41] is too abbreviated. It excludes arrests and convictions in which federal officers participated, but gives no indication of what is meant by participation. A new procedure inaugurated in one district for the careful checking of reports showed that past reports had been inaccurate. Local agencies were reporting cases which were properly federal cases. A single case might receive more than one reporting by one agency. When these misunderstandings were eliminated, the next report showed an appreciable drop in the number of offenses. Without carefully prepared guides and without meticulous scrutiny of reports, it is to be expected that the same situation obtains elsewhere.

Changes in the subject matter of the reports also contribute to comparison difficulty. Despite former practices to the contrary, Chicago reported arrests for addiction and possession of needles and other paraphernalia for the first time in 1960. Such

40. The tables furnished by the Narcotics Bureau to this project bear the following introductory note: "The following table shows the total narcotic and marijuana arrests and convictions, both Federal and local, reported to the Federal Bureau of Narcotics, for the calendar years 1953 through 1959."

41. See Appendix C, p. 195 *infra*.

a change, if published without an explanatory notation,[42] would make illicit activity in Chicago appear to have doubled in the last year when such is far from the case. Copies of the Cincinnati report for 1960 show that needle cases were also included in that city. A breakdown of all arrests reported showed 12 arrests for possession of needles. It also showed a total of 72 arrests, although the total on the form was only 68. When other materials were consulted, it was revealed that the breakdown actually referred to charges, not to arrests. The discrepancies are small in this case, but the possibility of immense multiplication across the country is overwhelming. With the breakdown and back-up papers from Cincinnati, it was possible to reconcile the differences, but when nothing is available except the report form, one can only conjecture as to what is intended.

A request to the Bureau of Narcotics for information on the sentences actually imposed upon narcotics violators brought the reply that the Bureau had no information. When one remembers that the Bureau of Narcotics is the staunchest proponent of severe mandatory sentences as an effective control measure, this reply is astounding. It was suggested that the Administrative Office of the United States Courts might be able to provide data for the federal courts. No source was suggested for information on the sentences imposed by state courts. The Federal Bureau of Prisons and the court administrator were able to provide several illuminating pieces of information.

Sentences in the Federal District Courts have increased markedly. The effect of the 1956 Narcotic Control Act is apparent. The mandatory sentence provisions have increased the average length of sentences by more than two years. Thus, while the number of commitments has declined from 1,531 to 1,190, the number of persons confined has increased from 3,241 to 3,672. Of the total confined, 2,129 are denied any pos-

---

42. At the time of this writing the 1960 figures have not been made available.

sibility of parole. The proportion of narcotics violators in the federal prison population has shown similar changes. Drug offenders constituted 8.7 percent of all commitments to federal prisons in 1960, but 17.4 percent of the prison population were serving drug sentences during 1960.[44]

Table 1.—Drug-Law Violators Received from Court and Confined in Federal Institutions

Fiscal Years Ended June 30, 1955 to 1959 [43]

Drug-law violators	1955	1956	1957	1958	1959	Percent change 1955–1959
Commitments	1,531	1,323	1,452	1,402	1,190	−22.3
Average sentence (months)	45.5	45.2	57.1	69.4	71.3	56.7
Confined at year-end	3,241	3,181	3,306	3,500	3,672	13.3
Average sentence (months)	55.5	58.9	66.4	75.7	81.3	46.5
Those confined under the provisions of the 1956 Narcotic Control Act who are ineligible for parole	0	0	479	1,394	2,129	. . .
Percent of total drug-law violators confined	0	0	14.5	39.8	58.0	. . .

An interesting sidelight to the sentencing data is the discrepancy in the average sentences being given in district courts in different circuits, and even in the same circuit.[45] In 122 convictions in the First Circuit, District Court judges gave an average of 48.6 months imprisonment. In 80 convictions in the Seventh Circuit, the average sentence was 100.4 months. Within the Seventh Circuit, average sentences ranged from 65.4 months for the Southern District of Indiana to 122.6 months for the

43. U.S. Dep't of Justice, Bureau of Prisons, Federal Prisons 1959, at 20 (1960).
44. Data supplied by the Federal Bureau of Prisons.

45. Data supplied by the Administrative Office of the United States Courts.

Northern District of Illinois. Probation followed the same scheme: First Circuit, 29.5 percent received probation; Seventh Circuit, 5.3 percent received probation.

The imposition of heavy sentences is regarded by many as the ultimate weapon against narcotics traffic and use. As discussed above, adequate data to support this contention are not available. However, using the statistics supplied by the Bureau of Narcotics for what they are worth, the following table of extracted data certainly raises a question as to the validity of the argument. The First Circuit, which has shown a markedly more lenient sentencing philosophy, has had a marked reduction in total narcotics arrests and convictions; the Seventh Circuit has had an increase.

Table 2.—Total Arrests and Convictions by Federal
Agencies in the States of the First and Seventh
Circuits, 1956 and 1959 [46]

	1956		1959	
	Arrests	*Convictions*	*Arrests*	*Convictions*
1st Circuit				
Mass.	18	19	7	5
Maine	2	2	0	0
N.H.	1	1	0	0
R.I.	2	2	3	0
Total	23	24	10	5
7th Circuit				
Ill.	230	146	396	180
Ind.	34	6	24	26
Wis.	0	0	0	2
Total	264	152	420	208

No great claims can emanate from a selected table such as this, but it can indicate that the results so often publicized are not a fully rounded picture of the effectiveness of incarceration

46. Data supplied by the Federal Bureau of Narcotics.

as a weapon against narcotics. The Federal Bureau of Narcotics published in 1958 a pamphlet of graphs purporting to show the results of mandatory penalties against peddlers under the Narcotic Control Act of 1956. The measure of results was the decrease in the number of *new addicts reported* in 1958 as contrasted with 1956. Taking the less manipulable figure of how many arrests were made for narcotics violations in the same states chosen for the Bureau's graphs, no such amazing improvements are shown. Translating the graphs to a table, following is the Bureau's summary of the results of the heavier penalties. The number of arrests have been inserted for comparative purposes. It will be readily noted that, except for Michigan, no state has shown a decrease in arrests comparable to the reported decline in addiction.

Table 3.—Arrests and New Drug Addicts Reported in Selected States for 1956 and 1958 [47]

State	1956		1958	
	Addicts	Arrests	Addicts°	Arrests
Dist. of Columbia	200	(218)	60	(174)
Ohio	92	(364)	37	(328)
Texas	523	(2,228)	175	(1,654)
La.	142	(321)	50	(758)
Mich.	543	(2,764)	264	(586)
N.Y.	4,138	(5,909)	2,836	(7,190)
Ill.	908	(9,301)	631	(9,351)
Calif.	1,568	(11,053)	1,276	(9,666)
Mo.	210	(401)	136	(571)

° Represents only first eleven months of 1958.

47. Data supplied by the Federal Bureau of Narcotics. It will be noted that discrepancies appear from time to time in the number of addicts reported for a given state in a given year. Such discrepancies are present in the source materials furnished by the Bureau. The number of new addicts ascribed to each state in the pamphlet (*supra* note 3) never agree with the figures in the materials supplied by the Bureau to this project, nor do they agree with the Bureau's official report. See U.S. TREASURY DEP'T, BUREAU OF NARCOTICS, TRAFFIC IN OPIUM AND OTHER DANGEROUS DRUGS 42 (1960).

According to data prepared by the Bureau of Narcotics, the number of drug addicts has gone down appreciably as a result of the mandatory penalties against peddlers, yet the number of narcotic offenses has increased appreciably in several of the jurisdictions. By adding 1953 to the comparison study, even more confusion results.

Table 4.–New Drug Addicts Reported in Selected States for the Calendar Years 1953, 1956, and 1958

State	Reported Addicts		
	1953	*1956*	*1958**
Dist. of Columbia	254	200	60
Ohio	362	92	37
Texas	362	523	175
La.	25	142	50
Mich.	425	543	264
N.Y.	2,975	4,138	2,836
Ill.	2,881	908	631
Calif.	388	1,568	1,276
Mo.	116	210	136

* Represents only first eleven months of 1958.

The fact that some states were showing a decrease before the Narcotics Control Act was passed would suggest that all the credit for the depicted "results" is not due to the Act.[48] Why the unknown factors contributing to this decrease were not operating in the six states showing an increase, is a compelling question. The penalty provisions of the Boggs Act, hailed as a great step forward, were in effect during this entire period. The most obvious answer to the questions posed by these figures is that the statistics are so unreliable, the criteria so ephemeral, and the selection so subject to conscious or unconscious bias, that they cannot be taken as answering anything.

The question of the addict population of this country is just

48. It might be pointed out that during the same time that the states selected for the graphic representation were showing decreases, eleven states adjacent to them were showing increases.

as subject to dispute today as it was when the earliest estimates were made. Unlike the early figures, today's statements on the extent of addiction are clothed in the impeccable raiment of "actual" counting of addicts. The completeness of the count is sustained by the oft-announced maxim that no illicit user can escape detection for more than two years. The accuracy of this statement cannot be easily determined, but it can be demonstrated that all of the addicts do not find their way so readily into the files of the Federal Bureau of Narcotics.

Many factors affect the discovery of addicts, not the least being the concentration of public attention and police activity on narcotics problems in a particular area. The Federal Bureau, for example, listed only 388 new narcotic addicts in California in 1953. Before that time, although California had been recognized as having a serious problem, it had never been considered in the same class with New York and Illinois. Then the California Citizens' Advisory Committee to the Attorney General began an investigation of narcotic addiction in the state. The Committee Report [49] disclosed that state criminal files reflected 10,000 addicts. The Committee believed that the illicit addict population of California was nearer 20,000, excluding 32,000 persons known to be using narcotics legally. The report was published in March 1954. The Federal Bureau's figure on new addicts reported in California began to climb immediately (Table 5).[50]

By 1959 California had replaced Illinois in the Bureau's statistics as having, after New York, the most severe addict problem in the United States. Nothing has appeared to explain the sudden rise in the addict population of California except the exposure made by the Citizens' Committee.

The comparison of reported addiction with reported offenses also raises questions about the accuracy of the addict census.

49. CITIZENS' ADVISORY COMMITTEE TO THE ATTORNEY GENERAL ON CRIME PREVENTION, NARCOTIC ADDICTION—REPORT TO ATTORNEY GENERAL EDMUND G. BROWN 22 (California, 1954).

50. Data furnished by the Federal Bureau of Narcotics.

Table 5.—New Drug Addicts Reported
in California, 1953—September 1960

1953	388
1954	893
1955	862
1956	1,567
1957	1,262
1958	1,436
1959	914
First 9 months of 1960	1,080

For example, the State of Utah is reported as having only one active narcotic addict as of the end of 1959. There have been only three reported addicts since 1953. Yet the Bureau's report of arrests and convictions in Utah for the same period show 117 arrests and 101 convictions for narcotics violations. While the arrests may be for many offenses which do not involve addiction, it is indisputable that traffic and related offenses exist to supply the demand of the addict. It strains credulity to suggest that an operation of this magnitude existed for the benefit of one addict. Similar but less dramatic situations exist in the following states: [51]

Table 6.—Arrests and New Addicts Reported
in Selected States, 1953–1959

State	Narcotic Arrests	Addicts Reported
Del.	87	20
Idaho	11	4
Mont.	38	10
Wis.	1,023	225
Wyo.	10	0

Conversely for the same periods New Hampshire and Mississippi had twice as many addicts reported as arrests for narcotics violations.

51. *Ibid.*

The addict statistics are inconsistent within themselves and inconsistent also with other narcotics experience. The Commissioner of Narcotics stated that sixty percent of the addicts reported once to the Bureau are never reported again.[52] This means either that these addicts are not again resorting to the use of drugs or that they are not being caught. If the addicts are abstaining from drug use, the hope for "cure" is certainly not so grim as argued by critics of the treatment approach to narcotics problems. If the addicts are not being reported, the whole narcotics census can be regarded only as a fragment of the total addict population. The lack of standards in reporting again becomes a nemesis. No agency interviewed had been advised of a criterion for reporting addicts. Some were not clear as to whether or not medical addicts coming to the attention of the police should be reported. Habitual users of cocaine and marijuana are not generally reported or included in the publications of the Bureau. The criteria for "active addiction" are not clearly drawn. From 1953 through September 1960, 62,036 persons were reported to the Bureau as new addicts. Yet the Bureau says that the total population of active addicts is 44,842. When queried on this point, Commissioner Anslinger replied that when the Bureau has heard nothing about an addict "for several years," and "investigation" fails to turn up anything about him, the addict is presumed to be no longer active and is removed from the list. Consider the following: In 1957 the total active addict population was reported to be 44,146. Since then 18,429 *new* addicts have been reported, but the total population has increased only 696. In less than three years nearly 18,000 addicts have disappeared.

There is no way known to check the completeness of the Bureau's figures. Nevertheless, when compiled by consistent reporting methods, the census can be valuable in gauging addiction in this country. Use of the census should be approached

52. U.S. Treasury Dep't, *op. cit. supra* note 47, at 12.

with care. Two points should be kept constantly in mind in any attempt to make evaluations based on the addict census. First, any comparison of reports of *known* addicts with early *estimates* will give a distorted picture of the effectiveness of legislation and enforcement policies. Second, decreases in the number of new addicts *reported* each year does not mean decreases in the number of new addicts *created* each year. As the enumeration of addicts continues and becomes more complete, the number of new addicts discovered each year will decrease even though the number of new addicts being created remains constant. A small number of new addicts in a given community after several years of reporting may indicate only that most of the addicts have been previously reported. It indicates nothing about the extent of the problem.

The activities of the Federal Bureau of Narcotics extend considerably beyond the administration of the federal laws. Advice is given freely by the Bureau as to proper methods of narcotic medication in the treatment of addiction as well as in the treatment of other illnesses requiring a pain reliever. A pamphlet dealing with the dispensing and prescribing of drugs [53] states that procedures described therein are intended only to advise medical practitioners, but the advice is buttressed with awesome citations of the legal consequences of departing from the suggested procedures. Recently the Bureau prepared the following draft resolution to be furnished to state medical societies, through which delegates to the American Medical Association would be instructed to oppose research into any methods of treatment not requiring institutional confinement during withdrawal.

WHEREAS the American Medical Association and the American Bar Association have had committees studying the problem of narcotic drug addiction, and

---

53. U.S. TREASURY DEP'T, BUREAU OF NARCOTICS, PRESCRIBING AND DISPENSING OF NARCOTICS UNDER THE HARRISON NARCOTIC LAW (Pamphlet No. 56, rev. 1938).

WHEREAS successful and humane *withdrawal* of individuals addicted to narcotics in the United States necessitates constant control under conditions affording a drug-free environment, and always requires close medical supervision, and

WHEREAS the successful treatment of narcotic addicts in the United States requires extensive post-withdrawal rehabilitation and other therapeutic services,

BE IT RESOLVED that the _____ expresses the opinion that maintenance of stable dosage levels in individuals addicted to narcotics is generally inadequate and medically unsound and that ambulatory clinic plans for the withdrawal of narcotics from addicts are likewise generally inadequate and medically unsound; and

BE IT FURTHER RESOLVED that the _____ delegates to the American Medical Association be instructed (a) to oppose the development of such ambulatory treatment plans, and (b) to support (1) after complete withdrawal, follow-up treatment, including that available at rehabilitation centers, (2) measures designed to permit the compulsory civil commitment of drug addicts for treatment in a drug-free environment, (3) the advancement of methods and measures towards rehabilitation of the addict under continuing civil commitment, and (4) the establishment of methods for the dissemination of factual information on narcotics addiction to members of the medical profession.

Sometimes the activities of the Bureau are more subtle and enigmatic. When the report of the Joint Committee of the American Bar Association and the American Medical Association on Narcotic Drugs was published by Indiana University Press, a Federal agent appeared at the University to make inquiries about the publication. The agent wanted to know about the reasons for publishing the book, the way it would be financed, and the number of copies to be printed. "He showed an amazing interest in financial details." [54] Commissioner Anslinger said that the agent had merely been instructed to

54. Washington Post, April 19, 1961, Sec. A, p. 3, col. 1.

buy a copy of the book,[55] but records of the press show that the Deputy Commissioner ordered the book for the Bureau on March 30, 1961. The Federal agent did not visit the Press until April 4.[56]

There is no question but that the Bureau of Narcotics has played a significant role in reducing the narcotics traffic in this country. It is equally beyond question that its efforts are necessary in any future program for control. The question is where those activities should be directed. Eliminating illicit access to drugs will certainly eliminate illicit addiction. This would seem to be the Congressional mandate to the Bureau. Attempts to formulate medical policy, to circumscribe treatment methods, to belittle the motives of those who seek new answers to narcotics problems, and to make "official" inquiries or investigations into sources of disagreement with Bureau policies—all these activities seem to fall outside the mandate to the Bureau and to create an unfavorable atmosphere for the concerted effort necessary to conquer addiction.

Discussion of the information available from the states is to a large extent repetitive of the matters referred to above in relation to the accumulation of federal information. For a clear picture of the problems involved in completing a study of the administration of the laws, however, certain distinguishing characteristics will be set out briefly.

California

FEW STATES have recognized the necessity for accumulating a whole body of information on the addict, his addiction, and the traffic which supplies him. California is one of the few. Beginning with the Citizens' Advisory Committee Report,[57] a series

55. Washington Post, April 21, 1961, Sec. B, p. 4, col. 4.
56. Communication to author from Alfred R. Lindesmith, Professor of Sociology, Indiana University.
57. CITIZENS' ADVISORY COMMITTEE TO THE ATTORNEY GENERAL ON CRIME PREVENTION, NARCOTIC ADDICTION—REPORT TO ATTORNEY GENERAL EDMUND G. BROWN (California, 1954).

of studies has been made aiming at understanding more of the complex factors in the narcotics problem.[58] This probing has produced more knowledge in the last two years about narcotics traffic in California than all previous investigation and study. Unfortunately, it is not possible to make an assessment of changes in the California situation because no such complete information exists prior to 1959.

The studies provide a great deal of valuable information about arrests—15,606 adult arrests during fiscal year 1960. This total included 12,365 different persons. Charted information is available as to the age, sex, previous criminal records, and particular offenses involved in the arrests made during the last nine months of the fiscal year, a total of 12,064. While the studies included dangerous drugs other than marijuana and the opiates, only 2,071 were involved in such offenses. Prior criminal records are surveyed from two points of view: general criminal record and narcotics criminal record.

Disposition of arrests made was left for later analysis. The present report, admittedly only a summary of narcotics statistics, unfortunately did not probe in depth. Dispositions are treated only as to types—prison, Youth Authority, probation, or jail; they are not broken down by particular offenses. It is anticipated that later reports will provide much more of the desired information.

Certain information contained in the Summary Report is interesting in the context of this study. Comparing 1954 and 1959, and taking population increases into account, the over-all felony rate increased 13 percent in the Los Angeles area and 6 percent in the rest of the state. The narcotics felony arrest rate increased 49 percent for Los Angeles and 7 percent elsewhere. Conviction rates were the reverse. In Los Angeles the

58. STATE DEP'T OF JUSTICE, BUREAU OF CRIMINAL STATISTICS, NARCOTICS ARRESTS IN CALIFORNIA (JULY 1, 1959–JUNE 30, 1960); STATE DEP'T OF JUSTICE, BUREAU OF CRIMINAL STATISTICS, SUMMARY NARCOTIC STATISTICS FOR CALIFORNIA (1954–1959).

rate of conviction for all felonies increased 22 percent; narcotics felony conviction rates increased only 3 percent.

As stated previously, the California effort is one of the most significant in the country. Comments by the compilers indicate a keen awareness of the weaknesses in the sources of information and the limited application which such studies should receive. At the same time there is an awareness of the necessity for truly comprehensive information. Complete information is not being received currently, but efforts are aimed at getting it. A study of the characteristics of the narcotics offender in prison and on parole was completed in 1960.[59] After three or four years the accumulated data should afford an excellent opportunity for the evaluation of narcotics policies in California. For the present, however, the studies can serve only to demonstrate incontrovertibly that past reporting methods have been so inadequate that the true state of California narcotics problems was never revealed.

District of Columbia

VERY LITTLE information is available aside from that reflected in the Federal Bureau's compilations. Information secured from the Metropolitan Police Department, however, shows some disagreement with that furnished by the Federal Bureau of Narcotics (see Table 7 below).

Certainly some of the difference can be explained by the fact that the Federal Bureau is not ordinarily interested in offenses except those involving actual narcotics. It would be expected nevertheless that arrests resulting in felony charges would find their way into annual compilations of "total narcotic and marijuana arrests" by the local authorities. It will be noted that in every year except 1959, felony arrests alone, as recorded by the police, exceeded the total arrests reported by the Federal Bureau.

59. CALIFORNIA DEP'T OF CORRECTIONS, CALIFORNIA NARCOTICS   OFFENDERS IN STATE PRISON AND ON PAROLE (1959, unpublished).

Table 7.—Comparison of Reported Arrests of Drug Law Offenders in the District of Columbia, 1953–1959

Year	Arrests by Local Authorities *			Arrests by Local Authorities **		
	Narcotics	Marijuana	Total	Felony	Misdemeanor	Total
1953	230	7	237	270	10	280
1954	164	17	181	215	6	221
1955	183	6	189	260	11	271
1956	167	9	176	186	44	230
1957	121	14	135	180	120	300
1958	110	24	134	187	57	244
1959	162	5	167	124	73	197

    * Source: Bureau of Narcotics.
    ** Source: D.C. Police Dept.

A similar comparison of statistics on new addicts reported, raises additional questions concerning reporting procedures, compilation techniques, and criteria for determination of active addiction.

Table 8.—Comparison of Reported New Narcotics Addicts in the District of Columbia, 1953–1960

Year	By Bureau of Narcotics	By D.C. Police Dept.
1953	254	366
1954	317	265
1955	278	188
1956	242	185
1957	175	150
1958	109	118
1959	125	102
1960	113 *	173
Total	1,613	1,547

* First 9 months of 1960.

These discrepancies are not large and are probably explained by the fact that some addicts were known previously to one agency and not to the other. Other questions are presented, however, when this information is taken together with statements about the total addict population in the District. Between the years 1955–1959, the District police discovered 743 new addicts. Department representatives interviewed, estimated the present population at between 700 and 1,100. During the same period of time the Federal Bureau reported 929 newly. discovered addicts. As of December 31, 1959, the Bureau placed the active population at 1,116.[60] But, on September 30, 1960, the Federal Bureau reported an amazing reduction. In nine months the addict population had declined to 521.[61]

What brought about this almost unbelievable change? The Narcotic Control Act had been in effect for over four years, and, while the number of new addicts reported declined in the years following its passage, still more than 700 new addicts were reported during 1956–1960. Civil commitment was available, but persons interviewed in Washington considered that its effect was nil. Of the 415 persons committed in the first nine months of fiscal year 1961, 403 had been released by May 1961. No significant changes in the personnel or policies of the District enforcement were reported, and no satisfactory explanation has appeared. Yet the District showed a decline of 695 addicts while the rest of the nation showed an increase of 386.

If records were available to conduct the kind of study envisioned by this project, it might be possible to determine why there was such an astounding decrease, or else to show that it did not exist. Unfortunately such records are not available.

Illinois

AVAILABLE information in Illinois is tantalizingly inadequate. During the period 1957–1959, the statutory structure for the control of narcotics traffic and use was overhauled after extensive study by a state commission.[62] A Division of Narcotic Con-

60. U.S. TREASURY DEP'T, *op. cit. supra* note 47.
61. Data supplied by the Federal Bureau of Narcotics.
62. ILLINOIS NARCOTICS AND DANGER-OUS DRUGS INVESTIGATION COMMISSION, REPORTS: March 25, 1957; May 15, 1959; May 31, 1961.

trol was established to aid in the enforcement of the law.[63] Among other duties the statute required that the division shall:

> ...advise and inform local and other State law-enforcement officers of various narcotic law-enforcement practices and shall establish a central office where local and other State law-enforcement officers may report narcotic violations and obtain information about narcotic violators. Every local and other state law-enforcement officer shall report any violation of the narcotic laws of this state to the Division.[64]

> The Superintendent shall in an annual report to the Governor, report the results obtained in the enforcement of this Act, together with such other information and recommendations as he deems proper.[65]

Unfortunately, so far as reported data reveal, the Division has concerned itself almost exclusively with its enforcement responsibilities. The especially unfortunate aspect of this development is that considerable data are available for the period before the establishment of the Division. But when the Division was created, the Crime Prevention Bureau which had previously compiled data for Chicago, ceased to do so, believing that the state agency would take over this task. The data compiled by the Crime Prevention Bureau, though it left many important questions unanswered, could have provided a satisfactory basis for some valid comparisons of the situation before and after the 1957 legislation. Persons interviewed in connection with narcotics control in Illinois expressed the opinion that the securing of convictions was fulfillment of its responsibilities. The Division was, of course, not created to provide statistical data to research projects, but it is difficult to understand how the Division can report the results obtained under the present program without obtaining data on the number of charges dismissed, the sentences given, the number suspended, the addicts

63. ILL. REV. STAT. ch. 127, §§ 55d–   64. Id. § 55h.
    55e (1959).   65. Id. § 55l.

treated, and follow-up studies of probation. If such records have been kept, they have been zealously guarded from public view.

The Chicago Police Department, though solely a law enforcement agency, provides a better source of information. The importance of extricating significant statistics from the mass of data in their files has been recognized and to some extent implemented. The files probably include a wealth of information of great utility in a comprehensive research effort, but such data are not easy to work with. The Chicago Police Department, like other purely enforcement agencies, does not have the responsibility to conduct statistical research, nor does it have the facilities to do so. Nevertheless, certain data have been extracted from the records which will prove to be of assistance. Sentence data on persons arrested by the Narcotics Section are available, though not correlated with the offense involved. Though in any given year the Department can tell how many arrests involved repeating offenders, it cannot be determined from the reports how many individuals were arrested nor how many times they had been arrested previously for narcotics offenses. Such information could be obtained from the more than 85,000 files maintained by the Department, but the effort would be monumental.

Age information is available in the reports of the Narcotics Section to the Superintendent of Police. A special report [66] for use in conjunction with the 1959 Annual Report contains especially illuminating data, which is reproduced in Table 9 below.

The table shows clearly that the ranks of narcotics offenders are not being replenished by young neophytes. The youngest group has shown a steady decline as its members moved into the 21–25 year category. This category experienced a rise in percentage as its ranks were swelled by incoming younger

66. CHICAGO POLICE DEPARTMENT, NARCOTICS SECTION, A SPECIAL REPORT IN SUMMATION OF NAR- COTIC PROBLEMS 2 (April 15, 1960).

Table 9.—Age of Persons Arrested for Narcotic Violations in Chicago, 1951, 1955, 1959

Year 1951 (Gross Arrests, 6,742)		Year 1955 (Gross Arrests, 7,454)		Year 1959 (Gross Arrests, 10,296)	
17–20 years	24.8%	17–20 years	10.7%	17–20 years	6.0%
21–25 years	39.6%	21–25 years	38.2%	21–25 years	26.5%
26–30 years	16.7%	26–30 years	31.2%	26–30 years	34.3%
31–35 years	7.2%	31–35 years	10.1%	31–35 years	20.6%
36–40 years	5.0%	36–40 years	4.9%	36–40 years	7.2%
41–45 years	2.4%	41–45 years	2.5%	41–45 years	2.5%
46–50 years	22.0%	46–50 years	1.0%	46–50 years	1.6%
51 years and over	2.3%	51 years and over	1.4%	51 years and over	1.3%
	100.0%		100.0%		100.0%

members, but then began a decline as offenders passed twenty-five. The 26–30 and 31–35 age groups have shown steady increases, but it is to be anticipated that the 26–30 age group will show a proportionate decline in the 1964 summary. Of course it may be pointed out that the gross arrests during the period have increased 52.6 percent, so that the absolute number of arrests has not fluctuated so markedly as the table suggests. What is not apparent, however, is that the repeat arrests arose from 38 percent in 1951 to 96 percent in 1959. This means that only 412 new offenders were involved in 1959 as contrasted with 4,180 in 1951. Unfortunately, no breakdown of new offenders by age groups is available.

An expression of firm conclusions from the data readily available in Illinois would require unwarranted extrapolation. Field studies of Chicago experience coupled with implementation of the responsibilities of the State Division could be very revealing.

Michigan

REQUESTS addressed to the officials responsible for the administration of the laws in Michigan elicited replies that the types of data desired in this project were not compiled in any one place and would have to be collected from the municipalities within the state. Some statistical records are kept by the Detroit police, but they reflect essentially the information reported to the Federal Bureau of Narcotics. These data have been discussed earlier in this report.

No state has gone along with the proponents of severe mandatory penalty legislation more strongly than Michigan. The penalty for the first offense of selling is a minimum of twenty years without possibility of suspension or probation. One would expect that the proponents of such legislation would cite Michigan as a glowing example of the changes wrought by the legislation. The fact that they do not can be readily appreciated because the legislation has not worked in Michigan.

> Graphic evidence as to what has happened under the strict Michigan laws to prosecutions of narcotics peddlers can be found in the statistics compiled by the Detroit Narcotics Squad since 1952. During the last eight years 1,005 defendants have been charged with narcotics violations. Out of this number only 30 individuals have been convicted of peddling narcotics. This represents about 3.3 percent of the total number of narcotics peddling cases filed. Most of the remainder of these cases resulted in guilty pleas to lesser offenses.[67]

The question is why? The California Commission in its study of Michigan concluded that the judges in Detroit felt that the law was too harsh and that it was unjust to deny judicial discretion in the sentencing of prisoners. They refuse to support a law which does not provide for consideration of the surrounding circumstances, the seriousness of the offense, or the amount of narcotics involved.[68] An as yet unpublished study by the Ameri-

67. California Special Study Com-   68. *Ibid.*
    mission on Narcotics, Interim
    Report 28–29 (1960).

can Bar Foundation of the administration of criminal justice reported that juries were unwilling to convict persons of sale of narcotics when the penalty was set so high.

Whatever the reason for the Michigan situation, it is clear that the legislation has not appreciably affected the problem in the state. With a population comparable to that of either Ohio or New Jersey, Michigan still has, after eight years of the mandatory penalty, more than four times as many addicts as Ohio and more than twice as many as New Jersey.[69] The reasons could doubtless be discovered in the policies of enforcement officers, prosecutors, and the judiciary, but it will require an intensive search of office records and the compiling of the data from scratch. Such an effort seems to be necessary. In answering the criticisms of the Michigan results, proponents of mandatory penalties reply that implicit in their proposals is the requirement of wholehearted cooperation and support from all branches concerned with the implementation of the law. The Michigan experience, if examined closely, may show that such cooperation is impossible to achieve. At least it demonstrates that there must be general sympathy among those responsible for the enforcement of legislation or it will not work.

Missouri

ASIDE from the material provided to the Federal Bureau of Narcotics and reflected in its records, virtually no information is available in Missouri. The Division of Health in the Department of Health and Welfare is charged by the state with responsibility for the implementation of the narcotics act. A reply from that agency indicated that the material asked for in connection with this project was not obtained or assembled by the Division. Similar requests to the police departments of St. Louis and

69. Data furnished by the Federal Bureau of Narcotics showed that as of September 30, 1960, Michigan had 2,196 addicts, Ohio had 454, and New Jersey had 921.

Kansas City elicited replies that the data were not available, though St. Louis is working on accumulating data on the drug problem in that city.

New Jersey

THE TOTAL retrievable information on narcotics use and traffic in New Jersey is published in the annual reports of the New Jersey Commission on Narcotic Control.[70] The six reports of the Commission are a welcome change from the usual paucity of information. The New Jersey Commission was created in 1953. It is not an enforcement body, but an organization charged with the responsibility of studying narcotics laws on a continuing basis and of recommending legislation which will improve the effectual control of illegal use. The reports of the Commission show an ever-increasing awareness of the intricate nature of the addiction and traffic problems. As a result the studies of the Commission have reached out farther to gather, correlate, and publish data on more and more aspects of the problem as it exists in New Jersey.

All narcotics offenders are required to register.[71] Another statute requires the clerks of all courts to report to the State Bureau of Identification the sentence or disposition in every case of an offense against the narcotics laws.[72] By this procedure it has been possible to obtain some information on the social characteristics of the addict group, including residential mobility, employment status, prior offense pattern, age, and marital status. It was not, however, a simple matter to secure the information. Neither was it possible to obtain as complete a picture of the registered offender as was desired. Data were extracted on each registered individual from his case folder as maintained by the State Police Narcotic Bureau. The result of this first study, published in the Sixth Report of the Commis-

---

70. The first through the sixth reports cover the years 1955–1960.

71. N.J. STAT. ANN. § 2A:169A (1940, Supp. 1960).

72. *Id.* § 53:1–18.2.

sion, contains some interesting summaries but, more importantly, it demonstrates that it is possible to obtain, correlate, and analyze the data without a tremendous outlay of money and time. The adaptation of data-collecting methods to the resources readily available can produce a rewarding picture of the local narcotics problem. The utilization of punched card automatic retrieval makes it possible to analyze group characteristics with ease. All available information can be entered upon the cards without reference to its presently understood pertinency. There will be created thereby a file of information in which, as the study progresses, new characteristics can be looked for without a new search of records.

The studies are not exhaustive, nor is it claimed by the Commission that they are, but each year's report shows additional steps toward a more complete revelation of the characteristics of the narcotics offender. For the present, it is not possible to correlate the severity of sentences with the offenses involved, though this information can be extracted to some extent from police records. It is not possible to correlate the severity of sentences with the past records of the offenders. While data are summarized on the prior offenses pattern, the information does not reveal how many of the offenders had prior narcotics offenses, how many had received penal sentences, and how many had received treatment, nor does it show the parole and probation experience of the offenders. When such information is available and is coupled with the social diagnosis, it may be possible to reach an honest and meaningful conclusion about the effectiveness of enforcement policies.

In New Jersey, as elsewhere, the available data demonstrate the individuality of problems associated with addicts and offenders. Unlike many others, New Jersey officials decline to indulge in sweeping generalizations about these problems. The last report indicates that the Commission will continue to examine and analyze data obtained from registrants and will publish the results of such studies when possible.

New York

OVER 40 percent of the reported addicts in the United States are located in New York State, chiefly in New York City. As a result, there has been more concern, more investigation, and more reporting in New York than in any other state. The most recent and thorough report was made by a joint legislative committee.[73] This document is a deep and penetrating inquiry into the narcotics problems of the state. It is not comparable to the data gathering efforts of New Jersey and California, but is rather an examination of the situation in New York: public attitude, treatment, and correctional facilities; proposals for dealing with the problem; and recommendations for immediate action. The tenor of the Report shows a determination to avoid mere parroting of well-worn legislative pronouncements concerning narcotics. The Report offers no panacea for the State, but calls for additional research and for cooperation between official and unofficial agencies in the struggle to find an answer to the dilemma posed by narcotics.

The members of the Committee did not suggest any radical reforms in the state penal structure. It was recommended that minimum sentences on first narcotics felony offenses be removed so that judges will have the discretion to determine the best means of rehabilitating an early offender without resorting to the deception of accepting pleas to lesser offenses, thereby creating a false record. The present penalty for third narcotics felony offenses is a mandatory fifteen years to life. The Committee found no reason why narcotics should be an exception to the general rule applying such sentences to fourth offenders. Accordingly, it was recommended that the exception be repealed. Despite the attitudes of the enforcement personnel concerning the existing statutory distinction between offenses based on the amount of drugs possessed, the Committee did not

73. STATE OF NEW YORK JOINT LEGIS-
    LATIVE COMMITTEE, REPORT ON
    NARCOTIC STUDY (1959).

suggest repeal. Instead, it recommended that the statute be amended to add a quality measure to the simple weight measure in determining the applicability of penalties.

From an examination of court records the Committee found that all Manhattan courts were showing an increasing volume of drug cases. Prima facie cases were made in a larger percentage of drug violations cases than in other offenses. Conviction rates were higher for drug cases than for other types of offenses. Confinement was ordered in a higher percentage of cases and probation used more sparingly when the offense was a violation of narcotics laws. Stricter disposition trends were noted for felonious offenses as compared with misdemeanor offenses in all of the courts.

The information provided in the Committee Report falls short of providing the kind of data which this project considers essential. However, the data collected by the Committee demonstrate that a thorough-going search in the records of the courts of New York City could provide much of the indispensable data.

New York provides the only fully described study of the efficacy of parole as a weapon in the fight against narcotics.[74] A three-year special project was set up to test experimental techniques on paroled drug offenders. The effort grew out of the increasing paroled addict caseload in some New York districts and the frustration experienced by parole workers as their charges reverted to drug use over and over again. Something had to be done. "Narcotic hospital facilities were limited, and it was recognized that return to the institution in some instances served little purpose since the addict's problem is basically a problem of living in the community." [75]

The experiment was set up with established criteria for the

74. NEW YORK STATE DIVISION OF PAROLE, AN EXPERIMENT IN THE SUPERVISION OF PAROLED OFFENDERS ADDICTED TO NARCOTIC DRUGS (Undated). This report covers the three-year period November 1, 1956, to October 31, 1959.

75. Id. at 13.

experimental group. A control group was selected according to the same criteria. The techniques of the project were not significantly different from those employed in the usual caseloads; it was a matter of degree rather than kind. Caseloads were kept smaller so that the parole worker could devote a much larger amount of time to each person under his supervision. Careful planning before the project was launched provided for the maximum utilization of community resources in the rehabilitation of the paroled addict. Authority to deal with violations of parole was kept at a maximum of flexibility to allow each situation to be treated on an individual basis, taking into account the good of the parolee and the danger to the community.

The project report described in detail the procedures employed in working with the paroled addicts as well as the considerations affecting a choice of procedure with different individuals. The contributions and importance of community resources and agencies in the attempt to rehabilitate drug users is discussed in the light of project experience. A series of appendices provide meticulous analyses of the activities and results.

During the three years of the project, 344 parolees were supervised. For the full three-year period, 35 percent were never delinquent for any reason whatsoever. Forty-five percent never reverted to the use of drugs. It is recognized that some of the parolees had not been in the project for an extended period at the time of the report, and some of them will doubtless revert to drug use. Even so, when the criteria of "success" and "failure" are understood, the percentages cited above should hold. Any person who used one injection of drugs was deemed a "failure" even though he thereafter managed to abstain for the remainder of his supervision. Also, a person who had managed to abstain for a long period of time and then relapsed to drug use for even a short time was considered a "failure." These considerations would seem to balance the scale against those who may revert in the future.

These success figures are highly encouraging glimmers in the normally gloomy forecast of treatment and rehabilitation success. They are especially encouraging in terms of cost to the public.

It has been estimated that the cost of maintaining an inmate in a correctional institution in New York State is in excess of $1,900, while the cost of supervising a parolee in our Project is approximately $250. When one remembers that as productive members of the community they are in a position to support their dependents, thereby obviating the need for public and private welfare support, the savings reach tremendous proportions.[76]

New York is also unique in the maintenance of a treatment facility for adolescent drug users at Riverside Hospital in New York City. The work of the hospital and the procedures employed in committing patients to its care have been fully explained in a recent exhaustive follow-up study of discharged patients.[77] Sadly, the results have not been encouraging in terms of satisfactory adjustment of discharged patients. It must be remembered, however, that Riverside is working with immature youths. The problems of dealing with drug addicts are aggravated by normal problems of adolescence. The *Trussell Report* found that 96 percent of the dischargees have failed to make a satisfactory adjustment to community living. This means that they have experienced some kind of difficulty, not necessarily narcotics, with community living. Only five percent of the dischargees interviewed [78] had abstained from drug use after discharge.[79] This percentage is tragically low. The report did show, however, that 24 percent of the dischargees had abstained for six months or more after leaving the hospital.

76. *Id.* at 25.
77. COLUMBIA UNIVERSITY SCHOOL OF PUBLIC HEALTH AND ADMINISTRATIVE MEDICINE, A FOLLOW-UP STUDY OF TREATED ADOLESCENT NARCOTICS USERS (Ray E. Trus- sell, M.D., ed.) (1959). [Hereinafter referred to as TRUSSELL REPORT.]
78. See discussion of techniques in Chapter Two, pp. 30–32 *supra.*
79. TRUSSELL REPORT 9.

Authorities interviewed at Riverside consider this a very important finding. The ability to refrain for six months is pointed to as a significant step toward eventual recovery. Certainly any prolonged period of abstinence is helpful in that it serves to break the living patterns out of which addiction grows, but it is questionable whether the expenditure of $10,000 per patient per year is justified by the result.

The keen awareness of the government of New York State of the extent and danger of the narcotics problem and the open-minded approach to finding a solution holds great promise. The study and effort by government and private agencies shows a determination to meet the problem face on. At present, the information is not available to answer all of the compelling questions. The *Trussell Report* answers many of them for a very small group of selected adolescents. The Parole Project answers many more for a very small group of selected parolees. But the data necessary for the analysis of New York narcotic addiction, traffic, crime, prosecution, disposition, and recidivism are still to be extracted from the records of the police, prosecutors, courts, and prison authorities.

Ohio

THE ADMINISTRATION of the narcotics laws in Ohio rests with the police. There is no commission charged with the enforcement of the laws or the study of the problems of control. Inspection responsibilities are delegated to the State Board of Pharmacy. Requests to a state narcotics inspector for the information sought in connection with this project brought the reply that it could be secured only by gathering it from each police department in each city in Ohio. There is at present no compilation of data on the state's experience with narcotic drug control except that accomplished by the Federal Bureau of Narcotics. The only data ever received from Ohio were copies of the annual reports submitted by the police departments to the Federal Bureau.

Statistics compiled by the Ohio Bureau of Research and Statistics reflect the activity of the criminal courts in Ohio.[80] From these compilations it is possible to discover the number of narcotics offenses charged, the number disposed of, and the type of sentence imposed. It is not possible to determine from the report what types of offenses were committed, nor the length of the sentences imposed. The statistics indicate a decline in the number of cases filed in the courts, but there is no breakdown even into felony–misdemeanor classifications. Similar information on both state and federal courts was obtained from the Federal Bureau of Prisons. The striking thing about a comparison of this information is that the reduction in state charges, while quite large, is completely overshadowed by the reduction in federal charges. For convenience, both absolute figures and percentages on these dispositions are set out in Tables 10a and 10b on pages 98 and 99.

The danger of taking data such as this and attempting to demonstrate the changing situation in a given area without a thorough study of all the factors contributing can easily be demonstrated. Judging from these figures, the problem in Ohio is more serious today than it was in 1951–1953, a period which had the rest of the nation in a near panic over the mounting drug problem. It is not that the situation worsened in 1953, but that the state began a vigorous drive against narcotics, which pushed its totals high in 1954 and 1955. New legislation was passed in 1955 which, claims the Federal Bureau of Narcotics, has resulted in an 80 percent decline in addiction. While it is impossible to prove or disprove this assertion, it is possible to prove that violations charged in court have not declined to the extent evidenced by Tables 10a and 10b.

It will be noted that the conviction rate has declined from a 91 percent high in 1955 to a 77 percent low in 1959. During this

80. Ohio Dep't of Mental Hygiene and Correction, Bureau of Research and Statistics, Ohio Judicial Criminal Statistics (1959).

Table 10a.—Number of Persons Charged with Narcotic Violations Disposed of in Federal and State Courts in Ohio, 1951–1959 [a]

(T = Total; F = Federal; S = State. Federal figures are based on fiscal years ended June 30; state figures are based on calendar years.)

Year [a]	Total defendants (1)			Not convicted (2)			Convicted (3)			Type of Sentence								
										Imprisonment (4)			Probation (5)			Other (6)		
	T	F	S [b]	T	F	S	T	F	S	T	F	S	T	F	S	T	F	S
1951	—	—	104	—	—	23	—	—	81	—	—	49	—	—	15	—	—	17
1952	—	—	154	—	—	33	—	—	121	—	—	79	—	—	25	—	—	17
1953	—	—	155	—	—	24	—	—	131	—	—	79	—	—	36	—	—	16
1954	337	112	225	41	9	32	296	103	193	213	95	118	72	8	64	11	—	11
1955	418	135	283	44	18	26	374	117	257	315	110	205	47	7	40	12	—	12
1956	259	43	216	48	12	36	211	31	180	155	26	129	38	5	33	18	—	18
1957	250	12	238	49	1	48	201	11	190	154	10	144	38	1	37	9	—	9
1958	216	16	200	35	4	31	181	12	169	116	10	106	58	2	56	7	—	7
1959	181	6	175	40	—	40	141	6	135	93	6	87	45	—	45	3	—	3

Numbers in parentheses are guides for computing percentages (See Table 10b). [a] Federal data unavailable for years 1951–1953. [b] Excludes defendants charged with narcotics violation and found guilty of another offense.

Table 10b.—Percent of Persons Charged with Narcotic Violations Disposed of in Federal and State Courts in Ohio, 1951–1959 [c]

(*T = Total; F = Federal; S = State. Federal figures are based on fiscal years ended June 30; state figures are based on calendar years.*)

	Total defendants [a]						Convicted and Sentenced [b]								
Year [c]	Not convicted (2)			Convicted and sentenced (3)			Imprisonment (4)			Probation (5)			Other (6)		
	T	F	S	T	F	S	T	F	S	T	F	S	T	F	S
1951	—	—	22	—	—	78	—	—	60	—	—	19	—	—	21
1952	—	—	21	—	—	79	—	—	65	—	—	21	—	—	14
1953	—	—	15	—	—	85	—	—	61	—	—	27	—	—	12
1954	12	8	14	88	92	86	72	92	61	24	8	33	4	—	6
1955	11	13	9	89	87	91	84	94	79	13	6	16	3	—	5
1956	19	28	17	81	72	83	73	84	72	18	16	18	9	—	10
1957	20	8	20	80	92	80	77	91	76	19	9	19	4	—	5
1958	16	25	16	84	75	84	64	83	63	32	17	33	4	—	4
1959	22	—	23	78	100	77	66	100	65	32	—	33	2	—	2

[a] Percentages in columns 2 and 3 are based on column 1 in table 10a.
[b] Percentages in columns 4, 5, and 6 are based on column 3 in table 10a.
[c] Federal data unavailable for years 1951–1953.

same period of time the percentage of cases receiving probation at the hands of the courts has more than doubled. It is difficult to reconcile the views of the proponents of severe mandatory penalty legislation in this context. The Bureau of Narcotics has extolled the virtues of the statute in Ohio and its administration.[81] In the same breath it has said that "all of [the state narcotic laws] should be made as strong as the Boggs-Daniel Law [Narcotic Control Act of 1956]." [82] If the enforcement personnel in Ohio are still enforcing the law as strictly as they were in 1955, the results are salutary. The experience with a Boggs-Daniel type law in Michigan has not produced nearly the same results.

81. U.S. Treasury Dep't, Bureau of Narcotics, Prevention and Control of Narcotic Addiction 29 (1960).

82. Id. at 26.

Another fact which may account for a considerable portion of the reduction in narcotics offenses in Ohio is that the offenders are in prison.

One known contributing factor is the number of persons in Ohio correctional institutions serving sentences for narcotic law violations, i.e., such persons are not at large and cannot violate narcotic laws. In 1949 there were 12 such persons, in 1954, 172 and in 1959 there were 464. Future statistics concerning narcotic law violations will be affected to a certain extent by the conduct following release of those persons presently serving prison sentences for drug law violations. There were 76 such persons released during 1959, 13 upon the expiration of their maximum sentence while the remaining 63 were released on parole.[83]

Applying the New York figures for cost of incarcerating an offender, a portion of the reduced offense rate for Ohio in 1959 was purchased at a cost of $881,600. Presumably there were savings to the community with respect to the depredations which would have been made by these individuals had they been at large. Also, presumably, there are additional costs to society in providing for the dependents of these persons while the violators are incarcerated. There are, certainly, other costs involved in the detection, preparation, and prosecution of offenses. There is no intention to suggest here that a balance sheet should be set up for determining whether or not an offender should be incarcerated, but it is suggested that when costs run into such amounts, legislatures should be willing to devote a relatively small sum of money to the continuing study of the causes and possible prevention of criminal activity.

Interviews with law enforcement personnel in Ohio disclosed that several factors have contributed to the decline of narcotics activity in Ohio. The police have been carefully trained in building cases against narcotics offenders. Prosecutors are able

83. OHIO DEP'T OF MENTAL HYGIENE
    AND CORRECTIONS, *op. cit. supra*
    note 80, at 8.

to enter court with strong evidence based on police efforts. A tacit understanding exists between the bar and the police on investigative arrests—police are allowed to hold suspects for 72 hours for questioning. During this time it is generally possible to secure from the suspect the necessary information to build a compelling case. Seizure of evidence and apprehension of suspects is greatly facilitated by a section of the act which removes the requirement of warrants.[84] Out of all this increased police activity has grown a large body of police informers. Cleveland narcotics agents estimated that nine out of ten persons involved in narcotics offenses at present are informers.

Table 11.—Criminal Cases Filed for Certain Types of Offenses in Ohio Common Pleas Court 1952–1959

Offense Charged	1952	1953	1954	1955	1956	1957	1958	1959
Robbery	617	773	907	841	799	853	1,045	900
Burglary	1,576	1,665	2,275	1,866	2,137	2,372	2,730	2,655
Larceny (non-auto) ...	919	867	1,030	834	914	838	1,026	998
Forgery and counterfeiting .	463	520	635	633	535	608	654	672
Embezzlement and fraud	841	873	996	924	1,002	1,122	1,276	1,248
Stolen property, buying, receiving, or possessing	112	81	126	108	110	119	141	200
Prostitution, commercialized vice	54	61	73	63	50	44	53	74

It is generally asserted that narcotic addicts are responsible for a large proportion of the crime in the United States—as much as fifty percent of the crime in large cities, argue some advocates of stiffer legislation. If this be so, the crime statistics for Ohio should reflect an appreciable drop as the number of addicts declines. Judging by cases filed in Ohio, the elimination of 80 percent of the addicts has not provided any relief.[85]

84. OHIO REV. CODE ANN. § 3719.22 (Baldwin 1958, Supp. 1960). 85. OHIO DEP'T OF MENTAL HYGIENE AND CORRECTIONS, *op. cit. supra* note 80, at 11.

Despite the lack of corroborating data, the experience of state and federal police officials in Ohio indicates that there has been a dramatic easing of the narcotics problems in that state. Repeatedly these officials state that it has become nearly impossible to purchase illicit drugs on the streets of the larger cities in the state. The concentration of drugs has declined markedly, and there has been an increase in attempts to secure drugs by forgery and fraud. These are all indications that the supply has become scarce and the distributors fewer. Granting that this is true, it is imperative, if Ohio's experience is to be translated to other states, that the importance of various contributing factors be assessed. It is not enough to say that the addict population of Ohio has declined a certain percentage. It is important to know how this decline was accomplished. How many are still in Ohio and are not using narcotic drugs? How many of those who are not using drugs have received some kind of treatment? How many are in jail? In ten years, the number of narcotics offenders in prison has increased over 4,000 percent. If most of these prisoners, regardless of the offense for which they were sentenced, were narcotic addicts, the demand may have so decreased that it was no longer profitable for the dope rings to operate. In such a case, it would not be the deterrent effect of the law which cut down on the traffic, but the lack of a market. If such be the case, it is doubtful whether the idyll will continue after the release of large numbers of the addicts. Also, it is important to know how many of the known addicts in 1955 are no longer present in Ohio and to determine where they went. To what extent did this 80 percent find its way into the addict populations of Chicago, Indianapolis, Buffalo, New York, and Pittsburgh?

No part of this data is available. It is not possible to duplicate the situation in Ohio in another state merely by legislating the same words. There must be a clear understanding of the exact dimensions and nature of the problem, the attitude of the public, the operation of the enforcement agencies and the courts, and the methods of rehabilitation. Only then can other states decide if the "Ohio system" is applicable to their own problems. In arguing against application of the British system in this country, the Federal Bureau and other proponents of stiff penalties constantly point out the sociological differences between Britain and the United States. Similar differences exist between states and regions of this country.

The above discussion is, of course, not exhaustive of all the material available in the states under consideration. It is simply a critical analysis of the shortcomings in the compiled material for the original purpose of this study: to assess the effectiveness of heavy penalty legislation. Other compiled material exists and a wealth of uncompiled material could be extracted by field studies in the records of state agencies. The point of the analysis is that the material is not presently available; it was not available to this study, and it was not available to those persons and organizations who have made unqualified pronouncements about the success or failure of preventive methods employed so far in this country. Adroit selection of statistics can make the experience of any of these states appear to prove a point or rebut a point. A look at all of the available information shows that there has never been a clear picture of narcotics traffic and use in this country, that there have been changes in habits and practices but the extent thereof is not known, and that even if these things were known, there is no clear understanding of the reasons for them. Until answers are found for these questions, any success will be an accident reached perhaps by many tragic failures.

Chapter Five

PROPOSED APPROACHES TO
NARCOTICS CONTROL

I N THE EFFORT to deal with narcotics in the United States, if there is anything more plentiful than problems, it is suggested solutions. Many are based on emotion, without reference to known facts. Others are based on incomplete facts, without a trace of humanity. Machiavelli, Freud, and Pollyanna could all find a proposal to suit their particular philosophies. Despite the difficulty presented by the inadequate information, there are some carefully thought-out plans. In every case, the proposals bear witness to dissatisfactions with the approach currently enjoying favor.

The analysis below of the most widely discussed proposals is drawn from numerous articles, reports, and interviews. The proposals are not always available in a carefully articulated plan such as that of the New York Academy of Medicine. More often they are the expressions of opinion by persons intimately associated with narcotics problems. Understandably, proposals are frequently colored by the aspect of the problem with which the particular proponent is associated. Even so, a careful study of such proposals reveals the foremost problems confronting the disciplines involved. Through such a study, research may be devised to assess the proposals in term of the actual needs of both the addict and the community.

Criminal Sanction

ESSENTIALLY the system currently operating in the United States, the application of criminal sanction calls for severe penalties for all violations of federal and state laws. Supporters argue that the narcotics traffic is a highly developed enterprise employing skilled maneuverers who operate in the underworld to keep the traffic flowing. These individuals are comparable to the key executives in a legitimate endeavor. They have experience and know-how that is difficult to replace; each time one is removed from circulation, a severe blow is struck at the mechanism of drug traffic. The application of long prison terms and heavy fines disrupts the operation and renders it unprofitable.

Neither the available literature nor interviews have given a clue to what the proponents of this approach consider the optimum penalty. The personnel of the Federal Bureau of Narcotics, chief spokesmen for increased penalties, indicate approval of the sanctions imposed by the Narcotic Control Act of 1956, but seem to look with a longing eye toward the Ohio and Michigan penalty structure which is considerably more severe in many cases. That these heavier state penalties are considered a better weapon is borne out by the increased number of cases taken into the state courts by the federal authorities.[1] How high these law enforcement people would desire the penalty to go is open to conjecture. Commissioner Anslinger has declined to advocate the death penalty, though he speaks of the excellent success of the Chinese with their heavy emphasis on executions.[2] Nowhere is there found among the advocates of criminal sanction an expression of concern for anything but freeing society from the depredations of drug

1. Many of the law enforcement people interviewed in the course of this project, both federal and local, stated that cases were jointly investigated and then prosecuted in the state courts because of the higher penalties available.

2. *Hearings on Scope of Soviet Ac-* *tivity in the United States Before the Subcommittee to Investigate the Administration of the Internal Security Act and Other Internal Security Laws of the Senate Committee on the Judiciary,* 85th Cong., 1st Sess., p. 3167 (February 28, 1957).

sellers and drug users. Concern over the causes of addiction and the plight of the addict find very little place in the criminal sanction approach. So long as the chief concern is "getting the addict off the street" and sending the peddlers to prison for long terms, the sky is the limit on what may be expected in the way of penalties.

The Federal Bureau of Narcotics and many state enforcement agencies believe that a law making a distinction between addicted and non-addicted offenders would be unworkable. Opposition to such distinction is implicit in the criminal sanction approach. It is contended that different treatment would place a premium on addiction, encouraging all traffickers to become addicts in order to receive more lenient treatment at the hands of the court. Some narcotics-enforcement officers would provide for compulsory treatment in lieu of prosecution in the case of addicts apprehended for mere possession, but as a rule the advocates of criminal sanction would afford commitment for treatment only to those persons who are not liable to prison sentences for any type of violation, narcotic or non-narcotic. None would permit relaxing the criminal sanctions applied against addicted peddlers, regardless of the extent of their selling activities.

Another facet of opinion expressed by a federal official, when coupled with the view outlined above, would appear to render talk of "compulsory hospitalization" as mere lip service to satisfy critics of the prevailing system. The opinion was offered that not only are virtually all sellers addicted, but also that there is practically no such thing as a non-selling addict. It therefore follows that everyone connected with the traffic, except possibly the "Big Men," is an addicted seller. If this be true, there will be no apprehended offenders eligible for treatment under the compulsory hospitalization procedures. However, such people could be treated while in prison if facilities were available. Unfortunately facilities are lacking. Even if treatment were available, the problem of motivation for the prisoner who is not eligible for parole, despite his best efforts, renders prospects for success very dim.

Obviously, to be effective, the application of criminal sanction as a deterrent must be fairly uniform throughout the country, else the traffickers will pick up their operations and move to the places where less severe treatment can be expected, and the addicts will follow the source of supply. Some enforcement people do not believe that such will be the case. They take the view that narcotics traffic is but a portion of the criminal activity of the Big Men who will give up their narcotics enterprises in order to continue other profitable criminal activities. It is argued that in Ohio, when penalties cut off the drug supply, the addicts simply gave up the drug. Such reasoning seems to deny the very fundamental definition of addiction—a compulsion to have the drug and to get it by any means. Critics of the Ohio experience say that there are three explanations of what happens when a police crackdown occurs: (1) Some addicts and sellers are sent away for long prison terms; (2) some leave for other places where "the heat is not on"; and (3) those remaining become more cautious and difficult to catch.

Criminal sanction obviously has a place in any effort to combat illicit traffic and to control drug use. The conclusion is inescapable, however, that the constriction now placed upon the laws by the Federal Bureau of Narcotics, taken together with their views on interrelation of addiction and traffic, make the criminal sanction approach an exclusive one. They argue that only those who are thoroughly familiar with the "true" nature and character of addicts should be attempting to devise methods of drug control, and that such knowledge is an attribute peculiar to enforcement agents.[3] There would appear to

3. This view was stated frequently during interviews for this project and is reflected throughout the Bureau of Narcotics reply to the Report of the Joint Committee. See U.S. TREASURY DEP'T, BUREAU OF NARCOTICS ADVISORY COMMITTEE, COMMENTS ON NARCOTIC DRUGS: INTERIM REPORT OF THE JOINT COMMITTEE OF THE AMERICAN BAR ASSOCIATION AND THE AMERICAN MEDICAL ASSOCIATION ON NARCOTIC DRUGS (1959).

be very little room for experimentation or modification by doctors, psychiatrists, social workers, or parole officials.

Narcotics clinics

THERE ARE two main objectives of the proposal calling for the establishment of clinics to dispense drugs free or at nominal cost. First, it is hypothesized that making legal drugs available to approved addicts will eliminate the illicit traffic in narcotics. Second, removing narcotics use from the aura of criminality will make it easier to effect cure and rehabilitation. Of course, numerous interrelated side effects are expected to follow implementation of the narcotics clinic proposals. The number of new addicts would decline because of the unavailability of illicit sources and the consequent elimination of peddler proselyting. The general crime rate would decline because the addict would be able to obtain his drugs at virtually no cost. Freed from the necessity to steal, sell his stolen goods, and find sources of supply, the addict could become a self-sustaining member of the community.

The advocates of narcotics clinics are not settled on any one plan, though the plan of the New York Academy of Medicine is the most elaborately worked out and the most widely discussed.[4] The Academy advocates the simultaneous establishment throughout the nation of narcotics clinics attached to general hospitals. The clinics would be open twenty-four hours a day, seven days a week. Registration, identity cards, and other safeguards would be set up to prevent addicts from obtaining drugs at more than one clinic. Initial hospitalization would be required in order to establish the existence of addiction, to allow for medical and psychiatric evaluation, and to determine "minimum needs for narcotics." Once this minimal need is es-

4. New York Academy of Medicine,   BULL. N.Y. ACAD. MED. 592
Subcommittee on Drug Addiction,   (1955).
Report on Drug Addiction, 31

tablished, the addict would be furnished the drug for self-administration, but not more than a two days supply. Addicts would be readmitted from time to time for re-evaluation of their needs in an effort to deal with the tolerance factor. Addicts discovered giving away or selling narcotics would be liable to commitment to a hospital for an attempt at rehabilitation. During the addict's association with the clinic, every effort would be expended to persuade him to undergo withdrawal and rehabilitation. The clinics would offer all sorts of medical, psychiatric, social, and rehabilitative services. Current enforcement machinery would be maintained to continue the suppression of illicit trafficking.

The objections to this proposed system of dealing with narcotics problems follow two main lines: one, it won't work; two, it is immoral. Will it work? Many informed people think it will not. The supplying of a minimum quantity of narcotics will not satisfy the addict unless the supply is sufficiently large not only to ward off withdrawal symptoms but also to provide the sought-after "thrill." It is easy to establish a level sufficient to keep the user free of discomfort. It is not presently possible to establish a level that will continue to produce euphoria, nor even to determine how much an addict needs to secure such pleasure at a given moment. The desire will always be for more. The plan, with its provisions to prevent multiple registration, recognizes that addicts would attempt to obtain additional drugs by going from hospital to hospital. If this is prevented, it is quite likely that they would turn to illicit sources of supply for additional drugs.

Unless the formation of new addicts is the result of proselyting by peddlers, and the evidence is against such a proposition, the establishment of the narcotics clinic would not reduce the number of persons who become addicted. In fact, the opponents suggest that if clinics were successful in cutting into the illicit market, the underworld might turn to deliberate attempts to create new addicts.

Have we the moral right to establish such a procedure? Supplying drugs will not alter the basic causes of the addict's problem. Despite the provision for attempts at persuading him to undergo treatment, clinics are mainly an effort to remove the problems created by drug addiction, not an effort to remove the problems which create addiction. The establishment of clinics will merely perpetuate the illness from which these people suffer. It will be, says one critic, like supplying an alcoholic with all the liquor he needs so he can face the next meeting of Alcoholics Anonymous.

There can be no reasonable expectation of cure so long as the addict is receiving drugs because he is not motivated to seek any kind of continuous treatment.[5] While it may be true that no permanent damage is caused by the use of narcotics, it is indisputably true that is causes undesirable physiological changes during long periods of heavy use. It also creates a false sense of security, diminishes drive and ambition, and inhibits reaction to problems and crises. No matter how effectively an addict may perform assigned tasks, he is not functioning normally when under the influence of drugs. To give legal and public sanction to the perpetuation of his abnormality is indefensible.

The American Medical Asociation Council on Mental Health reported that in its opinion such clinics should not be established at this time.[6] The Council recognized that opinion played a large part in its decision and adverted to the possibility of establishing an experimental clinic to test some of the hypotheses about its effectiveness. However, the report finds considerable objection to the initiation of even an experimental project.

---

5. "Usually when the addict is 'clean,' he sees no need for help—it's all a matter of will power. When he is hooked, he may want help, but, at that point, he is unable to make use of it." Bailey, *The Supervision of Paroled Drug Addicts,* 5 NAT'L PROB. & PAROLE ASS'N J. 53, 62 (1959).

6. American Medical Association, Council on Mental Health, *Report on Narcotics Addiction,* 165 J.A.M.A. 1970 (Dec. 14, 1957).

British system [7]

IN READING the legislative enactments on narcotics control, one would find little apparent difference between the American and British policies. But a great difference does exist. That difference is that in Great Britain the determination of proper treatment of addiction rests with the medical profession. When the question of proper professional practice arose in England, a committee of doctors was formed to determine the proper role of the physician in addiction problems. The committee set forth three circumstances under which drugs could be administered to addicts: (1) where the patient is under treatment by the gradual-withdrawal method with a view to cure; (2) where, after attempts at cure, it appears that the drug cannot be discontinued completely because of the severity of the withdrawal symptoms; and (3) where it has been demonstrated that the patient is capable of leading a relatively normal life if given drugs, and that he cannot do so without drugs. While the British statutes read very much like the Harrison Act in limiting prescription of drugs by physicians to the course of their professional practice only, the definition of professional practice was left to physicians. In the United States the definition was rigidly established by non-medical arbiters.

The advantages implicit in the British system of medical control are considered by many to be applicable to this country. This approach recognizes that addiction is a medical problem which should be handled by physicians. Under this procedure the addict must be under medical care if he is to receive licit drugs, which he will doubtless elect to do because of the nominal cost. Crime is thereby diminished and the illicit traffic forced out.

Critics point out that sociological differences between Great

7. For comprehensive discussion of the British system see Lindesmith, *The British System of Narcotics Control*, 22 LAW & CONTEMP. PROB. 138 (Winter 1957); Schur, *British Narcotics Policies*, 51 J. CRIM. L., C.&P.S. 619 (March–April, 1961).

Britain and the United States would not permit the successful functioning of the British system here. The most extensive examination of the British system finds that the system is the result of a small narcotics problem rather than the reverse.[8] This point is buttressed by evidence of the extensive narcotics problem in Hong Kong which operates under the same type of law.[9] Critics cast doubt upon the completeness of figures for addicts in Great Britain, saying the problem is really larger than is known.

Isolation [10]

MOTIVATED by evidence that narcotics addiction has aspects of "contagion," some persons have offered the suggestion that addicts be rounded up and confined to an addict colony, in what would be basically the same approach as that taken in the case of lepers. Narcotic addicts represent such a serious threat to the well-being of the community, they claim that isolation is justified to stop the spread of the disease.

Variations in method are not significant. In most cases, isolation advocates would provide opportunity for treatment and rehabilitation for addicts before determining whether the addict should be confined. Addicts who do not respond favorably to these ministrations would then be confined to the addict colony. Some proponents advocate a life-term confinement for "incurable addicts." Others propose a long period of confinement in the colony, with the state's right to return immediately any addict who reverts to drug use at any time subsequent to his release on long-time parole.

Objections, of course, are as plentiful as proposals. The isolation proposal is inhumane. The danger does not justify the means taken to combat it. The spread of narcotic addition is not

8. Larimore and Brill, *The British Narcotic System, Report of Study,* 60 N.Y. STATE J. MED. 107 (Jan. 1, 1960).
9. THE PROBLEM OF NARCOTIC DRUGS IN HONG KONG (A White Paper laid before the Legislative Council, November 11, 1959).
10. See discussion in MacDONALD (ed.), CURRENT LAW AND SOCIAL PROBLEMS 198 (1960).

the result of contagion. Long-term incarceration does not have an appreciable effect on abstention from the use of drugs. Also, like the clinic plan, the proposal has elements of shirking the larger responsibility of coping with the narcotics problem, namely, seeking to eradicate it. It is generally proposed as a correlative of the isolation theory that there will be an extensive and hard-hitting assault on the illicit traffickers. It must be admitted, however, that there is a point of irreducible minimum in drug activity as there is in nearly everything else. If so, there will continue to be some supply and some newly addicted persons. The plan offers nothing to strike at the causes of drug addiction which lie within the personality of the addiction-prone individual.

Institutionalization

PRESENT METHODS of treatment utilize institutionalization in a limited extent, as exemplified by the hospitals at Lexington, Ky., and Fort Worth, Texas, and by the facility for juveniles at Riverside Hospital, New York City. There is a scattering of patient facilities in state hospitals, but institutions built and operated for the treatment of addiction are practically non-existent.

Programs have been advocated, however, for building immense facilities for the handling of thousands of addicts at one time, in an all-out mass hospitalization effort designed to treat and rehabilitate addicts in sufficient numbers to limit the spread of addiction. One proposal [11] calls for building facilities near New York City to accommodate approximately 7,000 new patients a year, with a total capacity "far in excess of 10,000 addicts simultaneously removed from the community to rehabilitative institutions." [12] Similar facilities would be required in other areas of the country near the centers of heaviest addict

11. For discussion of the proposal known as the Hogan-Silver Plan see Kuh, *Dealing with Narcotics Addiction,* New York Law Journal, Part I, June 8, 1960, p. 2, col. 1; Part II, June 9, 1960, p. 2, col. 1; Part III, June 10, 1960, p. 2, col. 1. 12. *Id.* Part II.

concentration. Interstate compacts would be required so that all states would have facilities available, even though their own addiction problems did not justify the erection and maintenance of a drug treatment hospital.

Addicts would be confined for a year and in many cases considerably longer, with a five-year period of probation following discharge. Elaborate aftercare procedures would be established to nurture the withdrawn addict upon his return to his former environment. It is admitted that the cost would be enormous.

This proposal is in reality only an extension and rigidification of the recognized treatment procedures employed at the Public Health Service hospitals. It adds compulsory civil commitment to the means of getting the addicts into the facility, and provides for the aftercare which all treatment personnel have insisted is essential. It establishes a minimum period of confined hospitalization which can be extended "until cure is effected." The only radical aspect of the proposal is the immense size of the undertaking.

Criticism is, of course, directed at the visionary goal of incarcerating virtually all of the addict population of the country at one time. The problem does not merit the diverting of such huge sums of money from more compelling needs as would be required for this purpose. Civil commitment would be no more palatable to the addict than would criminal conviction. It would serve only to drive the addict further underground.

From an examination of much of the writing on narcotics treatment, it appears that provisions for a definite period of commitment of compulsory hospitalization are open to basic objection. Such commitment fails to take into account the individuality of each case of narcotic addiction as distinguished from any other types of disease. There appears to be no correlation between the length of time an individual is hospitalized or incarcerated and the likelihood of relapse. It is not possible to determine a general rule for the optimum period of hospitalization. The four and one-half months generally mentioned in connection with the treatment program at Lexington is drawn from the fact that the last vestiges of physiological changes, according to the most sophisticated method of detection, have disappeared by that time. In many patients it will be much earlier.[13] The establishment of a definite period of hospitalization is merely another case of substituting the opinion of lawyers, legislators, or enforcement agents for that of physicians.

13. A member of the staff at Lexington stated in an interview that occasionally the ripe time for a patient to leave is immediately after withdrawal. A person recently introduced to drugs may react so strongly to the experience of hospitalization and contact with long-time addicts that the best course is to capitalize on the reaction immediately.

Chapter Six

CONCLUSIONS AND
RECOMMENDATIONS

B^Y THIS POINT it is hoped that this study has demonstrated that the available evidence does not prove the claims made in behalf of the effectiveness of the American system of narcotics control. Neither is there adequate evidence on which to make a valid prognosis of the effect of suggested reforms. Certainly there are particular theses which may be offered, without a clear picture of what is happening in the country. It may be argued logically that without access to narcotic drugs there would be no addiction. With equal logic it can be asserted that if drugs were free, addicts would not have to commit crimes to obtain money for their purchase. These statements, offered as the cores of opposite extremes among the proposals for the control of addiction and traffic, beg the entire question at issue.

Total elimination of access to drugs through suppression of smuggling, illicit traffic, and diversion from legitimate channels must be recognized as an unrealistic, impossible, and visionary goal. Therefore, to state the first proposition as if it were a complete answer does nothing but delude the public. Strict law enforcement can cut down severely on the amount of drugs coming into the country, but what will happen to the traffic which does get through? Among the things necessary to know is the extent to which the price of drugs reflects the scarcity on the market. If the price goes up will predatory crime to support addiction increase? It seems apparent that unless enforcement is consistent in all areas of the country, the traffic will move from place to place, taking advantage of the most favorable conditions. Can enforcement consistent enough to avoid this danger be provided? If so, what would it take in terms of manpower, money, and police authority? The extent to which rigid control methods can diminish the narcotics problem is as yet an unknown quantity.

Similarly, the extent to which free distribution of drugs can reduce the problem is purely conjecture. Those persons who are receiving free drugs will not have to commit crime to support their habits. Such a statement is a truism, but to project that narcotics-associated crime will thereby disappear, necessarily relies on faulty syllogism. Critics aver that many addicts, for a variety of reasons, will not register, and that of those who do register and receive drugs, some will still purchase additional supplies from the underworld. It is known that some addicts, aside from their narcotics problems are criminals and probably would continue to obtain their supplies from criminal sources. The supplying of registered addicts with legal drugs might prompt the underworld to begin more active proselyting to develop drug-using tyros. The extent to which these considerations will affect the whole complexion of narcotic addiction in this country should be determined before dispensing clinics, other than in limited experimental settings, are established. Those proposing such approaches to the problem should not, however, have to meet the objection that they are throwing over a thoroughly proved system which is currently producing the best of all possible results. At least this requirement should not be imposed upon the reformers until the supporters of the present system are able to prove their claims. This research effort has uncovered no such proof.

Despite the lack of evidence supporting the effectiveness of the American system, and to some extent because of that lack, some general conclusions may still be reached validly. These conclusions group themselves naturally around two major premises:

    i Absent compelling considerations, thus far undemonstrated, those having the responsibility for dealing with narcotics problems should not be denied means found effective in other areas of criminal and anti-social behavior.

    ii Adoption of new, untried approaches to narcotics problems should be postponed until additional information has been systematically gathered which will enable enlightened planning and the avoidance of tragic missteps.

I

The United States has adopted and pursued a policy of narcotics control unlike that of almost every other nation in the world.[1] It is a policy, on the federal level at least, aimed at destroying the traffic by severe penalties applied uncompromisingly against all *purveyors* of illicit narcotics. Nearly all governments have established control procedures with the objective of curbing illegal traffic. Unfortunately, in America officials have deemed it impossible to make our system work without departing markedly from practices and principles well established in other areas of criminal law.

According to the proponents of the severe penalty approach, our system requires that the medical and psychiatric treatment of addiction must be afforded, but only *after* the enforcement and deterrent aspects have been satisfied. Judicial discretion, which enables a judge to make the punishment fit the crime, cannot be allowed, since all judges are not hard enough to

---

1. Joint Committee of the American Bar Association and the American Medical Association on Narcotic Drugs, Drug Addiction: Crime or Disease? 121–55 (Interim and Final Reports, 1961).

satisfy the requirements of our system. Parole, generally considered one of the most effective tools in the process of rehabilitation, cannot be permitted because only the absolute certainty of a long incarceration will deter offenders.

Certainly it must be conceded that experience may show any of the ordinary practices to be inapplicable or undesirable under certain conditions. However, such experience should be clear and convincing. The tasks of the physician, the psychiatrist, the judge, and the social worker are not easy. Their roles in the prevention and punishment of crime and the rehabilitation of the criminal offender are difficult and delicate. Their work is complementary to enforcement of the law, not antagonistic or secondary. Absent the most compelling reasons, they should not be denied the means generally available to them in their efforts to check crime and salvage the criminal.

This study has found no evidence which compels the conclusion that *all* narcotics offenses are so insidious or *all* narcotics offenders so incorrigible that those who work with them should be denied the means found effective in dealing with other types of anti-social behavior. On the contrary, addiction, which is the root of the narcotics problem, is so complex that every possible weapon should be brought to bear upon it at once.

What is needed basically is a recognition that the whole narcotics problem cannot be lumped together and given to legislators, enforcement agencies, hospitals, or doctors. There must be a realignment of responsibility and a genuine spirit of cooperation in areas which overlap in interest. Enforcement needs to concern itself with illicit traffic. Legislators need to concern themselves with controls which are more permissive and less directive to the medical profession. Doctors need to concern themselves with the causes and treatment of drug addiction, rather than with means for decreasing or limiting traffic. Certainly, anyone as an individual has a right to concern himself with whatever aspects of the problem he pleases, but the professions represented should devote their efforts to that field where their experience and skills are most called for.

The first step should be to recognize that the treatment of addiction and research into possible preventive medicine are medical problems and should be dealt with as such. This does not mean that enforcement officials and legislators should recite in unison that the treatment of addiction is a medical problem and then continue to legislate and regulate the practice of medicine. Neither does it mean that the ultimate disposition of addicted offenders against the criminal laws should be determined by physicians. There must be a clear recognition that the enforcement of narcotics laws and the treatment of narcotic addiction are dichotomous functions. Certainly, every activity touching upon narcotics will have areas of interest common to all; but not to the point that enforcement officials determine what is good medical practice or that legislators prescribe the course of medical treatment.

There is not necessarily any particular method of treatment implicit in the designation "medical approach," but rather a recognition of the doctor's right and duty to treat a narcotic addict as he has the right and duty to treat any diseased person. The medical profession must be free to search for and find the most effective means of treating addiction, and must be free to adapt the methodology to fit the patient, his disease, his environment, and any other factor which may appear to have significant bearing on the prospect of recovery. The medical approach does not necessarily mean that ambulatory treatment will or should be the rule, or that supportive doses of narcotics should be administered to the addict during treatment, or that some or any addicts should be given maintenance doses indefinitely. Neither does the recognition of medical responsibility imply that the findings of medical researchers shall supplant social judgment. It may well be that the most successful therapy for the individual would still be objectionable to society for moral reasons, or because of the danger which it presents to society. It does mean, however, that the medical profession is the only body capable of making decisions as to the therapeutic efficacy and desirability of treatment procedures. The social efficacy and desirability of such procedures then becomes a question for all the disciplines affected by the narcotics problem, and for the public generally.

It is not regarded as a salient argument that the American Medical Association made a statement of policy on some of these points nearly forty years ago. No other situation comes to mind where a decision in medicine has had the force of *stare decisis*. Medical men, acting in good faith, must exercise their prerogatives constantly as practitioners of the healing arts to re-examine therapeutic approaches to narcotic addiction in the light of changing conditions and changing knowledge. Neither does the fact that the Public Health Service has a generally agreed upon policy as to the treatment of addiction militate against the continuous reappraisal by the medical profession of the application of that policy to other efforts. The Public Health Service operates facilities under governmental sanction and control. They are operated primarily as a facility for treatment and rehabilitation of federal prisoners, which to a large extent dictates what custodial policies will be, as well as other aspects of institutionalization.

In short, a medical approach to addiction should mean the same thing that a medical approach to any disease means. Today doctors may work with many people, such as alcoholics or sexual deviates, whose activities transgress the mores of society as expressed in the law. Only in the case of narcotic addiction have the legislator and the law enforcement officer set out to limit the scope of research or prescribe the manner of treatment.

Judges should be accorded the right to individualize sentences. Utilizing the facts presented by the law enforcement agencies, psychiatrists, and social workers, the judge should be free to draw upon his experience to find the sentence which will afford society the best protection and the offender the best chance of rehabilitation. These objectives are not antagonistic, for each holds within itself the germ of the other.

A group of distinguished judges, in a conscientious effort to share their experiences and to formulate guides for sentencing, considered the problem of narcotics offenders.

> The narcotic peddler and narcotic addict present entirely different problems, particularly if the peddler is not an addict. Some addicts do a small amount of peddling to help finance their addiction; they should be treated in the same manner as non-peddling addicts are.
>
> . . . .
>
> Just as a distinction should be made between the peddler and the addict, a distinction should also be made between persons who are primarily criminal and only incidentally addicted to narcotics, and those who are primarily addicted and commit crimes to secure the wherewithal for supporting the addiction.
>
> In determining disposition in a narcotics case, therefore, the judge should ask: "What is the basic problem? Is it addiction, peddling, or a background of criminality? What is the behavior of the defendant as a result of the addiction?" [2]

The majority of statutes today do not permit the judge to weigh these considerations. They require that illegal possession shall be punished by a stated number of years, regardless of the facts which may come to the attention of the judge. In many cases that number of years is the same whether the offender is an addict with a capsule obviously for his own use, or a non-addict with two pounds of heroin obviously intended for distribution.

Such indiscriminate application of penalties probably does increase the deterrent effect of the law, but at the expense of other values. It denies the possibility of a sentence designed to effect rehabilitation of the offender. Moreover, it is patently

---

2. NATIONAL PROBATION AND PAROLE ASSOCIATION, ADVISORY COUNCIL OF JUDGES, GUIDES FOR SENTENCING 59–60 (1957).

unjust. As Aristotle declared, "There can be no greater injustice than to treat unequal things equally." Much of the narcotics legislation today requires our judges, against their wisdom, experience, and inclination, to pronounce judgments of such injustice upon those before the bench.

Parole and probation should be utilized in narcotics offenses as they are in other criminal offenses. Parole, particularly, can play an important part in the correctional process when dealing with narcotic addicts. It is generally accepted that addiction is largely the result of personal inadequacy, emotional instability, and social maladjustment.[3] It is also known that 95 percent of persons confined are eventually released with or without parole.[4] When the possibility of parole is denied, it means that these people who particularly need supervision are returned to the environment which spawned their troubles without any assistance whatever. It is argued that addicted offenders have a high recidivism rate, and do not warrant the risk involved in releasing them on parole. If parole meant merely release, the argument might be salient; but parole is much more than a conditional release from confinement. It is a rehabilitation process which envisions assisting the offender to adjust to social responsibility.[5]

If parole were merely conditional release without after-care, one should always have to be restricted to those prisoners who might be able to get along without supervision, i.e., the so-called "good risks." This, however, would mean that the very men who had lapsed into criminality because they needed care and did not get it, should never be paroled, which would not only be unjust, but dangerous as well.

It is, thus, understandable as well as justifiable that with the development of after-care, parole has also been extended to

3. Such causal factors actually play a large part in most criminal activity. See McGee, *The Administration of Justice: The Correctional Process,* 5 NAT'L PROB. & PAROLE ASS'N J. 225 (1959).

4. NATIONAL CONFERENCE ON PAROLE, PAROLE IN PRINCIPLE AND PRACTICE, A MANUAL AND REPORT 90 (1957).

5. McGee, *supra* note 3, at 225.

prisoners not belonging in the "best risks" category. In former times, eligibility for parole was very limited. Often, also, parole-granting authorities were afraid to accept a certain amount of risk, *overlooking the fact that risks are inevitably much more serious if the weak prisoner afterwards has to be released without parole and after-care, and yet be exposed to the same unfavourable influence.* Often, agencies stressed too much the showing of favourable statistics.[6] [Emphasis added.]

The power to consider for parole does not mean that parole must be granted. It means only that parole authorities may select those persons most likely to benefit from parole supervision and attempt to return them to the community in the manner best calculated to insure their successful adjustment. When this power is placed in the parole authority, it may be exercised on an individualized basis. Unequal things may be treated unequally. When the power is denied by legislation, the chance to create a good citizen by guidance and supervision is lost. Such legislation is really a denial of the concept of parole.[7]

The National Conference on Parole made the following statement in its report:

The laws under which offenders are sentenced may determine in large measure the effectiveness of parole. Statutes whose provisions permit release on parole when optimum response to the correctional-educational program of the institution indicated the offender is ready to be returned to society are most conducive to parole effectiveness.

The following statement of basic criteria is limited to adult felony-type offenders not handled in specialized courts:

1. Sentencing structure should provide a wide spread between minimum and maximum length of sentence within which the board of parole may operate.

6. UNITED NATIONS, DEPARTMENT OF SOCIAL AFFAIRS, PAROLE AND AFTER-CARE 10–11 (1954).

7. NATIONAL CONFERENCE ON PAROLE, *op. cit. supra* note 4, at 73.

2. The court should, within the maximum sentence prescribed by law, select and impose a maximum sentence.

3. Mandatory minimum sentences should not be established by legislation.

The group did not reach agreement for or against the impositions of minimum sentences but did adopt the following principle:

If, however, the court is authorized by statute to impose a minimum sentence, it is vital that the law require a broad spread between the minimum and the maximum and that the minimum be short enough to permit sound release decisions.[8]

Nothing has been demonstrated to show why narcotics offenders should be excluded from the application of procedures known to be desirable and effective when applied to other criminal offenders. In fact, many facets of narcotics problems suggest that these procedures are indispensable if we are going to achieve anything better than a stalemate in dealing with narcotic addiction.

II

Narcotics use and traffic is clouded with misconception, both accidental and carefully instilled. It is imperative that the misconceptions be removed by clear demonstrative evidence of what is real and what is myth in the practice and effect of narcotics use. The need for demonstrative evidence is not satisfied by testimony of the defenders of the status quo nor by the emotion-riddled writings of the postulators of reform. Neither is it sufficient to provide negative evidence demonstrating the inadequacy of one system. The body of knowledge to be accumulated must be capable of supporting decisions to cut away certain control procedures as well as to adopt new procedures. If there be deficiencies in the present system, it will have taken half a century to /expose them and bring about a change.

8. *Id.* at 72–73.

Another fifty years should not be gambled upon a new system until the most penetrating study has dealt with every foreseeable problem in the light of available scientific knowledge. This does not mean an absolute assurance of success, but it does mean that all information now available or practically obtainable should be evaluated to avoid as many pitfalls as possible. Research is slow, but not near so slow as social reform. The time to perfect the basis for any new system is now.

The first step in a program of accumulating definitive information should be the establishment of responsibility for the program. A national agency should be given the responsibility for accumulating the information. No single agency represents all the disciplines involved in this complex problem. In view of the data to be gathered, the propositions to be studied, and the dissemination to be accomplished, the Department of Health, Education and Welfare would appear to be the best choice. While the branch charged with this responsibility would work closely with the Public Health Service, it should be given adequate funds and personnel to function as an independent unit. This branch would be responsible for creating a set of standards to be used by the agencies reporting to it, so that the comparability of reported data could be relied upon. The branch would re-examine the method and content of reports from time to time, in the light of accumulated information, to determine what elaborations are needed in order to obtain a more complete understanding of narcotics use and traffic.

Similar fixing of responsibility should be made in the states. Whether such responsibility should be allocated to existing agencies or whether a new agency should be created expressly for the purpose would depend largely upon the extent of the problem in each state. In any event, as with the national agency, great care should be taken to assure that the agency evaluating the problems should not be wedded to the agency responsible for enforcement. Building upon the national reporting standards, the state bureau should establish procedures for reporting by local agencies. Such procedures must keep two objectives clearly in mind: first, to obtain information on all salient aspects of addiction and traffic; and second, to assure complete reporting from all agencies concerned with the problem.

The determination of what information is essential is the most difficult part in the development of a data-gathering program. In the case of narcotics, it would be a mistake to embark upon the program without extensive consultation with those agencies now gathering information and with representatives of those disciplines substantially concerned with the problem. Law enforcement officers, lawyers, judges, physicians, psychiatrists, penologists, probation officers, sociologists, and social workers fall within this group. Such consultation will help to provide information, the lack of which has prevented these disciplines from reaching more significant conclusions on narcotics in the past. Certain minimal requirements should be established by the national bureau to which localities may add requirements according to local problems. These requirements would include at least the following categories.

PERSONAL STATISTICS (*to be obtained by arresting officer*). Name, address, age, race, nationality, education, and employment history. The place of birth and a record, with dates, of places of residence will help to determine a great deal about the mobility of the addict population. Thorough information on the family of the offender should be obtained, including the number, age, and sex of siblings, the age of parents and whether they are living together. If parents are not living together, it is important to know when they parted and with whom the offender resided thereafter.

PRESENT OFFENSE (*to be provided by the arresting officer*). This information should include the offense charged and the drug involved, the place of the offense, the place of the arrest, and other persons involved in the offense.

NARCOTICS HISTORY (*to be obtained from the offender by the arresting officer*). The report should show when the offender claims to have first used narcotics, where this occurred, what drug was used, and the method of introduction. Subsequent history should be elicited and reported as fully as possible. This history should include the subject's evaluation of when he first became a regular user, what his preferences of drugs have been, how heavy his present habit is, and the causes of his addiction. Experience with prior treatment should be explored to discover attempts at self-treatment, voluntary commitment, involuntary commitment, and the subject's evaluation of the success of any treatment experiences. Periods of abstinence after inception of the habit should be identified.

CRIMINAL RECORD (*to be obtained from police files*). Though the subject may be asked about his criminal records, it is not sufficient to rely upon his account. This information should be as exhaustive as possible, utilizing state and local criminal files as well as those of the Federal Bureau of Investigation and the Federal Bureau of Narcotics.

DISPOSITION (*to be obtained from police and the courts*). If the arrestee should be released for any reason short of court action, the arresting agency should be required to report such disposition to the bureau collecting information for the state. Disposition by the court should be reported by the clerk of the court. The report should include the offense charged; the offense of which convicted, if any; the sentence; and the conditions of suspension or probation, if any. If the sentence was based on evidence of prior convictions, that information should also be supplied.

PRISON HISTORY (*to be obtained from penal authorities*). Prison officials should be required to report the receipt of all persons incarcerated for narcotics violations, any medical or psychiatric treatment afforded such persons, and the date and conditions of the offender's release. Any unusual problems or behavior should also be reported.

PROBATION RECORD (*to be obtained from probation officers*). The record and experience with all persons turned over to probation officers, either by the court or by a parole board, should be reported to the state agency. Such record should include the time under supervision, any relapses to use of drugs and action taken thereon, any violations of the law during probation, and the date and conditions of discharge. Additional information on the employment record of the individual and his adjustment to community living and personal problems is of vital concern. A large part of reporting in this area must be left to the determination of the state agency and the reporting officers.

The complete reporting of narcotics activity can be assured only by a uniform requirement for reports from all agencies in a well-established routine. Arresting officers should be required to fill out a personal history at the time the offender is booked. Insofar as possible, this form should provide for answering questions by checking blocks rather than filling in blanks. Experience of those now collecting data indicates that narration frequently makes for incomplete answers to questions. The form should be sent to the state criminal identification bureau where a copy of the offender's criminal record will be attached before the form is forwarded to the state narcotics agency. Such a method is not a serious addition to the present duties of police in narcotics cases. Histories are generally taken in connection with narcotics arrests though not in the detail which would be required by this proposal. The use of multiple copy forms would reduce the amount of extra effort required.

In New Jersey, the legislature requires the clerks of all courts in the state to report to the Narcotics Commission the disposition of all narcotics cases. Similar requirements would probably be needed in other states to insure that complete information is received by the state agency. Such legislation might well provide for the reporting at all levels—police, courts, prisons, probation officers, and other agencies concerned in the problem.

It is highly desirable to utilize automatic punched card systems for storing the information obtained by the state agency. Generally within the state government establishment, such equipment will be available, the use of which can obviate a large outlay of money and save on clerical assistance. The desirability of using such systems is readily apparent. All of the information received can be punched into the cards without regard to its presently understood pertinency. Thereafter, searches for characteristics, trends, age studies, drug preferences, recidivism rates, recovery rates, and all types of combinations can be made with a minimum of difficulty. If a particular trend is noted in one area, it can be checked immediately against another without the immense task of examining files and records on each offender. Such flexibility would be especially useful because of the changing character of traffic in narcotics. To have been able to determine immediately the trend of burgeoning teen-age drug use after World War II, might have been of tremendous value. Preventive efforts could perhaps have nipped that outbreak before it had time to spread so widely.

The information suggested herein is a bare minimum necessary for the most basic appraisal of the narcotics problem in this country. It is anticipated that the suggested consultation with experts in the fields concerned with narcotic addiction and traffic will add considerably to the list of essential information. Questions of cost in the implementation of such a data-gathering system are readily answered with another question—what is it worth to the American public? We are told that half the crime in large cities is the result of narcotics. Figures in the hundreds of millions are cited as the cost of addiction. Maintenance of narcotics offenders in prisons costs about five dollars per day; in the hospital at Lexington, about nine dollars per day, and in Riverside Hospital, more than thirty dollars per day. Add to this the cost of law enforcement and support of dependents by social welfare agencies, and the total reaches enormous proportions. Any reasonable effort with any reasonable prospects of success will be worth considerable investment by the public.

Until a carefully planned systematic collection of information is launched, every effort to draw adequately supported conclusions will fail. Research studies either will come to the conclusions which this study has reached, or they will be answered by another study based on differing data supporting opposite conclusions. Medical, economic, and humanitarian considerations demand that the collection of information be postponed no longer. If the importance of this information to an understanding of narcotics problems is not appreciated, in another thirty years another research effort will again echo the astonishment of Dr. Terry that so little is known and that so much is written without a basis in fact.

POSTSCRIPT

SOCIAL CHANGE is extremely difficult to measure. The changes in American social policy concerning narcotic drug control since the first edition of this book are no exception. In the five years since publication of the first edition of this book, however, there has occurred a sequence of events that provides us with a primitive yardstick.

In the interval since the first edition, two commissions were appointed to advise the government on the best approach to serious social problems. One commission was charged solely with investigation of narcotics problems; the other considered the narcotics problem in the larger context of crime. Both had expert assistance from consultants and witnesses. Both perceived their responsibilities to include making an assessment of the dimensions of the problem and its seriousness and making recommendations for coping with it. One commission reported in 1963 and the other in 1967. The near identity of task and method for the two commissions makes it possible to use their reports to compare conditions at two points in time. There is, of course, no way to demonstrate that either commission was close to absolute truth, but it is reasonable to assume that, with similar approaches to

In preparation of this postscript and in revision of Appendix B the author was greatly assisted by Batya Miller and Peter Levin, student researchers from the University of Chicago Law School.

responsibility, similar resources, similar methods, and highly qualified personnel in both instances, there should be a substantially similar sensitivity to conditions and to change in conditions.

The measure of change in objective

IN SEPTEMBER 1962, a White House Conference on Narcotic and Drug Abuse was convened in Washington by President Kennedy.[1] More than six hundred persons were invited to participate in the meeting and . . . "suggest new solutions to old problems and let strong light dispel the appearances of controversy that have surrounded these problems."[2] Out of the conference grew the President's Advisory Commission on Narcotic and Drug Abuse; in November 1963, the final report of the Advisory Commission appeared.[3] The commission reviewed the polar views marking the range of response to the narcotic problem and then carefully set a course between them, shifting now slightly toward one side and now slightly toward the other, but keeping to a careful middle course. The general philosophy was stated as follows:

1. The illegal traffic in drugs should be attacked with the full power of the federal government. The price for participation in this traffic should be prohibitive. It should be made too dangerous to be attractive.

2. The individual abuser should be rehabilitated. Every possible effort should be exerted by all governments — federal, state, and local — and by every community toward this end. Where necessary to protect society, this may have to be done

1. See PROCEEDINGS OF THE WHITE HOUSE CONFERENCE ON NARCOTIC AND DRUG ABUSE (1962).
2. Message from President Kennedy to the conferees, *id.* at iii.

3. PRESIDENT'S ADVISORY COMMISSION ON NARCOTIC AND DRUG ABUSE, FINAL REPORT (1963). (Hereinafter referred to as 1963 Commission and 1963 Report.)

at times against the abuser's will. Pertinent to all, the causes of drug abuse must be found and eradicated.

3. Drug users who violate the law by small purchases or sales should be made to recognize what society demands of them. In these instances, penalties should be applied according to the principles of our present code of justice. When the penalties involve imprisonment, however, the rehabilitation of the individual, rather than retributive punishment, should be the major objective.[4]

In line with its general philosophy, the Advisory Commission made twenty-five recommendations covering a wide range of activities, with an equally wide range of specificity. The recommendations seem to reflect a conviction of the commission that more knowledge about drug abuse and more resources for curbing it were the prime order of the day. The commission devoted six recommendations to improvements in the organization and coordination of activities aimed at controlling drug practices in this country. These included dividing the responsibilities of the Federal Bureau of Narcotics between the Department of Justice and the Department of Health, Education, and Welfare; appointing a special White House assistant on drug abuse and a permanent citizens' advisory panel; and increased involvement by all federal executives. Four recommendations called for increased research, information compilation, and educational programs for the public and for officials. Two recommendations called for an expansion of the pharmacopoeia of dangerous drugs subject to federal regulation, and three more recommended an extension of international controls through the United Nations and through treaties. Three recommendations

4. *Id.* at 3-4.

called for increased personnel and other resources for the law enforcement agencies. Finally, seven of the recommendations, in various forms, urged a greater degree of flexibility in punishment, treatment, and rehabilitation programs, including a civil commitment program and a new definition of legitimate medical practice in regard to dispensing narcotics and treating addicts, the definition to be determined primarily by the medical profession.

Despite the commission's recognition of the inadequacy of knowledge in the whole area of drug abuse and addiction, and despite the call for extensive research, there is a curious avoidance of examining the prime objectives of the drug control program and the basic values undergirding those objectives. The section of the report dealing with research[5] does raise some questions: What is the ultimate fate of the drug abuser? What should be the definition of a "cure"? Can an addict ever be pronounced "curable" or "incurable"? The commission's response to such questions is, quite properly, a call for more research. Yet all its other recommendations are made with an apparent assurance that these disturbing questions have no real relevance except to the problem of treatment. The impression is created that a great deal of research is needed to enable those having the responsibility for treatment to offer greater assistance in terminating drug use, but that validity of the basic objective of eliminating drug use except for the relief of physically caused pain would be unaffected by the answers to those questions. The decision that drug use must be terminated is not subject to enlightenment—only the ways of bringing about termination are considered open.

5. *Id.* at 21-30.

This attitude is difficult to comprehend, considering the resources at the disposal of the commission, the questions that were raised by the participants in the White House conference, and the working papers prepared for the conferees by the ad hoc panel. Without examination, without explanation, the commission has, for most purposes, equated drug use and drug abuse. The goal has been set at termination of drug use rather than at a satisfactory social adaptation of those persons presently considered to be abusing drugs. While it may well be that satisfactory social adaptation can never be achieved by any individual under any circumstances without the termination of drug use, that point is certainly not yet resolved. The commission lost a significant opportunity to say to the American public that the real goal might be to meliorate the high social costs resulting from drug abuse. Termination of drug use may be the best means, or indeed the only means, to that end, but it is a means, not the end itself. Nowhere is this clearly or even tacitly recognized by the commission. Consequently, all its deliberations and recommendations are apparently aimed at the refinement of a means without an examination of the end.

Whatever its shortcomings may have been, the White House conference and the subsequent commission report form an assessment of conditions and proposals for improvement that serve as the initial point of our five-year yardstick. The nearer point of the measure is marked by the report of the President's Commission on Law Enforcement and Administration of Justice, published in 1967,[6] particularly that part dealing with narcotics and drug abuse.[7]

6. PRESIDENT'S COMMISSION ON LAW ENFORCEMENT AND ADMINISTRATION OF JUSTICE, THE CHALLENGE OF CRIME IN A FREE SOCIETY (1967). (Hereinafter referred to as 1967 Commission and 1967 Report.)

7. *Id.* at 211-31.

The commission made seven recommendations, divided between improvements in the operation of law enforcement and expansion of the programs of research and education. Summarizing its own recommendations the commission said:

> The growing problem of narcotics and drug abuse in this country must be attacked by strengthening all approaches: Law enforcement, rehabilitation and treatment of drug users, and public education on the dangers involved. This is partly a matter of increased resources, such as for customs control; for the Bureau of Narcotics (especially to strengthen its long-range intelligence); and for expansion of treatment. There is also need for intensified research, and for careful implementation, and coordination of the many new and promising programs for control.[8]

There are two striking things in the summary that deserve comment. First, five years after the White House recommendations, a new commission characterizes narcotics and drug abuse in this country as a "growing problem." The report does not elaborate on the current dimensions of the narcotic problem, but all the figures today are of the same order as those of 1962.[9] Further, we are safe in assuming that the commission was characterizing the problem on the basis of the extensive evidence presented to it by those who

8. *Id.* at 299.
9. Total active addicts in the United States known to the Federal Bureau of Narcotics was 44,906 at the end of 1960. See U.S. Treasury Department, Bureau of Narcotics, Traffic in Opium and Other Dangerous Drugs 28 (1961). At the end of 1965, the latest report available, the total was 57,199. U.S. Treasury Department, Bureau of Narcotics, Traffic in Opium and Other Dangerous Drugs 17 (1966). All interim reports show a steady increase over this period. For a discussion of the inadequacy of Bureau statistics, see Eldridge, *Statistical Analyses of the Drug Abuse Problem*, Proceedings of the White House Conference on Narcotics and Drug Abuse 139 (1962); Chein, *Some Needed Research on Opiate Addicts*, *id.* at 131. While the criticisms remain valid, an increase of nearly 30% in Bureau statistics over a five-year period is disquieting.

deal with the problem every day. Undoubtedly they see a growth in the problem.

There is, certainly, one aspect of the problem that is unquestionably growing. The shopper for artificial paradises has a greater selection today than ever before. Widening use of "old" drugs such as amphetamines and barbituates and new drugs such as LSD presents serious problems. Whether or how much the number of users has increased we do not know. But, in any event the enterprising search for new ways of achieving pleasures is creating holes in the dikes faster than the government can supply fingers.[10]

Second, despite some differences in the tone of the report, the recommendations are the same as those of five years ago — reflecting a continued focus on means of achieving an unexamined or at least inadequately examined objective. But this time, at least, the elementary questions were raised by some members of the commission. In an appendix of "Additional Views of Individual Commission Members"[11] four members[12] expressed their disappointment that in the area of narcotics, alone among the subjects treated, the commission had been unable to face the fundamental questions. "Instead, for reasons that are quite understandable but in our view not justifiable, it

10. Occasional fads have presented problems beyond the law's capacity. When the pleasure seeker turns to prosaic everyday sources, the control procedures are plainly inadequate. Some half-hearted efforts were made to limit the availability of acetone glues when glue-sniffing emerged as a new and threatening gimmick, but no really concentrated control program has been invoked. The latest innovation, smoking the dried shreds of banana peels, unless ignored, may involve the control structure in riduculous extremes. The humor potential has already proved irresistible to several popular comedians.

11. *Op. cit. supra* note 6, at 302-3.

12. Kingman Brewster, Jr., President of Yale University; Judge Charles D. Breitel, New York Court of Appeals, Julia Davis Stuart, President, League of Women Voters of the United States; and Whitney M. Young, Jr., Executive Director, National Urban League.

assumes that the laws and the traditional methods of enforcement which have obtained for over 50 years are the only proper ways in which to meet the problem."[13] These members found particularly striking the contrast between this attitude and the commission's open-minded, penetrating approach to so many other problems. Reasons abound for the difference, but as the dissenting members pointed out, the reasons provide only an understanding, not a justification.

The commission did make one significant break with past traditions; it decided that research should be undertaken on marijuana aimed at answering whether marijuana belongs within the general system for controlling narcotics use. This could be an extremely important step, representing as it does the first break with the idea that "a drug is a drug is a drug . . .," and that any socially unapproved use is an undiluted evil. This recommendation, even though it is only for research, recognizes that there is a possibility of question. Whatever the outcome of the research, the commission has said, at least with regard to one drug, that scientific evidence is relevant to a study of the law regulating the use of that drug and "the propositions on which they are based."[14]

If the two commission reports constitute a valid measure of change, as suggested earlier, a careful examination of both leads us to two conclusions:

1. There has been little change in the nature or the dimensions of the narcotic problem in the United States over the past five years.
2. There has been little change in the way of looking at the problem, including a continued failure

13. *Op. cit. supra* note 6, at 302.   14. *Id.* at 225 (emphasis added).

to look at the fundamental questions of objective
by even the best qualified public bodies.

The measure of change in method

FIVE YEARS AGO, this study found the nation committed to the premise that control of narcotic addiction and narcotic abuse depended upon a severe and
repressive system of punishment—chiefly long prison
terms without possibility of probation or parole. The
premise underlay the approach to all forms of narcotic
violation—smuggling, selling, dispensing, possession,
record-keeping, treatment. The proponents have often
said that narcotics involvement must be made so risky
and so expensive that it will lose its attractiveness.
Possibly this could be accomplished for the commercial operations, since they do, after all, operate according to market principles. It is patent, however,
that risk of punishment has almost no impact on the
essentially compulsive behavior of the drug user. In
fact, the compulsion of the narcotic addict, the "willingness to do anything to get the drug," forms a part
of the definition of addiction. Yet, the hard-line enforcement people, oblivious to the inconsistency,
have unrelentingly urged more severe sentences in
order to deter user as well as seller.[15]

The 1963 commission recognized the dubiety of the
premise.

The Bureau of Narcotics maintains that the present severe
penalties act as a powerful deterrent. The Commission does

---

15. The inconsistency involved in the definition and punishment of the narcotics addict bears close analogy to the problems of handling the public inebriate. Where the public drunk is demonstrably an alcholic, which is defined in terms of inabil- ity to control the desire for alcohol, courts have ruled that he cannot be criminally punished for appearing in public since that activity is a necessity if the compulsive craving is to be satisfied. See Driver v. Hinnant, 356 F.2d 761 (1966).

not agree. As the Commission pointed out in its introduction, it is difficult to believe that a narcotic addict who is physically and psychologically dependent on a drug will forego satisfaction of this craving for fear of a long prison sentence, or that a marihuana user obsessed by the "high" sensation of marihuana will think of the penalty that awaits him if he is caught possessing it. The weakness of the deterrence position is proved every day by the fact that the illicit traffic in narcotics and marihuana continues.[16]

The commission went on to disagree with the basic theory of penal provisions which treats narcotic offenses as of equal gravity. The commission then divided the various offenses into three categories: (1) smuggling, trafficking, or possessing large quantities for sale, (2) smuggling, selling, and giving away small quantities, and (3) possession without intent to sell.[17] As to each category the commission made a recommendation of appropriate criminal penalties. Of particular interest are the second category and its recommended penalty. It was recognized that the small-scale seller is most often an addict who is supporting his habit, or he may even be giving the drug away "to accommodate a fellow addict who will in turn reciprocate on occasion." Despite its rejection of the deterrent power of imprisonment when applied to addicts, the commission recommended that offenders in the second category "should receive some measure of imprisonment." The commission believes that such offenders should be subject to a fixed maximum sentence and be denied any suspension of sentence but should not be subject to a mandatory minimum sentence and not be denied the hope of parole.[18] Whatever disappointment the proponents of the deterrent

16. *Op. cit. supra* note 3, at 40. 18. *Id.* at 42.
17. *Ibid.*

approach may have felt at the rejection of their position must have been substantially assuaged by the succeeding paragraphs.

The recommendations for decreased penalties for offenses of lesser gravity were addressed directly to the federal penalty structure, but their applicability to state penalties was strongly implied. The recommendations have not been followed in the federal law.[19] The marked increases in the severity of penalties in the 1951 and 1956 federal laws[20] have not been modified to take account of the distinctions between possession for use and possession for sale, nor the significance of the quantity of narcotics involved, nor the difference between marijuana and the opiates. State legislatures have likewise remained unresponsive to the Commission's recommendations. Most of the state penalties remain the same, but nearly a fourth of the states have increased the severity of penalties for violation of one or more provisions of state narcotics laws.[21]

The 1963 Commission recommended a slight easing of the restraints on judicial discretion in sentencing narcotic offenders. The recommendation has been ignored by Congress and the state legislatures. The Commission on Law Enforcement and Administration of Criminal Justice goes far beyond the earlier recommendations, urging that the discretion of a judge to sentence narcotic offenders should be governed by the general rules that govern his discretion in other offenses.[22] There is certainly nothing in the experience of the last five years to cause the advocates

---

19. *Op. cit. supra* note 3, at 223.
20. 65 Stat. 767, 21 U.S.C. 174 (1952); 70 Stat. 570, 21 U.S.C. 174 (1956).
21. Current penalty legislation is set forth in the charts beginning at page 178.
22. *Op. cit. supra* note 3, at 223. See also 141-43.

of greater permissiveness to take heart from the new recommendations.

While there is nothing in the penalty structure to suggest any change in the basic approach to control, there is here, again, one innovation that suggests the possibility of a shift in public attitude and an attempt to respond. Two states and the federal government have established "civil commitment" of narcotic addicts.[23] Little in the experience of medicine or law enforcement leads one to expect substantially improved results from the civil commitment program. Rather, the determination to establish the programs, notwithstanding the lack of such evidence, suggests that the programs are a response to the frustrations of the criminal approach and the public's growing dissatisfaction with the old methods.

Criticisms of the civil commitment programs come from all sides.[24] Many of the objections are valid beyond question, and some probably are not; but the validity of the objections is beside the point here. A response has been made to a change of public sentiment, and though that response may be inadequate or even wrong, and though it certainly represents a compromise between opposing points of view, it nevertheless stands as an attempt, at the very least, to avoid *classifying* the narcotics user as a criminal on the basis of narcotics use alone.

There are, of course, many dangers in such a step. First, under the guise of a non-criminal procedure, the addict may be processed and treated exactly as he has been treated before, but without the protective shield

---

23. CAL. WELFARE & INST. CODE §§ 3000-3201 (Supp. 1965); N.Y. MENTAL HYGIENE LAW, Art. 9, § 208 *et seq.* 80 STATE 1438-48 (1966).

24. *Op. cit. supra* note 6, at 229 and LINDESMITH, THE ADDICT AND THE LAW 290-94 (1965).

of the due process requirements of criminal law. Second, from the addict's point of view, the procedure may be considerably worse; at the hands of those who want to "do for" him instead of "do to" him, he may spend more time confined and under supervision than his less favored associate who grinds his way through the conventional penal mill. Third, and most serious, the concerned segment of the public may congratulate itself for having provided a humane and enlightened system without looking further to see if that system is in fact operating according to expectation.

All these dangers, however, are not inherent in the civil commitment approach. They are chiefly dangers resulting from the fickleness of public opinion and the shallowness of concern on the part of reformers. The dangers should not prevent taking what is probably the only meliorative step currently realizable, but they should alert citizen and reformer to the necessity for constant vigilance to assure that the program is adequately evaluated.

Thus with method as with objective the 1962 status quo is essentially descriptive of 1967. In both instances we see evidence of a certain restlessness growing out of the frustration of trying to deal with the narcotic problem. In neither case has the restlessness borne significant result, but it may, if properly nourished, create for the first time a climate favoring open-minded and careful evaluation of the results of some current experiments in narcotic treatment.

The Vanguard of Experiment

Aldous Huxley has said that it is very unlikely that humanity at large will ever be able to dispense with artificial paradises. Looking at man's past and present, we have almost no ground on which to dispute the proposition. The widespread social approval of, or at least social indifference to, the use of alcohol suggests the extent of tacit acceptance of Huxley's view. But to accept the proposition is not to accept all its manifestations. No matter how cogent the arguments analogizing the use of narcotics to the use of alcohol, or even to tobacco and coffee, the use of narcotics, by and large, exceeds social tolerance.[25] Whatever the reasons — social, scientific, emotional, religious — the public is strongly united in its opposition to drug use and in its demand for prevention and control.[26]

The public is unusually solid in its condemnation of drug use, and the government is almost unquestioning in its adherence to termination of drug use as the prime objective, but here the solidarity ends.[27] Repeated failure of repressive police methods and conventional medical methods has encouraged the proliferation of proposed approaches to the problem. Five years ago, there were almost no programs or experiments in operation that deviated from conventional institutionalized treatment. Criticisms of existing programs and proposals for new experiments were plentiful, but legal and medical inertia and caution

25. A recent study of social tolerance of criminal activity showed drug addiction as the subject of the harshest public attitude. When rated on a scale ranging from 5 (strongly against liberalization of present policies) to 20 (strongly in favor of present policies), social tolerances for three "victimless crimes" were as follows: abortion, 15.7; homosexuality, 12.4; drug addiction, 10.6. See Rooney and Gibbons, *Social Reactions to 'Crimes Without Victims'*, 13 SOCIAL PROBLEMS 400-410 (Spring 1966).

26. Whether public attitude shapes or is shaped by governmental policy is a question on which we have seen no research. Replication of the Rooney and Gibbons study, *ibid.*, in a country with a less vigorous propaganda effort in support of control policies could shed interesting light on this question.

27. See Frankel, *Narcotic Addiction, Criminal Responsibility, and Civil Commitment*, UTAH L. REV. 581 (1966).

presented serious obstacles to transforming any of the proposals into workable programs.

Today we see, at last, a discernible shift. There is a widening range of experimentation and, even more significantly, there is an encouraging trend visible in the willingness of narcotics authorities to evaluate objectively and even to participate in innovative experimentation. The experiments do not extend into the furthest reaches of programs espoused by the avant garde; there are still no dispensing clinics and no ambulatory treatment of drug-using patients, though there are experiments involving the continued administration of substitute drugs. There are still no official programs of completely open institutions, but there are programs with wide latitude for patients. Most important, more and more experiments are based on a recognition that drug-use problems require the development of specialized and individualized techniques; that rehabilitation may not be possible for those who have never been "habilitated" in the first place.

The four approaches to be discussed below have been chosen to represent the kind of experimentation currently directed at the narcotics problem. Two are governmental and two are private. At some points the implicit philosophies of these efforts agree, and at other points they are in irresolvable conflict. Some are obviously suited for only a portion of the total addict population. Others are viewed, by their proponents at least, as promising in all cases. If addiction is, indeed, a highly individualized condition, it is possible that the developing array of treatment methodology may offer something for everybody.

Civil commitment

THE THREE GOVERNMENTAL JURISDICTIONS that face the largest problems—California, New York, and the federal government—have all adopted civil commitment programs.[28] The basic programs are the same but with some variation in each jurisdiction.

Basically, the civil commitment programs are aimed at providing institutional care and therapy for addicts who have run afoul of the narcotic or other criminal laws without classifying the addicts as criminals and without confining them in penal facilities. These programs, however, are based on the conviction that addicts will not be self-motivated toward rehabilitation and that any governmental program of institutionalization must be one based upon coercion.

ELIGIBILITY. Eligibility for the programs varies among the three jurisdictions. California excludes persons convicted of certain offenses unless the court, with consent of the prosecutor and defendant, finds that the interests of justice require civil commitment.[29] In New York an addict charged with crime is ineligible if he has been convicted previously of a felony or if he has been committed previously as an addict. Where the addict is charged with a felony carrying a penalty of death or life imprisonment, he is not eligible for civil commitment. Moreover, in any case where the addict is charged with a felony, he will be excluded from the civil commitment program unless the prosecutor consents to commitment.[30] The

28. CAL. WELFARE AND INST. CODE §§ 5625-5635 (1966); N.Y. PUBLIC HEALTH LAW §§ 3360-3366 (1954); PUBLIC HEALTH AND WELFARE, 42 U.S.C.A. §§ 257, 258, 260, 260a, 261a (1956).

29. CAL. WELFARE AND INST. CODE §§ 3051, 3052 (Supp. 1965).
30. N.Y. MENTAL HYGIENE LAW § 210 (Supp. 1967).

federal program excludes persons charged with crimes of violence, with unlawfully importing, selling, or conspiring to import or sell narcotic drugs; persons against whom a prior felony charge is pending or who have not fully served any sentence from prior convictions; persons who have two or more previous convictions on felony charges; and persons who have had three or more civil commitments for narcotics addiction under federal or state programs.

PROCEDURES. In California a judge may adjourn criminal proceedings, after conviction and before sentencing, to hold a hearing on whether the defendant is an addict or in danger of becoming one. The hearing procedure provides for the full complement of due process safeguards including representation by counsel and the right to jury trial. If the defendant is found to be addicted or in danger of becoming addicted, he may be committed to a narcotics detention, treatment, and rehabilitation center for a maximum of seven years and a minimum of six months. (Volunteers may be committed for a maximum of two and one-half years.) Parole is available and includes close supervision, periodic and surprise testing for narcotics use, counseling, and return to inpatient status where considered necessary. Patients may be discharged from the program after not less than three years on parole. Finally, whether the original charges against the defendant shall be dismissed rests with the court in which he was tried.

The New York system is quite similar to the California program, but with the following important procedural differences: criminal proceedings are suspended while a suspected addict undergoes medical examination. If found to be addicted, the defendant is immediately detoxified. Eligible addicts are given a choice of proceeding with the criminal trial or being committed civilly for treatment. Commitment and aftercare range from three to five years; successful completion abates the criminal proceeding. Charges are reinstated against addicts who fail to complete the program, but the sentence is reduced by the time served in civil commitment.

The federal program is the most elaborate. It provides for both pretrial and posttrial commitment. Under the pretrial provision, addicts are committed to the custody of the Surgeon General for a maximum of three years allocated between hospitalization and aftercare in the Surgeon General's discretion. Addicts committed after trial are in custody of the Attorney General for an indeterminate period, not to exceed ten years or the maximum sentence for the addict's offense.

In the pretrial procedures, the addict may choose to submit to medical examination. If he so elects, the criminal charges are held in abeyance. Having agreed to initiation of the procedures, the addict may not voluntarily withdraw from examination or the treatment program that follows. If after treatment the Surgeon General certifies to the court that the individual has successfully completed the program, the court discharges the defendant from custody. If the Surgeon General is unable to certify successful completion, the criminal proceeding is resumed, with the defendant receiving credit against his sentence for time spent in commitment.

Addicts may also be committed under the federal legislation though not charged with any criminal

offense.[31] "Related individuals" may file a petition
with the United States Attorney to have an alleged
addict committed. A physician then makes a determination of addiction and the likelihood of rehabilitation through treatment. The court also must find, upon
a hearing, that the addict is likely to be rehabilitated
through treatment before committing him to the program. The alleged addict is entitled to have all relevant evidence heard, to testify, and to present and
cross-examine witnesses. All orders of commitment
are subject to appellate review. Non-criminal addicts
may be committed to a hospital for a maximum of six
months and to the custody of the Surgeon General for
posthospitalization treatment for a maximum of three
years.

TECHNIQUES. During hospitalization, emphasis is on
group therapy, educational services, marital and family counseling, sheltered work programs, and recrea-
tional activities. Also, close supervision upon release
from the hospital is stressed, and efforts are made to
reintegrate the individual gradually into his outside
environment.

Once the addict is received at the rehabilitation
unit, he is given a physical examination and psychiatric screening. Through administration of a battery of
tests, an investigation into the addict's social and
criminal history, and various interviews, the counseling staff attempts to develop an individualized treatment program.

RESULTS. Assessment of the accomplishment of all

31. New York and California statutes   (Supp. 1967); CAL. WELFARE AND
    have similar provisions. N.Y.   INST. CODE §§ 5625-5635 (1966).
    MENTAL HYGIENE LAW § 206

narcotic programs is difficult. Since narcotic treatment is necessarily of long duration, the difficulty of evaluation is heightened when dealing with new programs.

In New York, the meagerness of data makes assessment of the programs impossible at the present point. It appears that the election of treatment option afforded to the addict under the New York plan has not worked satisfactorily. "[T]he Metcalf-Volker Law did not demonstrate that permitting the arrested narcotic addict to choose civil commitment and a course of treatment and rehabilitation in lieu of prosecution could serve as the basis for a broad and comprehensive approach to New York's narcotic addiction problem."[32] The experience with the Metcalf-Volker Law, however, has provided the base for new legislation.[33] The implication throughout reports on the New York program is that civil commitment can help drug users over a period of time and that preliminary experience warrants continuation and expansion of the program.

In California, there is considerably more data available on the programs in progress under civil commitment laws, but here again, the short duration of the program makes evaluation difficult. The reports emanating from the California program reflect a cautious but increasing tone of optimism. A 1966 report covering the preceding five years stated: "Experience within the Department of Corrections in handling narcotic addicts has supplied no cures, but has not been completely negative."[34] In the same report, the author writes that the program has "demonstrated that there

---

32. Letter from Dr. Harold Meiselas of the Narcotic Addiction Control Commission to the author, dated January 3, 1967.

33. N.Y. MENTAL HYGIENE LAW §§ 200-213 (C.L.S. Supp. 1966).

34. WOOD, THE CIVIL NARCOTICS PROGRAM—A FIVE YEAR PROGRESS REPORT 28 (Cal. Rehabilitation Center, Oct. 27, 1966).

is hope for the addict. The addict can be successfully treated in a non-punitive setting."[35] The Third Annual Report of the Narcotics Rehabilitation Advisory Council reflects current appraisal of program results. "The civil addict program has continued to make consistent progress with each year of operation. When 1966 results are compared with prior years, better results are being achieved . . . with more difficult people . . . in a shorter period of institution stay . . . for less money."[36]

As pointed out earlier, statistical comparison is very difficult, potentially misleading, and always confusing. In the administration of a program that must take a long-range view—ten years or more—and that must consider recidivism a natural and inherent aspect of the disease being treated, great care must be taken in evaluating its results. The number of addicts continuing drug-free must be expected to decline as the time out of the institution lengthens. The measure of success should be against other experience with other methods, not against an absolute scale. Further, any successful program will reach out to accept commitments reflecting greater risk as the program operators accumulate greater experience and confidence. This also, predictably, will affect the ratio of "successes" to "failures." Probably the only meaningful universal measure of successful programs is the number of drug-free days experienced by addicts at what cost. A drug-free day represents a benefit to the addict and to the community. To count as failure three years of abstinence followed by a relapse to drug use is absurd.

35. *Id.* at 1.
36. Draft of the Third Annual Report, dated May 1, 1967, provided to the author by Roland W. Wood, Superintendent of the California Rehabilitation Center at Corona, California.

The author has seen no reports of government programs couched in terms of drug-free days.[37]

Synanon House

ONE OF THE MOST interesting programs for treating narcotic addicts is Synanon, the therapeutic community run by former addicts in Santa Monica, California.[38] Data on treatment at Synanon is scanty, due in large part to the antipathy of Synanon leaders to statistical evaluation.[39] There have been glowing claims by, for, and about Synanon, and even skeptical observers concede that the program has had substantial success in freeing its residents from addiction.[40]

Basically, Synanon is a community run by the formerly addicted for the currently addicted. No efforts are made to recruit new members; the addict must find Synanon and convince its members that he should be permitted to enter. At the outset, applicants are carefully screened in an interview of brutal directness. Synanon demands of any inhabitant or applicant full recognition of his problem and its seriousness. Withdrawal is immediate, without medi-

37. For those interested in probing the statistics, the following sources are recommended: *op. cit. supra* note 33; California Rehabilitation Center, Civil Addict Program, Statistical Review, *Narcotics Rehabil. Advis. Coun., 2d Annual Report* (Cal. Youth and Adult Corrections Agency, 1966); *Narcotics Rehabil. Advis. Coun., 3d Annual Report* (1967). Some data on the New York experience is reported in 112 CONG. REC. 24416 (Daily ed., Oct. 6, 1966).

38. The most extensive and sympathetic treatment of Synanon can be found in DANIEL CASRIEL, SO FAIR A HOUSE: THE STORY OF SYNANON (1963). See also Lewis Yablonsky, *The Anti-Criminal Society*, 26 FEDERAL PROBATION 50 (Sept. 1962).

39. Gilbert Geis, *Narcotic Treatment Programs in California*, PERSPECTIVES ON NARCOTIC ADDICTION (Chatham Conference, Mass., 1963). Charles Diederick, founder of Synanon, explains his opposition to counting in Casriel, *op. cit. supra* note 38, at 175-79.

40. See, *e.g.*, Steinberg, *Synanon House—A Consideration of Its Implications for American Correction*, 54 J. CRIM. L., C. & P.S. 447 (Dec. 1963).

cation, and in full view of the others. Synanon attempts to aid the addict in recognizing the problems
underlying his addiction and to build a protective
society in which he can live. The first objective is
implemented by a kind of group therapy seminar,
called the "small-s synanon"; these are wide-open
sessions drawing the line only at physical violence.
Ridicule, cross-examination, and hostile verbal attack
are the weapons of therapy.

The second objective — creation and maintenance
of a supportive community — has produced the most
severe and telling attacks from the critics. Synanon
residents are not encouraged to leave the community,
an approach that flies in the face of all American correctional philosophy.[41] One writer views the process
as the "Synanon Syndrome," replacing one form of
addiction (narcotics) with another (protective community).[42] Indeed, the inward orientation of Synanon
does qualify its success and raise doubts as to its
applicability on a broad scale and as to its accept-
ability to society. If we wish to return the addict to
society as an autonomous individual capable of living
within social norms, yet free to exercise his creative
capabilities, then Synanon has thus far offered limited
hope of widespread impact.[43] The individual in Synanon is still isolated from society, albeit in a voluntary and sometimes productive manner.

Aside from serious questions about its objectives,
the methodology of Synanon is probably an absolute

41. *Ibid.*
42. *Ibid.*
43. Of course, an important word in this evaluation is "return." Many addicts have *never* been functioning autonomous individuals in society. In many cases they have never experienced the security of family or group acceptance. Thus, Synanon's senior members would say that the protective community is equipping them for their first entry into society, not a return, and that this process is long, difficult, and delicate.

limitation on the quantitative impact of the program. First, Synanon requires forceful leadership able to convey with unequivocating assurance the rightness and righteousness of its mission.[44] Second, it has worked with a highly selected population screened by "inmates," not by outsiders or administrators. The selectivity of Synanon has been motivated primarily by its limited resources and a desire to allocate those resources where the members feel they will be most useful. The result, nevertheless, has been to work with prime candidates for Synanon-style therapy. Third, and perhaps most important, is Synanon's corporateness and privacy. Public money, and the resulting taint of the establishment, might destroy the very basis of the Synanon program. If the money did not, the increased size of the communities might.

Despite the limitations, Synanon remains a promising program. It shares with society the view that a day without drugs is better than a day with drugs. If society is able to accomplish drug-free days only through imprisonment or commitment, Synanon's way seems much preferable, even if it means that the addict never returns to society as a functioning individual.

Daytop Village

THERE ARE SOME who believe that the Synanon approach can be made to work under a program of governmental support and sanction, and an experiment has begun in New York to substantiate this. Daytop Village, originally called Daytop Lodge (the name is an acronym for Drug Addicts Treated on Probation), was established by the Probation Depart-

---

44. Geis, *op. cit. supra* note 38.

ment of the Supreme Court of New York City under a grant from the National Institute of Mental Health.[45] All residents of Daytop are paroled there by the New York City courts. In order to be referred (residence at the Lodge takes the place of serving a sentence), the addicted criminal offender must demonstrate to the court an interest in rehabilitation, besides meeting more specific requirements as to age, sex, literacy, intelligence, etc. Admission is not insured by referral. Once he arrives at the house, having traveled there unaccompanied, the candidate must convince the admission committee (composed of ex-addicts, many from Synanon) that he is truly motivated by a desire for rehabilitation, not merely detoxification, and that he will abide by the rules of the house: complete abstinence from all drugs, no physical violence, and assumption of his share of the work and responsibility for the house and the program. The rules are identical to those of Synanon House.

The program has three phases: (1) full-time residence at the house for ten months, (2) work in the outside community while residing at the house, and (3) work and residence in the home community while on probation from the court. The goals are identical to those of Synanon, though the external support and involvement in Daytop doubtless causes the greater emphasis on speedy return to the community. The techniques also are those developed at Synanon— small-s synanons, group therapy marathons, lectures, and dressing down before the group.

45. For a more complete presentation on the Daytop program see: Shelly and Bassin, *Daytop Lodge Halfway House for Drug Addicts*, 28 FEDERAL PROBATION 46 (Dec. 1964); Shelly and Bassin, *Daytop Lodge—A New Treatment Approach for Drug Addicts*, 11 CORRECTIVE PSYCHIATRY 186 (July 1965); Casriel and Deitch, *Permanent Cure of Narcotic Addicts*, PHYSICIANS PANORAMA (Oct. 1966).

Few data are yet available on Daytop experience, but those associated with the project give an impression of satisfaction with progress so far. Of all those who enter the program, 60 percent remain for the duration of treatment.[46] Sufficient time has not yet elapsed to permit revealing follow-up studies, but New York is proceeding with plans for identical establishments in all boroughs of the city. There are also plans for establishing branch villages in other states.[47]

Maintenance therapy

THE MOST CONTROVERSIAL development in the treatment of narcotic addiction has been the maintenance therapy program. Maintenance therapy involves the administration of a synthetic narcotic substitute, in this case methadone, which blocks the euphoria produced by heroin, eliminates the craving for heroin, and avoids the developing of a craving for the substitute.

The experimental maintenance therapy program was begun in January of 1964 by Dr. Marie Nyswander and Dr. Vincent Dole of Rockefeller University. The program was expanded with the establishment of a wing of Manhattan General Hospital in January of 1965, and more recently at Harlem Hospital.

The treatment program consists of three phases. First is a six-week period of hospitalization during which blockade is induced. During this time, the patient is allowed extensive freedom; the ward is never locked, and he is permitted to leave during the day for approved activities such as a job, shopping, school, museums, or visits to family. In the second

46. Casriel and Deitch, *op. cit. supra* note 44.   47. New York Times, June 26, 1966, p. 53, col. 1.

phase, the addict is an out-patient returning to the hospital daily to receive medication and leave urine specimens. This is the most difficult time for the patient; he is returning to a strange and often friend-less world, the familiar world of the addict no longer being available to him. Besides receiving his daily medication at the hospital, the addict also receives support and encouragement from older patients and from the staff, though no formal psychotherapy is offered. Phase three is reached when the patient is living a responsible life, self-supporting, and requir-ing little or no social help from the institution or the staff. During this phase, the need for continuing medi-cation is periodically reviewed by the staff physician. Thus far blockade has not been discontinued in any patient.[48]

As of March, 1966, 120 patients had been admitted to the program, of which 13 had been discharged because of psychopathic behavior, intractable con-tinuing addiction to non-narcotic substances such as alcohol and barbiturates, or psychosis. Of the remain-ing 107 in the program, none had returned to the use of heroin. As of March, 1966, 79 of the patients had been in the program for more than three months; 71 percent of these were employed in a steady job, going to school, or both. (Employment and education being used as measures of social rehabilitation, these patients are considered to be leading socially useful lives.) Here again the data is meager, but what is available is encouraging.

Predictably, this program has evoked violent re-

48. See Dole and Nyswander, *Reha-bilitation of Heroin Addicts after Blockade with Methadone*, 66 N. Y. J. OF MEDICINE 2011 (Aug. 1, 1966); Dole, Nyswander, and Kreek, *Narcotic Blockade*, 118 ARCHIVES OF INTERNAL MEDICINE 304 (Oct. 1966).

actions on the part of many people concerned with the problems of addiction. Opponents argue that maintenance therapy is simply the substitution of one addiction for another and fails to get at the basic causes of addiction. In rebuttal of this viewpoint, the program's defenders reply that the argument is irrelevant, that what really counts is that people who were formerly useless to themselves and to society are now productive and relatively happy individuals. In the words of the program's foremost pioneer:

> What it comes down to . . . is that we take care of the pharmacological problems, leaving the addict and everyone else free to turn his attention to other problems. It does not strike me as relevant whether these patients ever get off methadone. . . . What is relevant is that a treatment can be developed so that the addict can become a socially useful citizen, happy in himself and society.[49]

It seems to this writer that the real criticism is not of a failure to get at the basic causes of addiction but a failure to get the addict to respond to those causes in the same way the critic does. There currently exists a pretty good picture of the stresses and pressures that give rise to addiction, although there is not a good understanding of why some people respond by escaping through drugs, while others respond in ways which society accepts or at least tolerates. Thus the critic of maintenance therapy and the critic of Synanon are both saying that anything short of a full acculturation to society's norms by society's methods is a crutch or, more dramatically, another form of addiction.

Like Synanon, maintenance therapy probably has

---

49. Interview with Marie Nyswander, NEW YORKER, June 26, 1965, p. 54.

a limited role in the over-all control of addiction. It requires a high degree of motivation and determination and it is not aimed at those individuals who are using narcotics to meet basic psychological needs. If motivations to change the pattern of living is as rare among addicts as we have been told, there are few who will or can benefit from the maintenance program.

It is quite true that there is not now, nor does it appear likely that there ever will be, a single universal answer to the problems of narcotic addiction. There are, however, hopeful signs that the multifaceted problem may be resolved with multifaceted responses. For the many addicts who clearly are not sufficiently motivated to enter any voluntary program, coercion seems to offer a possible answer. It must be remembered that coercion has a place in any organized society, and that through its careful use, the civil commitment program may be shaped into an effective and humane instrument providing the authority structure these addicts seem to need. It is also clear that some addicts are not going to respond to authority — indeed it may be authority against which their addiction is a defense — and for them, developments like Synanon and maintenance therapy may hold the answer. The great key in any program, private or governmental, is somehow, at some stage, to reach the addict in terms of motivation. He must be helped to see that he is more than the object of experimentation. He must be aided to see that there are other ways than his way. If he can be helped to see that there are other ways, and yet rejects them, then it is time for the rest of us to question what is wrong with the norm society insists upon.

Appendix A

UNIFORM NARCOTIC DRUG ACT *

An Act defining and relating to narcotic drugs and to make uniform the law with reference thereto.

1932 Act

Be it enacted . . . .

§ 1. *Definitions.*

The following words and phrases, as used in this act, shall have the following meanings, unless the context otherwise requires:

(1) "Person" includes any corporation, association, copartnership, or one or more individuals.

* Prepared by the National Conference of Commissioners on Uniform State Laws. Reprinted here by permission.

(2) "Physician" means a person authorized by law to practice medicine in this state and any other person authorized by law to treat sick and injured human beings in this state and to use narcotic drugs in connection with such treatment.

(3) "Dentist" means a person authorized by law to practice dentistry in this state.

(4) "Veterinarian" means a person authorized by law to practice veterinary medicine in this state.

(5) "Manufacturer" means a person who by compounding, mixing, cultivating, growing, or other process, produces or prepares narcotic drugs, but does not include an apothecary who compounds narcotic drugs to be sold or dispensed on prescriptions.

(6) "Wholesaler" means a person who supplies narcotic drugs that he himself has not produced nor prepared, on official written orders but not on prescriptions.

(7) "Apothecary" means a licensed pharmacist as defined by the laws of this state and, where the context so requires, the owner of a store or other place of business where narcotic drugs are compounded or dispensed by a licensed pharmacist; but nothing in this act shall be construed as conferring on a person who is not registered nor licensed as a pharmacist any authority, right, or privilege, that is not granted to him by the pharmacy laws of this state.

(8) "Hospital" means an institution for the care and treatment of the sick and injured, approved by [Insert here proper official designation of state officer or board] as proper to be entrusted with the custody of narcotic drugs and the professional use of narcotic drugs under the direction of a physician, dentist, or veterinarian.

(9) "Laboratory" means a laboratory approved by [Insert here proper official designation of state officer or board] as proper to be entrusted with the custody of narcotic drugs and the use of narcotic drugs for scientific and medical purposes and for purposes of instruction.

(10) "Sale" includes barter, exchange, or gift, or offer therefor, and each such transaction made by any person, whether as principal, proprietor, agent, servant, or employee.

(11) "Coca leaves" includes cocaine and any compound, manufacture, salt, derivative, mixture, or preparation of coca leaves, ex-

cept derivatives of coca leaves which do not contain cocaine, ecgonine, or substances from which cocaine or ecgonine may be synthesized or made.

(12) "Opium" includes morphine, codeine, and heroin, and any compound, manufacture, salt, derivative, mixture, or preparation of opium, but does not include apomorphine or any of its salts.

(13) "Cannabis" includes all parts of the plant Cannabis Sativa L., whether growing or not; the seeds thereof; the resin extracted from any part of such plant; and every compound, manufacture, salt, derivative, mixture, or preparation of such plant, its seeds, or resin; but shall not include the mature stalks of such plant, fiber produced from such stalks, oil or cake made from the seeds of such plant, any other compound, manufacture, salt, derivative, mixture or preparation of such mature stalks (except the resin extracted therefrom), fiber, oil, or cake, or the sterilized seed of such plant which is incapable of germination.

(14) "Narcotic drugs" means coca leaves, opium, cannabis, and every other substance neither chemically nor physically distinguishable from them; any other drugs to which the Federal Narcotic Laws may now apply; and any drug found by the (State Commissioner of Health or other competent state officer), after reasonable notice and opportunity for hearing, to have an addiction-forming or addiction-sustaining liability similar to morphine or cocaine, from the effective date of determination of such finding by said (State Commissioner of Health or other competent state officer).

(15) "Federal Narcotic Laws" means the laws of the United States relating to opium, coca leaves, and other narcotic drugs.

(16) "Official Written Order" means an order written on a form provided for that purpose by the United States Commissioner of Narcotics, under any laws of the United States making provision therefor, if such order forms are authorized and required by federal law, and if no such order form is provided, then on an official form provided for that purpose by [Insert here proper official designation of state officer or board].

(17) "Dispense" includes distribute, leave with, give away, dispose of, or deliver.

(18) "Registry number" means the number assigned to each per-

son registered under the Federal Narcotic Laws. As amended August 1942; September 1952.

§ 2. *Acts Prohibited.*

It shall be unlawful for any person to manufacture, possess, have under his control, sell, prescribe, administer, dispense, or compound any narcotic drug, except as authorized in this act.

§ 3. *Manufacturers and Wholesalers.*

No person shall manufacture, compound, mix, cultivate, grow, or by any other process produce or prepare narcotic drugs, and no person as a wholesaler shall supply the same, without having first obtained a license so to do from the [Insert here proper official designation of state officer or board].

§ 4. *Qualification for Licenses.*

No license shall be issued under the foregoing section unless and until the applicant therefor has furnished proof satisfactory to [Insert here proper official designation of state officer or board].

(a) That the applicant is of good moral character or, if the applicant be an association or corporation, that the managing officers are of good moral character.

(b) That the applicant is equipped as to land, buildings, and paraphernalia properly to carry on the business described in his application.

No license shall be granted to any person who has within five years been convicted of a willful violation of any law of the United States, or of any state, relating to opium, coca leaves, or other narcotic drugs, or to any person who is a narcotic drug addict.

The [Insert here proper official designation of state officer or board] may suspend or revoke any license for cause.

§ 5. *Sale on Written Orders.*

(1) A duly licensed manufacturer or wholesaler may sell and dispense narcotic drugs to any of the following persons, but only on official written orders:

(a) To a manufacturer, wholesaler, or apothecary.

(b) To a physician, dentist, or veterinarian.

(c) To a person in charge of a hospital, but only for use by or in that hospital.

(d) To a person in charge of a laboratory, but only for use in that laboratory for scientific and medical purposes.

(2) A duly licensed manufacturer or wholesaler may sell narcotic drugs to any of the following persons:

(a) On a special written order accompanied by a certificate of exemption, as required by the Federal Narcotic Laws, to a person in the employ of the United States Government or of any state, territorial, district, county, municipal, or insular government, purchasing, receiving, possessing, or dispensing narcotic drugs by reason of his official duties.

(b) To a master of a ship or a person in charge of any aircraft upon which no physician is regularly employed, or to a physician or surgeon duly licensed in some State, Territory, or the District of Columbia to practice his profession, or to a retired commissioned medical officer of the United States Army, Navy, or Public Health Service employed upon such ship or aircraft, for the actual medical needs of persons on board such ship or aircraft, when not in port. *Provided:* Such narcotic drugs shall be sold to the master of such ship or person in charge of such aircraft or to a physician, surgeon, or retired commissioned medical officer of the United States Army, Navy, or Public Health Service employed upon such ship or aircraft only in pursuance of a special order form approved by a commissioned medical officer or acting assistant surgeon of the United States Public Health Service.

(c) To a person in a foreign country if the provisions of the Federal Narcotic Laws are complied with.

(3) Use of Official Written Orders. An official written order for any narcotic drug shall be signed in duplicate by the person giving said order or by his duly authorized agent. The original shall be presented to the person who sells or dispenses the narcotic drug or drugs

named therein. In event of the acceptance of such order by said person, each party to the transaction shall preserve his copy of such order for a period of two years in such a way as to be readily accessible for inspection by any public officer or employee engaged in the enforcement of this act. It shall be deemed a compliance with this subsection if the parties to the transaction have complied with the Federal Narcotic Laws, respecting the requirements governing the use of order forms.

(4) Possession Lawful. Possession of or control of narcotic drugs obtained as authorized by this section shall be lawful if in the regular course of business, occupation, profession, employment, or duty of the possessor.

(5) A person in charge of a hospital or of a laboratory, or in the employ of this state or of any other state, or of any political subdivision thereof or a master of a ship or a person in charge of any aircraft upon which no physician is regularly employed, or a physician or surgeon duly licensed in some State, Territory, or the District of Columbia, to practice his profession, or a retired commissioned medical officer of the United States Army, Navy, or Public Health Service employed upon such ship or aircraft who obtains narcotic drugs under the provisions of this section or otherwise, shall not administer, nor dispense, nor otherwise use such drugs within this state, except within the scope of his employment or official duty, and then only for scientific or medicinal purposes and subject to the provisions of this act. As amended August 1942.

§ 6. *Sales by Apothecaries.*

(1) An apothecary, in good faith, may sell and dispense narcotic drugs to any person upon a written prescription of a physician, dentist, or veterinarian, dated and signed by the person prescribing on the day when issued and bearing the full name and address of the patient for whom, or of the owner of the animal for which, the drug is dispensed, and the full name, address, and registry number under the Federal Narcotic Laws of the person prescribing, if he is required by those laws to be so registered. If the prescription be for an animal, it shall state the species of animal for which the drug is prescribed. The person filling the prescription shall write the date of

filling and his own signature on the face of the prescription. The prescription shall be retained on file by the proprietor of the pharmacy in which it is filled for a period of two years, so as to be readily accessible for inspection by any public officer or employee engaged in the enforcement of this act. The prescription shall not be refilled.

(2) The legal owner of any stock of narcotic drugs in a pharmacy, upon discontinuance of dealing in said drugs, may sell said stock to a manufacturer, wholesaler, or apothecary, but only on an official written order.

(3) An apothecary, only upon an official written order, may sell to a physician, dentist, or veterinarian, in quantities not exceeding one ounce at any one time, aqueous or oleaginous solutions of which the content of narcotic drugs does not exceed a proportion greater than twenty per cent of the complete solution, to be used for medical purposes.

§ 7. *Professional Use of Narcotic Drugs.*

(1) Physicians and Dentists. A physician or a dentist, in good faith and in the course of his professional practice only, may prescribe, administer, and dispense narcotic drugs, or he may cause the same to be administered by a nurse or interne under his direction and supervision.

(2) Veterinarians. A veterinarian, in good faith and in the course of his professional practice only, and not for use by a human being, may prescribe, administer, and dispense narcotic drugs, and he may cause them to be administered by an assistant or orderly under his direction and supervision.

(3) Return of Unused Drugs. Any person who has obtained from a physician, dentist, or veterinarian any narcotic drug for administration to a patient during the absence of such physician, dentist, or veterinarian, shall return to such physician, dentist, or veterinarian any unused portion of such drug, when it is no longer required by the patient.

§ 8. *Preparations Exempted.*

Except as otherwise in this act specifically provided, this act shall not apply to the following cases:

Administering, dispensing, or selling at retail any medicinal preparation that contains in one fluid ounce, or if a solid or semi-solid preparation, in one avoirdupois ounce, not more than one grain of codeine or of any of its salts, or not more than one-sixth grain of dihydrocodeine or any of its salts.

The exemption authorized by this section shall be subject to the following conditions: (1) that the medicinal preparation administered, dispensed, or sold, shall contain, in addition to the narcotic drug in it, some drug or drugs conferring upon it medicinal qualities other than those possessed by the narcotic drug alone; and (2) that such preparation shall be administered, dispensed, and sold in good faith as a medicine and not for the purpose of evading the provisions of this act.

Nothing in this section shall be construed to limit the quantity of codeine or of any of its salts that may be prescribed, administered, dispensed, or sold, to any person or for the use of any person or animal, when it is prescribed, administered, dispensed, or sold, in compliance with the general provisions of this act. As amended August 1942; September 1952.

§ 9. *Record to be Kept.*

(1) Physicians, Dentists, Veterinarians, and Other Authorized Persons. Every physician, dentist, veterinarian, or other person who is authorized to administer or professionally use narcotic drugs, shall keep a record of such drugs received by him, and a record of all such drugs administered, dispensed, or professionally used by him otherwise than by prescription. It shall, however, be deemed a sufficient compliance with this subsection if any such person using small quantities of solutions or other preparations of such drugs for local application, shall keep a record of the quantity, character, and potency of such solutions or other preparations purchased or made up by him, and of the dates when purchased or made up, without keeping a record of the amount of such solution or other preparation applied by him to individual patients.

Provided: That no record need be kept of narcotic drugs administered, dispensed, or professionally used in the treatment of any one patient, when the amount administered, dispensed, or professionally used for that purpose does not exceed in any forty-eight consecutive hours (a) four grains of opium, or (b) one-half of a grain of morphine or of any of its salts, or (c) two grains of codeine or of any of its salts, or (d) one-fourth of a grain of heroin or of any of its salts, or (e) a quantity of any other narcotic drug or any combination of narcotic drugs that does not exceed in pharmacologic potency any one of the drugs named above in the quantity stated.

(2) Manufacturers and Wholesalers. Manufacturers and wholesalers shall keep records of all narcotic drugs compounded, mixed, cultivated, grown, or by any other process produced or prepared, and of all narcotic drugs received and disposed of by them, in accordance with the provisions of subsection 5 of this section.

(3) Apothecaries. Apothecaries shall keep records of all narcotic drugs received and disposed of by them, in accordance with the provisions of subsection 5 of this section.

(4) Vendors of Exempted Preparations. Every person who purchases for resale, or who sells narcotic drug preparations exempted by Section 8 of this act, shall keep a record showing the quantities and kinds thereof received and sold, or disposed of otherwise, in accordance with the provisions of subsection 5 of this section.

(5) Form and Preservation of Records. The form of records shall be prescribed by the [Insert here proper official designation of state officer or board]. The record of narcotic drugs received shall in every case show the date of receipt, the name and address of the person from whom received, and the kind and quantity of drugs received; the kind and quantity of narcotic drugs produced or removed from process of manufacture, and the date of such production or removal from process of manufacture; and the record shall in every case show the proportion of morphine, cocaine, or ecgonine contained in or producible from crude opium or coca leaves received or produced and the proportion of resin contained in or producible from the plant Cannabis Sativa L. The record of all narcotic drugs sold, administered, dispensed, or otherwise disposed of, shall show the date of selling, administering, or dispensing, the name and address of the person to whom, or for whose use, or the owner and species of animal for which the drugs were sold, administered or dispensed, and the kind and quantity of drugs. Every such record

shall be kept for a period of two years from the date of the transaction recorded. The keeping of a record required by or under the
Federal Narcotic Laws, containing substantially the same information as is specified above, shall constitute compliance with this
section, except that every such record shall contain a detailed list of
narcotic drugs lost, destroyed, or stolen, if any, the kind and quantity of such drugs, and the date of the discovery of such loss, destruction, or theft. As amended August 1942.

§ 10.   *Labels.*

(1) Whenever a manufacturer sells or dispenses a narcotic drug,
and whenever a wholesaler sells or dispenses a narcotic drug in a
package prepared by him, he shall securely affix to each package in
which that drug is contained a label showing in legible English the
name and address of the vendor and the quantity, kind, and form
of narcotic drug contained therein. No person except an apothecary
for the purpose of filling a prescription under this act, shall alter,
deface, or remove any label so affixed.

(2) Whenever an apothecary sells or dispenses any narcotic drug
on a prescription issued by a physician, dentist, or veterinarian, he
shall affix to the container in which such drug is sold or dispensed,
a label showing his own name, address, and registry number, or the
name, address, and registry number of the apothecary for whom he
is lawfully acting; the name and address of the patient or, if the
patient is an animal, the name and address of the owner of the
animal and the species of the animal; the name, address, and registry number of the physician, dentist, or veterinarian, by whom the
prescription was written; and such directions as may be stated on
the prescription. No person shall alter, deface, or remove any label
so affixed.

§ 11.   *Authorized Possession of Narcotic Drugs by*
Individuals.

A person to whom or for whose use any narcotic drug has been
prescribed, sold, or dispensed, by a physician, dentist, apothecary, or
other person authorized under the provisions of Section 5 of this
act, and the owner of any animal for which any such drug has been

prescribed, sold, or dispensed, by a veterinarian, may lawfully possess it only in the container in which it was delivered to him by the person selling or dispensing the same.

§ 12. *Persons and Corporations Exempted.*

The provisions of this act restricting the possessing and having control of narcotic drugs shall not apply to common carriers or to warehousemen, while engaged in lawfully transporting or storing such drugs, or to any employee of the same acting within the scope of his employment; or to public officers or their employees in the performance of their official duties requiring possession or control of narcotic drugs; or to temporary incidental possession by employees or agents of persons lawfully entitled to possession, or by persons whose possession is for the purpose of aiding public officers in performing their official duties.

§ 13. *Common Nuisances.*

Any store, shop, warehouse, dwelling house, building, vehicle, boat, aircraft, or any place whatever, which is resorted to by narcotic drug addicts for the purpose of using narcotic drugs or which is used for the illegal keeping or selling of the same, shall be deemed a common nuisance. No person shall keep or maintain such a common nuisance.

§ 14. *Narcotic Drugs to be Delivered to State Official, etc.*

All narcotic drugs, the lawful possession of which is not established or the title to which cannot be ascertained, which have come into the custody of a peace officer, shall be forfeited, and disposed of as follows:

(a) Except as in this section otherwise provided, the court or magistrate having jurisdiction shall order such narcotic drugs forfeited and destroyed. A record of the place where said drugs were seized, of the kinds and quantities of drugs so destroyed, and of the time, place, and manner of destruction, shall be kept, and a return under oath, reporting said destruction, shall be made to the court or magistrate and to the United States Commissioner of Narcotics, by the officer who destroys them.

(b) Upon written application by the State [Commissioner of Public Health], the court or magistrate by whom the forfeiture of narcotic drugs has been decreed may order the delivery of any of them, except heroin and its salts and derivatives, to said State [Commissioner of Public Health], for distribution or destruction, as hereinafter provided.

(c) Upon application by any hospital within this State, not operated for private gain, the State [Commissioner of Public Health] may in his discretion deliver any narcotic drugs that have come into his custody by authority of this section to the applicant for medicinal use. The State [Commissioner of Public Health] may from time to time deliver excess stocks of such narcotic drugs to the United States Commissioner of Narcotics, or may destroy the same.

(d) The State [Commissioner of Public Health] shall keep a full and complete record of all drugs received and of all drugs disposed of, showing the exact kinds, quantities, and forms of such drugs; the persons from whom received and to whom delivered; by whose authority received, delivered, and destroyed; and the date of the receipt, disposal, or destruction, which record shall be open to inspection by all Federal or State officers charged with the enforcement of Federal and State narcotic laws.

§ 15. *Notice of Conviction to be Sent to Licensing Board.*

On the conviction of any person of the violation of any provision of this act, a copy of the judgment and sentence, and of the opinion of the court or magistrate, if any opinion be filed, shall be sent by the clerk of the court, or by the magistrate, to the board or officer, if any, by whom the convicted defendant has been licensed or registered to practice his profession or to carry on his business. On the conviction of any such person, the court may, in its discretion, suspend or revoke the license or registration of the convicted defendant to practice his profession or to carry on his business. On the application of any person whose license or registration has been suspended or revoked, and upon proper showing and for good cause, said board or officer may reinstate such license or registration.

§ 16. *Records Confidential.*

Prescriptions, orders, and records, required by this act, and stocks of narcotic drugs, shall be open for inspection only to federal, state, county and municipal officers, whose duty it is to enforce the laws of this state or of the United States relating to narcotic drugs. No officer having knowledge by virtue of his office of any such prescription, order, or record shall divulge such knowledge, except in connection with a prosecution or proceeding in court or before a licensing or registration board or officer, to which prosecution or proceeding the person to whom such prescriptions, orders, or records relate is a party.

§ 17. *Fraud or Deceit.*

(1) No person shall obtain or attempt to obtain a narcotic drug, or procure or attempt to procure the administration of a narcotic drug, (a) by fraud, deceit, misrepresentation, or subterfuge; or (b) by the forgery or alteration of a prescription or of any written order; or (c) by the concealment of a material fact; or (d) by the use of a false name or the giving of a false address.

(2) Information communicated to a physician in an effort unlawfully to procure a narcotic drug, or unlawfully to procure the administration of any such drug, shall not be deemed a privileged communication.

(3) No person shall willfully make a false statement in any prescription, order, report, or record, required by this act.

(4) No person shall, for the purpose of obtaining a narcotic drug, falsely assume the title of, or represent himself to be, a manufacturer, wholesaler, apothecary, physician, dentist, veterinarian, or other authorized person.

(5) No person shall make or utter any false or forged prescription or false or forged written order.

(6) No person shall affix any false or forged label to a package or receptacle containing narcotic drugs.

(7) The provisions of this section shall apply to all transactions relating to narcotic drugs under the provisions of Section 8 of this act, in the same way as they apply to transactions under all other sections.

§ 18. *Exceptions and Exemptions not Required to be Negatived.*

In any complaint, information, or indictment, and in any action or proceeding brought for the enforcement of any provision of this act, it shall not be necessary to negative any exception, excuse, proviso, or exemption, contained in this act, and the burden of proof of any such exception, excuse, proviso, or exemption, shall be upon the defendant.

§ 19. *Enforcement and Cooperation.*

It is hereby made the duty of the [Insert here proper official designation of state officer or board], its officers, agents, inspectors, and representatives, and of all peace officers within the state, and of all county attorneys, to enforce all provisions of this act, except those specifically delegated, and to cooperate with all agencies charged with the enforcement of the laws of the United States, of this state, and of all other states, relating to narcotic drugs.

§ 20. *Penalties.*

Any person violating any provision of this act shall upon conviction be punished, for the first offense, by a fine not exceeding (   ) dollars, or by imprisonment in (jail) for not exceeding (   ), or by both such fine and imprisonment, and for any subsequent offense, by a fine not exceeding (   ) dollars, or by imprisonment in (state prison) for not exceeding (   ), or by both such fine and imprisonment.

§ 21. *Effect of Acquittal or Conviction under Federal Narcotic Laws.*

No person shall be prosecuted for a violation of any provision of this act if such person has been acquitted or convicted under the Federal Narcotic Laws of the same act or omission which, it is alleged, constitutes a violation of this act.

§ 22. *Constitutionality.*

If any provision of this act or the application thereof to any person or circumstances is held invalid, such invalidity shall not affect other provisions or applications of the act which can be given effect without the invalid provision or application, and to this end the provisions of this act are declared to be severable.

§ 23. *Interpretation.*

This act shall be so interpreted and construed as to effectuate its general purpose, to make uniform the laws of those states which enact it.

§ 24. *Inconsistent Laws Repealed.*

All acts or parts of acts which are inconsistent with the provisions of this act are hereby repealed.

§ 25. *Name of Act.*

This act may be cited as the Uniform Narcotic Drug Act.

§ 26. *Time of Taking Effect.*

This act shall take effect [Insert here statement of time when the act is to take effect].

Appendix B

SUMMARY OF STATE PENALTIES

FOR NARCOTICS VIOLATIONS

The charts in this appendix provide a self-contained summary of the penalty provisions for violations of state narcotics laws. The chart form facilitates a comparison of the penalties in all the states on a given violation, as well as all the penalties in one state on differing violations. It is thus possible to ascertain extremes in the application of sanctions on an interstate or intrastate approach.

The column, "General Penalty Provisions," sets forth the general penalty clause in each state narcotics act. Except in the case of addiction, the general penalty will apply to all other offenses named in the column headings, unless a different penalty appears. No penalty attaches to addiction unless an entry appears in the "Addiction" column.

The column, "Other Offenses," will show entries in two cases: (1) If the offense described appears in the Uniform Narcotic Drug Act and has a penalty different from the General Penalty, or (2) if the offense described is one not appearing in the Uniform Act.

This Appendix is current through June 1967.

GENERAL PENALTY PROVISIONS	ADDICTION	POSSESSION	POSSESSION FOR SALE	SALE AND SIMILAR TRANSACTIONS
ALABAMA ° 1				
1st offense, $50 - $200 a/o NMT 6 mos *2nd offense,* $100 - $500 a/o NMT 6 mos *Subsequent,* NLT $500 and NMT 6 mos		*1st offense,* 2 - 10 yrs and may be fined NMT $20,000 *2nd offense,* 5 - 20 yrs and may be fined NMT $20,000 *Subsequent,* 10 - 40 yrs and may be fined NMT $20,000		*1st offense,* 5 - 20 yrs and may be fined NMT $20,000 *Subsequent,* 10 - 40 yrs and may be fined NMT $20,000
ALASKA ° 2				
1st offense, NMT $5000 and 2 - 10 yrs *2nd offense,* NMT $7500 and 10 - 20 yrs *Subsequent,* NMT $10,000 and 20 - 40 yrs				
ARIZONA ° 3				
Superior court may fine NMT $50,000 for each offense in addition to terms of imprisonment	*1st offense,* 90 days - 1 yr or 90 days and 5 yr probation *2nd offense,* 2 - 10 yrs *3rd offense,* 5 - 20 yrs	*1st offense,* 2 - 10 yrs *2nd offense,* 5 - 20 yrs *Subsequent,* 15 - life	*1st offense,* 5 - 15 yrs *2nd offense,* NLT 10 yrs *Subsequent,* NLT 15 yrs	*1st offense,* 5 - life *2nd offense,* 10 - life *Subsequent,* 15 - life

NLT — Not Less Than   NMT — Not More Than   a/o — and or   ° — Uniform Narcotic Drug Act

178

PENALTIES FOR VIOLATIONS

SALE TO MINOR BY ADULT	OTHER OFFENSES	MITIGATION OF SENTENCE		
		SUSPENSION	PROBATION	PAROLE
0 - 40 yrs and may be fined NMT $20,000; if heroin, life imprisonment or NLT 10 yrs or death if jury so directs and may be fined NMT $20,000		Prohibited after first offense not involving sale	Same	
		Prohibited on any offense of selling	Same	
		Prohibited in any marijuana offense	Same	
st offense, 0 - 30 yrs and $5000 - $10,000 *2nd offense,* 5 - 30 yrs and NMT $25,000 *Subsequent,* life in prison	Violation of record keeping provision: $500 - $5000 a/o 1 - 5 yrs	Prohibited except in first offenses not involving sale	Same	Same
nducing minor to violate drug law *1st offense,* 10 - life *2nd offense,* 10 - life *Subsequent,* 15 - life	Furnishing or possessing peyote or mescal buttons is a misdemeanor ——— Possession of marijuana: *1st offense,* 1 - 10 yrs or NMT $1000 *2nd offense,* 2 - 20 yrs *Subsequent,* 5 - life ———	Prohibited for any but first offender Prohibited absolutely where offense is sale or inducement to minor (marijuana excepted)	Same	Not available until minimum sentence served (slightly more lenient in marijuana offenses)

GENERAL PENALTY PROVISIONS	ADDICTION	POSSESSION	POSSESSION FOR SALE	SALE AND SIMILAR TRANSACTIONS

ARIZONA *(Cont.)*

SALE TO MINOR BY ADULT	OTHER OFFENSES	MITIGATION OF SENTENCE		
		SUSPENSION	PROBATION	PAROLE
	Possession for sale (marijuana): *1st offense,* 2 - 10 yrs *2nd offense,* 5 - 15 yrs *Subsequent,* 10 - life			
	Sale of marijuana: *1st offense,* 5 - life *2nd offense,* 5 - life *Subsequent,* 10 - life			
	Hiring, using and inducing minor to use marijuana: *1st offense,* 10 - life *2nd offense,* 10 - life *Subsequent,* 15 - life			
	Minors inducing minors to violate law (other than marijuana): *1st offense,* NLT 5 yrs *2nd offense,* NLT 10 yrs			
	Obtaining narcotics by fraud or deceit: 1 - 10 yrs			

GENERAL PENALTY PROVISIONS	ADDICTION	POSSESSION	POSSESSION FOR SALE	SALE AND SIMILAR TRANSACTIONS
ARKANSAS ° 4 *1st offense,* NMT $2000 and 2 - 5 yrs *2nd offense,* NMT $2000 and 5 - 10 yrs *Subsequent,* NMT $2000 and 10 - 20 yrs				
CALIFORNIA 5 $30 - $500 a/o 15 - 180 days in jail Extra $20,000 fine may be imposed by trial court for each offense	90 days - 1 yr Up to 5 yrs probation conditioned on 90 days mandatory confinement	*1st offense,* 2 - 10 yrs *2nd offense,* 5 - 20 yrs *Subsequent,* 15 - life	*1st offense,* 5 - 15 yrs *2nd offense,* NLT 10 yrs *Subsequent,* NLT 15 yrs	*1st offense,* 5 - life *2nd offense,* 10 - life *Subsequent,* 10 - life

NLT — Not Less Than   NMT — Not More Than   a/o — and or   ° — Uniform Narcotic Drug Act

SALE TO MINOR BY ADULT	OTHER OFFENSES	MITIGATION OF SENTENCE		
		SUSPENSION	PROBATION	PAROLE
	Obtaining exempt preparations by fraud or deceit: *1st offense,* NMT $25 *2nd offense,* NMT $50 *Subsequent,* NMT $100	Prohibited, except for first offenses, until statutory minimum served	Same	Same
Inducing minor to violate any provision *1st offense,* 10 - life *2nd offense,* 10 - life *Subsequent,* 15 - life	Possession of marijuana: *1st offense,* 1 - 10 yrs *2nd offense,* 2 - 20 yrs *Subsequent,* 5 - life ———— Possession for sale (marijuana): *1st offense,* 2 - 10 yrs *2nd offense,* 5 - 15 yrs *Subsequent,* 10 - life ———— Sale of Marijuana: *1st offense,* 5 - life *2nd offense,* 5 - life *Subsequent,* 10 - life ———— Inducing minor to violate marijuana provisions:	Prohibited after first offense of possession, sale, inducing minor to violate narcotic laws, maintaining nuisance, or forging prescription (Prohibited absolutely where minor involved — marijuana excepted)	Same[7]	Generally available after statutory minimum served

GENERAL PENALTY PROVISIONS	ADDICTION	POSSESSION	POSSESSION FOR SALE	SALE AND SIMILAR TRANSACTIONS

CALIFORNIA *(Cont.)*

COLORADO ° [8]

1st offense, NMT $10,000 and 1 - 5 yrs *2nd offense,* NMT $10,000 and 2 -10 yrs *Subsequent,* NMT $10,000 and 5 - 20 yrs	6 mos -1 yr	*1st offense,* NMT $10,000 and 2 -15 yrs *2nd offense,* NMT $10,000 and 5 - 20 yrs *Subsequent,* NMT $10,000 and 10 - 30 yrs	*1st offense,* 10 - 20 yrs *2nd offense,* 15 - 30 yrs *Subsequent,* 20 - 40 yrs	*1st offense,* 10 - 20 yrs *2nd offense,* 15 - 30 yrs *Subsequent,* 20 - 40 yrs

NLT—Not Less Than   NMT—Not More Than   a/o—and or   °—Uniform Narcotic Drug Act

184

SALE TO MINOR BY ADULT	OTHER OFFENSES	MITIGATION OF SENTENCE		
		SUSPENSION	PROBATION	PAROLE
	1st offense, 10 - life *2nd offense,* 10 - life *Subsequent,* 15 - life			
	Minor soliciting minor to violate act: *1st offense,* NLT 5 yrs *2nd offense,* NLT 10 yrs			
	Forging or alter-ing prescription: *1st offense,* county jail 6 mos - 1 yr or state prison NMT 6 yrs *Subsequent,* NMT 10 yrs[6]			
	Using minor (under 25) in traffic, inducing violation by minor, inducing unlawful use: *1st offense,* life *Subsequent,* life in prison or death			On all offenses except stealing from lawful possessor, of-fender is not eligible for parole until minimum is served
	Common nuisance: *1st offense,* NMT $10,000 and 2 - 15 yrs			

185

GENERAL PENALTY PROVISIONS	ADDICTION	POSSESSION	POSSESSION FOR SALE	SALE AND SIMILAR TRANSACTIONS

COLORADO *(Cont.)*

CONNECT-ICUT ° 9

1st offense,
$500 - $3000
a/o 5 - 10 yrs
2nd offense,
$2000 - $5000
a/o 10 - 15 yrs
Subsequent,
15 - 25 yrs[10]

NMT 5 yrs; Court
may commit
addict to proba-
tion officer or to
hospital for
treatment

DELAWARE ° 11

NMT $3000 a/o
NMT 10 yrs [12]

Commitment in
hospital or in-

1st offense,
$500 - $3000 and

1st offense,
$500 - $3000 and

NLT—Not Less Than   NMT—Not More Than   a/o—and or   °—Uniform Narcotic Drug Act

SALE TO MINOR BY ADULT	OTHER OFFENSES	MITIGATION OF SENTENCE		
		SUSPENSION	PROBATION	PAROLE
	2nd offense, NMT $10,000 and 5 - 20 yrs *Subsequent,* NMT $10,000 and 10 - 30 yrs			
	Stealing from lawful possessor: *1st offense,* 2 - 15 yrs *2nd offense,* 5 - 20 yrs *Subsequent,* 10 - 40 yrs			
1st offense, 20 - 30 yrs *Subsequent,* life in prison	Failure to keep record *1st offense,* NMT $500 *2nd offense,* NMT $1000 a/o 30 days *Subsequent,* NMT $2000 a/o NMT 1 yr			
	Sale of non-narcotic as narcotic: general penalty provisions			
	Unlawful sale or dispensing of a			

GENERAL PENALTY PROVISIONS	ADDICTION	POSSESSION	POSSESSION FOR SALE	SALE AND SIMILAR TRANSACTIONS
DELAWARE *(Cont.)*	stitution until cured	3 - 10 yrs *2nd offense,* $1000 - $3000 and 7 - 12 yrs *Subsequent,* $2000 - $5000 and 10 - 20 yrs		3 - 10 yrs *2nd offense,* $1000 - $3000 and 7 - 12 yrs *Subsequent,* $2000 - $5000 and 10 - 20 yrs
DISTRICT OF COLUMBIA ° [13] *1st offense,* $100 - $1000 a/o NMT 1 yr *Subsequent,* $500 - $5000 a/o NMT 10 yrs	Vagrant Narcotic Drug User: NMT $500 a/o 1 yr; may be suspended conditioned upon treatment			
FLORIDA ° [14] *1st offense,* NMT 5 yrs a/o NMT $5000 *2nd offense,* NMT 10 yrs and may be fined NMT $10,000 *Subsequent,* NMT 20 yrs and may be fined NMT $20,000	Commitment in hospital or institution until treatment no longer needed			*1st offense,* NMT 10 yrs and may be fined NMT $10,000 *2nd offense,* 10 - 20 yrs and may be fined NMT $20,000 *Subsequent,* 20 yrs - life and may be fined NMT $20,000
GEORGIA ° [15] *1st offense,* NMT $2000	Commitment in hospital or			

NLT — Not Less Than   NMT — Not More Than   a/o — and or   ° — Uniform Narcotic Drug Act

PENALTIES FOR VIOLATIONS *(Cont.)*

SALE TO MINOR BY ADULT	OTHER OFFENSES	MITIGATION OF SENTENCE		
		SUSPENSION	PROBATION	PAROLE
	hypodermic needle is a misdemeanor			
	Interfering with service of search warrant: NMT $1000 or NMT 2 yrs			
1st offense, 5 yrs - life and may be fined NMT $10,000 *2nd offense,* 10 - life and may by fined NMT $20,000 *Subsequent,* 20 yrs - life and may be fined NMT $20,000		Prohibited except in first offenses	Same	
1st offense, life unless jury		Prohibited in any offense of	Same	Same

GENERAL PENALTY PROVISIONS	ADDICTION	POSSESSION	POSSESSION FOR SALE	SALE AND SIMILAR TRANSACTIONS
GEORGIA *(Cont.)*				
and 2 - 5 yrs *2nd offense,* NMT $3000 and 5 - 10 yrs *Subsequent,* NMT $5000 and 10 - 20 yrs	institution until treatment no longer needed			
HAWAII ° [17]				
1st offense, NMT $1000 or NMT 1 yr *Subsequent,* NMT $2000 and NMT 1 yr	Commitment in hospital or institution until cured followed by NMT 2 yrs probation[18]	*1st offense,* NMT 5 yrs *Subsequent,* NMT 10 yrs	*1st offense,* NMT $1000 and NMT 10 yrs *Subsequent,* NMT $2000 and NMT 20 yrs	*1st offense,* NMT $1000 and NMT 10 yrs *Subsequent,* NMT $2000 and NMT 20 yrs
IDAHO ° [19]				
1st offense, NMT $1000 a/o 1 - 14 yrs *Subsequent,* NLT $1000 a/o 5 - 14 yrs [20]	Commitment is under law covering insane persons			

NLT – Not Less Than   NMT – Not More Than   a/o – and or   ° – Uniform Narcotic Drug Act

SALE TO MINOR BY ADULT	OTHER OFFENSES	MITIGATION OF SENTENCE		
		SUSPENSION	PROBATION	PAROLE
recommends 10 - 20 yrs which judge may accept *Subsequent,* death unless mercy is recommended; if 10 - 20 yrs recommended, judge may impose 10 - 20 yrs or life[16]		selling to minor Prohibited after first offense of other violations	Same	Same
1st offense, NMT $1000 and NMT 20 yrs *Subsequent,* NMT $2000 and prison for life	maintain nuisance: NMT $1000 or NMT 1 yr or both Resort thereto: NMT $500 or NMT 1 yr or both Failure of physician to report addict: NMT $500			Prohibited after 1st offense of sale or possession for sale until 5 yrs are served; after 1st offense of sale to minor until 10 yrs are served

GENERAL PENALTY PROVISIONS	ADDICTION	POSSESSION	POSSESSION FOR SALE	SALE AND SIMILAR TRANSACTIONS
ILLINOIS ° 21				
	90 days - 1 yr Up to 5 yrs probation conditioned upon treatment; in any case, 90 days confinement is mandatory 22	*1st offense,* NMT $5000 and 2 - 10 yrs *Subsequent,* 5 yrs - life in prison		*1st offense,* 10 yrs - life in prison *Subsequent,* life in prison
INDIANA ° 24				
NMT $1000 and may be imprisoned 1 - 5 yrs	NMT $300 and may be confined NMT 180 days25	*1st offense,* NMT $1000 and 2 - 10 yrs *Subsequent,* NMT $2000 and 5 - 20 yrs	*1st offense,* NMT $2000 and 5 - 20 yrs *Subsequent,* NMT $5000 and 20 yrs - life in prison	*1st offense,* NMT $2000 and 5 - 20 yrs *Subsequent,* NMT $5000 and 20 yrs - life in prison

NLT—Not Less Than   NMT—Not More Than   a/o—and or   °—Uniform Narcotic Drug Act

SALE TO MINOR BY ADULT	OTHER OFFENSES	MITIGATION OF SENTENCE		
		SUSPENSION	PROBATION	PAROLE
	Inducing minor to violate act: 2 - 5 yrs	Prohibited in cases involving sale		
	Acquisition of drugs by fraud: 1 - 3 yrs	Prohibited in subsequent offenses of possession[23]		
	Violation of prescription law: *1st offense,* NMT $1000 a/o NMT 1 yr *Subsequent,* NMT $3000 a/o NMT 5 yrs			
	Pretending to furnish narcotics: 1 - 10 yrs			
	Violation of hypodermic law: *1st offense,* NMT $1000 a/o NMT 1 yr *2nd offense,* NMT $2000 a/o NMT 1 yr *Subsequent,* NMT 2 yrs			
	Obtaining by fraud: *1st offense,* NMT $1000 and 2 - 10 yrs *Subsequent,* NMT $2000	Prohibited in cases of sale to minor Prohibited in subsequent offenses of any type until	Same	Same

GENERAL PENALTY PROVISIONS	ADDICTION	POSSESSION	POSSESSION FOR SALE	SALE AND SIMILAR TRANSACTIONS

INDIANA *(Cont.)*

IOWA ° 26

1st offense, NMT $2000 and 2 - 5 yrs	Commitment until cured
2nd offense, NMT $2000 and 5 - 10 yrs	
Subsequent, NMT $2000 and 10 - 20 yrs	

NLT—Not Less Than   NMT—Not More Than   a/o—and or   ° — Uniform Narcotic Drug Act

PENALTIES FOR VIOLATIONS *(Cont.)*

SALE TO MINOR BY ADULT	OTHER OFFENSES	MITIGATION OF SENTENCE		
		SUSPENSION	PROBATION	PAROLE
	and 5 - 20 yrs _____	minimum sentence served		
	Possession of paraphernalia, maintaining common nuisance: *1st offense,* NMT $1000 and 1 - 5 yrs *Subsequent,* NMT $2000 and 2 - 10 yrs _____			
	Violation of prescription provisions *1st offense,* NMT $1000 and 1 - 5 yrs *2nd offense,* NMT $2000 and 5 - 15 yrs *Subsequent,* NMT $5000 and 10 - 25 yrs			
5 - 20 yrs	Theft of drugs to be punished under general penalty pro- vision _____	Prohibited until minimum is served		
	Failure to keep records or prop- erly label punished under general penalty provision			

	GENERAL PENALTY PROVISIONS	ADDICTION	POSSESSION	POSSESSION FOR SALE	SALE AND SIMILAR TRANSACTIONS
KANSAS ° 27	NMT 7 yrs				
KENTUCKY ° 29	*1st offense,* NMT $20,000 and 5 - 20 yrs *Subsequent,* NMT $20,000 and 10 - 40 yrs	NMT 12 mos; probation may be granted if addict enters hospital for treatment	*1st offense,* NMT $20,000 and 2 - 10 yrs *2nd offense,* NMT $20,000 and 5 - 20 yrs		
LOUISIANA ° 32	5 - 15 yrs	*1st offense,* Probation for treatment at USPHS hospital *Subsequent,* No probation, general penalty applies	5 - 15 yrs		10 - 50 yrs
MAINE ° 33	*1st offense,* NMT $1000 and 2 - 8 yrs *2nd offense,* NMT $2000 and 5 - 15 yrs				

NLT – Not Less Than   NMT – Not More Than   a/o – and or   ° – Uniform Narcotic Drug Act

PENALTIES FOR VIOLATIONS *(Cont.)*

SALE TO MINOR BY ADULT	OTHER OFFENSES	MITIGATION OF SENTENCE		
		SUSPENSION	PROBATION	PAROLE
	Violation of administrative provisions: $100 - $1000 a/o NMT 1 yr	[28]		
NMT $20,000 and 20 yrs - life in prison [30]	Refusing to permit authorized inspection of prescription records or narcotic stocks: *1st offense,* $100 - $500 *2nd offense,* NLT $500 and 90 days	Prohibited in cases of sale to minor	Same	
		Prohibited after first offense in other cases[31]	Same	
Death, unless jury recommends mercy, in which case 30 - 99 yrs	Sale by minor: 5 - 15 yrs	Available for first offenders except those convicted of selling narcotics	Same	Same
NMT $1000 and NMT 20 yrs		Prohibited after first offense	Same	Prohibited until minimum sentence served

GENERAL PENALTY PROVISIONS	ADDICTION	POSSESSION	POSSESSION FOR SALE	SALE AND SIMILAR TRANSACTIONS
MAINE *(Cont.)* *Subsequent,* NMT $5000 and 10 - 20 yrs				
MARYLAND ° 34 *1st offense,* NMT $1000 and 2 - 5 yrs *2nd offense,* NMT $2000 and 5 - 10 yrs *Subsequent,* NMT $3000 and 10 - 20 yrs				
MASSA-CHUSETTS ° 35 *1st offense,* NMT $2000 a/o NMT 2 yrs *Subsequent,* 5 - 10 yrs	Commitment NMT 2 yrs	Other than heroin, NMT $1000 or NMT 3½ yrs ───── Heroin: *1st offense,* $500 - $5000 or 2½ - 5 yrs *Subsequent,* 5 - 15 yrs ───── Violation of licensed manufacture and wholesale provisions: *1st offense,* $500 - $1000 or 6 mos - 2 yrs *2nd offense,* $500 - $2000 or	*1st offense,* 5 - 10 yrs *Subsequent,* 10 - 25 yrs	*1st offense,* 5 - 10 yrs *Subsequent,* 10 - 25 yrs ───── Sale by licensee to unauthorized person or violation of written order provisions: *1st offense,* $500 - $1000 or 6 mos - 2 yrs *2nd offense,* $500 - $2000 and 5 - 10 yrs *Subsequent,* $2000 and 10 - 20 yrs

NLT — Not Less Than   NMT — Not More Than   a/o — and or   ° — Uniform Narcotic Drug Act

SALE TO MINOR BY ADULT	OTHER OFFENSES	MITIGATION OF SENTENCE		
		SUSPENSION	PROBATION	PAROLE
5 - 20 yrs, and NMT $1000	Possession of paraphernalia is punished under general penalty	Prohibited after first offense	Same	Same
1st offense, 10 - 25 yrs *Subsequent,* 20 - 50 yrs	Stealing drugs: *1st offense,* 5 - 10 yrs *Subsequent,* 10 - 25 yrs ———— Violation of oral prescription regulations: NMT $25 for each offense ———— Conspiring to violate drug laws, or being where drugs are illegally kept or possessed: NMT 5 yrs or $500 - $5000[36]	Prohibited after first offense of sale, using a minor in drug traffic, inducing a minor to use drugs, inducing any violation of the narcotic laws, possession for sale, stealing drugs or any offense covered by the general penalty	Same	Same

GENERAL PENALTY PROVISIONS	ADDICTION	POSSESSION	POSSESSION FOR SALE	SALE AND SIMILAR TRANSACTIONS
MASSA-CHUSETTS *(Cont.)*		5 - 10 yrs *Subsequent,* $2000 and 10 - 20 yrs		
MICHIGAN ° 37	NMT $2000 a/o NMT 1 yr[38]	*1st offense,* NMT $5000 and NMT 10 yrs		20 yrs - life in prison

NLT — Not Less Than   NMT — Not More Than   a/o — and or   ° — Uniform Narcotic Drug Act

SALE TO MINOR BY ADULT	OTHER OFFENSES	MITIGATION OF SENTENCE		
		SUSPENSION	PROBATION	PAROLE
	Obtaining drugs from two or more physicians without disclosure: NMT 5 yrs			
	Use of exempt preparations for other than relief of pain: $200 - $2000 or NMT 2 yrs			
	Violation of hypodermic provisions: NMT $500 a/o NMT 2 yrs			
	Violation of labeling provisions: same as violations of written order provisions			
	Using minor in traffic or inducing anyone to use narcotics: *1st offense,* 10 - 25 yrs *2nd offense,* 20 - 50 yrs			
	Violation by a licensed person of any			

39

GENERAL PENALTY PROVISIONS	ADDICTION	POSSESSION	POSSESSION FOR SALE	SALE AND SIMILAR TRANSACTIONS
MICHIGAN *(Cont.)*				
		2nd offense, NMT $5000 and NMT 20 yrs *Subsequent,* NMT $5000 and 20 - 40 yrs		
MINNE-SOTA ° 40 *1st offense,* NMT $10,000 and 5 - 20 yrs *Subsequent,* subject to habitual offender statute				
MISSIS-SIPPI ° 41 *1st offense,* NMT $2000 and 2 - 5 yrs *2nd offense,* NMT $2000 and 5 - 10 yrs *Subsequent,* $2000 and 10 - 20 yrs				*1st offense,* NMT $2000 and 5 - 10 yrs *Subsequent,* $2000 and 10 - 20 yrs

NLT — Not Less Than   NMT — Not More Than   a/o — and or   ° — Uniform Narcotic Drug Act

PENALTIES FOR VIOLATIONS *(Cont.)*

SALE TO MINOR BY ADULT	OTHER OFFENSES	MITIGATION OF SENTENCE		
		SUSPENSION	PROBATION	PAROLE
	provision governing legitimate traffic: NMT $10,000 a/o NMT 10 yrs			
	Fraudulent procurement of drugs is a felony			
NMT $20,000 and 10 - 40 yrs	Person three times convicted within 5 yrs of furnishing or using narcotics is habitual offender and may be imprisoned NMT 3 yrs			
NMT $10,000 a/o NMT 30 yrs[42]		Prohibited for any offense until minimum sentence served	Same	Same

GENERAL PENALTY PROVISIONS	ADDICTION	POSSESSION	POSSESSION FOR SALE	SALE AND SIMILAR TRANSACTIONS
MISSOURI ° [43]				
1st offense, NMT 20 yrs in prison, or NMT 1 yr in jail, or NMT $1000, or both confinement and fine. *2nd offense,* 5 - 30 yrs *3rd offense,* 10 - 50 yrs *Subsequent,* 25 yrs - life in prison	Commitment until cured			
MONTANA ° [45]				
1st offense, 1 - 5 yrs *Subsequent,* 5 - 20 yrs[46]				
NEBRASKA ° [47]				
1st offense, NMT $3000 and 2 - 5 yrs *2nd offense,* NMT $5000 and 5 - 10 yrs *Subsequent,* NMT $5000				

NLT—Not Less Than   NMT—Not More Than   a/o—and or   °—Uniform Narcotic Drug Act

204

PENALTIES FOR VIOLATIONS *(Cont.)*

SALE TO MINOR BY ADULT	OTHER OFFENSES	MITIGATION OF SENTENCE		
		SUSPENSION	PROBATION	PAROLE
NMT $10,000 and 10 yrs - life in prison; or, if the jury so directs, death	Possessing paraphernalia is punished under general penalty ———— Stealing drugs under $50: *1st offense,* NMT $1000 a/o NMT 1 yr *2nd offense,* NMT $1000 a/o NMT 1 yr *3rd offense,* same penalty as stealing drugs over $50, i.e., 2 - 10 yrs in state prison or NMT 1 yr in county jail a/o NMT $1000	44		
5 yrs - life in prison	Maintaining common nuisance: NMT $500 or NMT 6 mos			

GENERAL PENALTY PROVISIONS	ADDICTION	POSSESSION	POSSESSION FOR SALE	SALE AND SIMILAR TRANSACTIONS

NEBRASKA *(Cont.)*
and 10 - 20
yrs

NEVADA ° 48

1st offense, NMT $2000 and 2 - 5 yrs *2nd offense,* NMT $2000 and 5 - 10 yrs *Subsequent,* NMT $2000 and 10 - 20 yrs	90 days - 1 yr. May be placed on probation up to 5 yrs, but in any case must be confined 90 days			*1st offense,* $10,000 and 20 - 40 yrs *2nd offense,* $10,000 and 40 - life in prison

SALE TO MINOR BY ADULT	OTHER OFFENSES	MITIGATION OF SENTENCE		
		SUSPENSION	PROBATION	PAROLE
$10,000 and life in prison	Cultivating, planting, processing marijuana: *1st offense,* 2 - 5 yrs *2nd offense,* 5 - 10 yrs	Prohibited after first offense in offenses not involving sale or supply	Same Prohibited in any offense of sale or supply[49]	Same Same
	Supplying drugs to person who intends to transfer same to a person over 21 yrs: *1st offense,* 30 - 60 yrs *2nd offense,* life in prison			
	Same, to a person under 21 yrs: life in prison			
	Possession of paraphernalia punished under general penalty			
	Maintaining or frequenting nuisance is a misdemeanor			

GENERAL PENALTY PROVISIONS	ADDICTION	POSSESSION	POSSESSION FOR SALE	SALE AND SIMILAR TRANSACTIONS
NEW HAMP-SHIRE ° [50]				
1st offense, NMT $2000 and 2 - 5 yrs *2nd offense,* NMT $2000 and 5 - 10 yrs *Subsequent,* $2000 and 10 - 20 yrs				*1st offense,* NMT $2000 and 5 - 10 yrs *Subsequent,* $2000 and 10 - 20 yrs
NEW JERSEY ° [51]				
1st offense, NMT $2000 and 2 - 15 yrs *2nd offense,* NMT $5000 and 5 - 25 yrs *Subsequent,* NMT $5000 and 10 - life in prison	NMT $1000 a/o NMT 1 yr [52]			

PENALTIES FOR VIOLATIONS *(Cont.)*

		MITIGATION OF SENTENCE		
SALE TO MINOR BY ADULT	OTHER OFFENSES	SUSPENSION	PROBATION	PAROLE
		Prohibited after first offense; where sale provision is violated, minimum sentence must be served	Same	Same
$2000 - $10,000 and 2 yrs - life in prison	Failure of physician to report cases of addiction shall result in such physician's being adjudged a disorderly person			
	Inducing unlawful use is high misdemeanor			
	Possessors of paraphernalia are disorderly persons			
	Conspiracy to violate act is a high misdemeanor			

GENERAL PENALTY PROVISIONS	ADDICTION	POSSESSION	POSSESSION FOR SALE	SALE AND SIMILAR TRANSACTIONS
NEW MEXICO ° 53				
NMT $1000 a/o NMT 1 yr	NMT $1000 a/o NMT 1 yr; or commitment to a state hospital	*1st offense,* NMT $2000 and 2 - 10 yrs *2nd offense,* NMT $2000 and 5 - 20 yrs *Subsequent,* NMT $2000 and 10 - 40 yrs	*1st offense,* NMT $2000 and 2 - 10 yrs *2nd offense,* NMT $2000 and 5 - 20 yrs *Subsequent,* NMT $2000 and 10 - 40 yrs	*1st offense,* NMT $2000 and 2 - 10 yrs *2nd offense,* NMT $2000 and 5 - 20 yrs *Subsequent,* NMT $2000 and 10 - 40 yrs
NEW YORK ° 55				
1st offense, NMT $500 a/o NMT 1 yr *2nd offense,* 6 mos - 1 yr		3 - 10 yrs	5 - 15 yrs	5 - 15 yrs
NORTH CAROLINA ° 59				
1st offense, NMT $1000 a/o NMT 5 yrs				

NLT—Not Less Than   NMT—Not More Than   a/o—and or   °—Uniform Narcotic Drug Act

PENALTIES FOR VIOLATIONS *(Cont.)*

SALE TO MINOR BY ADULT	OTHER OFFENSES	MITIGATION OF SENTENCE		
		SUSPENSION	PROBATION	PAROLE
NMT $10,000 and 10 yrs - life in prison <hr> "Knowingly," NMT $20,000 and 10 - life imprisonment unless jury directs death[54]	Maintaining common nuisance: *1st offense,* NMT $300 or NMT 2 yrs *2nd offense,* NMT $1000 a/o NMT 5 yrs *Subsequent,* NMT 10 yrs <hr> Resort thereto: NMT $300 a/o NMT 6 mos	Prohibited in cases of sale, possession, or possession with intent to sell, except for first offenses	Same	Same
7 - 15 yrs	Using minor in drug traffic: 2½ - 5 yrs[56] <hr> Unlawful sale of hypodermics is a misdemeanor <hr> Visiting or maintaining public nuisance is a misdemeanor[57] <hr> Conspiracy is a felony[58]			
NMT $3000 and 10 yrs - life in prison	Maintaining common nuisance: general	Prohibited in cases of sale to minors	Same	

GENERAL PENALTY PROVISIONS	ADDICTION	POSSESSION	POSSESSION FOR SALE	SALE AND SIMILAR TRANSACTIONS
NORTH CARO-LINA *(Cont.)* *2nd offense,* NMT $2000 and 5 - 10 yrs *Subsequent,* NMT $3000 and 15 yrs - life in prison				
NORTH DAKOTA ° [60] $100 - $1000 a/o 1 - 3 yrs		NMT $10,000 a/o 99 yrs	NMT $10,000 a/o 99 yrs	NMT $10,000 a/o 99 yrs
OHIO ° [61]		*1st offense,* NMT $10,000 and 2 - 15 yrs *2nd offense,* NMT $10,000 and 5 - 20 yrs *Subsequent,* NMT $10,000 and 10 - 30 yrs[62]	*1st offense,* 10 - 20 yrs *2nd offense,* 15 - 30 yrs *Subsequent,* 20 - 40 yrs	20 - 40 yrs

NLT — Not Less Than   NMT — Not More Than   a/o — and or   ° — Uniform Narcotic Drug Act

212

SALE TO MINOR BY ADULT	OTHER OFFENSES	MITIGATION OF SENTENCE		
		SUSPENSION	PROBATION	PAROLE
	penalty pro-visions	Prohibited after first offense of sale or posses-sion for sale	Same	
	Maintaining or resorting to common nuisance: *1st offense,* $200 - $1000 and 90 days - 1 yr *2nd offense,* 1 - 2 yrs			In cases of sale to minor, no ap-plication for parole, reprieve or commutation can be made until 20 yrs have been served
	Sale of peyote: NMT $500 or NMT 6 mos or both			
30 yrs - life in prison	63	64		

GENERAL PENALTY PROVISIONS	ADDICTION	POSSESSION	POSSESSION FOR SALE	SALE AND SIMILAR TRANSACTIONS
OKLA-HOMA ° 65				
1st offense, NMT $1000 a/o NMT 5 yrs *2nd offense,* NMT $3000 or 5 - 10 yrs *Subsequent,* NMT $5000 or 10 - 20 yrs	Misdemeanor, *1st offense,* NLT 90 days *Subsequent,* NLT 6 mos Penalty for use: NMT 6 mos			
OREGON ° 66				
NMT $5000 or NMT 10 yrs or both	Jail 90 days - 1 yr Probation al-lowed but only after 90 days have been served			

NLT—Not Less Than   NMT—Not More Than   a/o—and or   °—Uniform Narcotic Drug Act

SALE TO MINOR BY ADULT	OTHER OFFENSES	MITIGATION OF SENTENCE		
		SUSPENSION	PROBATION	PAROLE
Heroin: death or prison NLT 10 yrs	Any violation relating to marijuana: NMT $5000 a/o NMT 7 yrs	Prohibited in cases of addiction	Same	Same
———— Marijuana: *1st offense,* NMT 20 yrs *2nd offense,* 5 yrs - life in prison		Prohibited after first offense in all other cases	Same	Same
	Causing addiction:NMT 10 yrs			
	———— Causing addiction of minor: *1st offense,* NMT 10 yrs *2nd offense,* up to life in prison			
	———— Maintaining or frequenting common nuisance is a misdeameanor			
	———— Furnishing prison inmates with drugs NMT $1000 a/o NMT 5 yrs			
	———— Violation of prescription provisions NMT $200 a/o			

GENERAL PENALTY PROVISIONS	ADDICTION	POSSESSION	POSSESSION FOR SALE	SALE AND SIMILAR TRANSACTIONS

OREGON *(Cont.)*

PENNSYL-VANIA [67]

1st offense, NMT $5000 a/o NMT 1 yr[68] 2nd offense, NMT $25,000 a/o NMT 3 yrs		1st offense, NMT $2000 and 2 - 5 yrs 2nd offense, NMT $5000 and 5 - 10 yrs 3rd offense, NMT $7500 and 10 - 30 yrs		1st offense, NMT $5000 and 5 - 20 yrs 2nd offense, NMT $15,000 and 10 - 30 yrs 3rd offense, NMT $30,000 and life in prison

RHODE ISLAND ° [69]

NMT $1000 or NMT 1 yr or both	State hospital NLT 1 yr	1st offense, NMT $10,000 and 2 - 15 yrs 2nd offense, NMT $10,000 and 5 - 20 yrs Subsequent, NMT $10,000 and 10 - 30 yrs	1st offense, 10 - 20 yrs 2nd offense, 15 - 30 yrs Subsequent, 20 - 40 yrs	20 - 40 yrs

NLT—Not Less Than   NMT—Not More Than   a/o—and or   °—Uniform Narcotic Drug Act

PENALTIES FOR VIOLATIONS *(Cont.)*

SALE TO MINOR BY ADULT	OTHER OFFENSES	MITIGATION OF SENTENCE		
		SUSPENSION	PROBATION	PAROLE
	NMT 6 mos			
	Obtaining drugs by fraud NMT $500 a/o NMT 1 yr			
	Maintaining or frequenting "opium joint," possessing or using smoking opium: NMT $500 a/o NMT 1 yr	Prohibited in cases involving sale Prohibited after first offense of possession	Prohibited after first violation of sale or possession provisions	Same Same
	Possessing opium apparatus: NMT $500 a/o NMT 1 yr			
30 yrs - life in prison	Possession of paraphernalia *1st offense,* NMT $500 or 1 - 5 yrs *Subsequent,* $200 - $1000 or 1 - 5 yrs		Prohibited where sale to minor involved	
	Maintaining common nuisance: *1st offense,* NMT $500 or 1 - 5 yrs			

GENERAL PENALTY PROVISIONS	ADDICTION	POSSESSION	POSSESSION FOR SALE	SALE AND SIMILAR TRANSACTIONS

RHODE ISLAND *(Cont.)*

SOUTH CAROLINA ° 70
1st offense,
NMT $2000
a/o NMT 2 yrs
2nd offense,
$2000 - $5000
a/o 2 - 5 yrs
3rd offense,
10 - 20 yrs

SOUTH DAKOTA ° 71
1st offense,
NMT $500 a/o
NMT 90 days
2nd offense,
NMT $1000
a/o NMT 2 yrs

NMT 20 yrs

TENNES-SEE ° 72
1st offense,
$500 and

NLT—Not Less Than   NMT—Not More Than   a/o—and or   °—Uniform Narcotic Drug Act

PENALTIES FOR VIOLATIONS *(Cont.)*

SALE TO MINOR BY ADULT	OTHER OFFENSES	MITIGATION OF SENTENCE		
		SUSPENSION	PROBATION	PAROLE
	Subsequent, $200 - $1000 or 1 - 5 yrs			
	Visiting a common nuisance: $50 - $300 a/o 3 mos - 1 yr			
1st offense, $5000 a/o 5 yrs *2nd offense,* 10 yrs	Violation of records provisions: *1st offense,* NMT $500 a/o NMT 6 mos *2nd offense,* NMT $1000 a/o NMT 1 yr	Prohibited on second offense of sale to minor Prohibited on third offense under general penalty provisions until 10 yrs served	Same Same	
Imprisonment at hard labor up to life				
		Prohibited after first offense[73]		

GENERAL PENALTY PROVISIONS	ADDICTION	POSSESSION	POSSESSION FOR SALE	SALE AND SIMILAR TRANSACTIONS
TENNESSEE (*Cont.*)				
2 - 5 yrs *2nd offense,* $500 and 5 - 10 yrs *Subsequent,* $500 and 10 - 20 yrs				
TEXAS ° [74]				
1st offense, 2 yrs - life in prison *2nd offense,* 10 yrs - life in prison	NMT 3 yrs[75]			*1st offense,* 5 yrs - life in prison *2nd offense,* 10 yrs - life in prison
UTAH ° [77]				
1st offense, NLT $1000 a/o NMT 5 yrs *2nd offense,* NLT $5000 a/o 5 yrs up to life in prison at discretion of court	All addicts may be punished as vagrants or under the addiction and use penalty: 90 days - 6 mos or probation up to 6 mos conditioned upon 90 days confinement or upon treatment			

PENALTIES FOR VIOLATIONS *(Cont.)*

SALE TO MINOR BY ADULT	OTHER OFFENSES	MITIGATION OF SENTENCE		
		SUSPENSION	PROBATION	PAROLE
1st offense, NLT 5 yrs - life in prison *2nd offense,* Death, life in prison or NLT 10 yrs	Using minor in drug traffic: same penalties as sale to minor	Prohibited[76]		
	Failure to preserve written orders, to return unused drugs, to retain drugs in original containers; or to dispense prescriptions which show evidence of alternation, or to obtain drugs by fraud are punishable as misdemeanors			
	Maintaining or frequenting opium den is a felony			

GENERAL PENALTY PROVISION	ADDICTION	POSSESSION	POSSESSION FOR SALE	SALE AND SIMILAR TRANSACTIONS
VERMONT ° [78] $100 - $500 or 1 - 5 yrs or both				
VIRGINIA ° [79] *1st offense,* NMT $1000 or 3 - 5 yrs *2nd offense,* NMT $2000 and 5 - 10 yrs *Subsequent,* NMT $3000 and 10 - 20 yrs		More than 25 grs or 8 oz: NMT $5000 and 20 - 40 yrs		
WASH- INGTON ° [81] *1st offense,* NMT $10,000 a/o 5 - 20 yrs[82] *2nd offense,* NMT $10,000 and 10 - 20 yrs *Subsequent,* NMT $25,000 and 15 - 40 yrs	Addiction or habitual use is a gross misde- meanor			
WEST VIRGINIA ° [84] *1st offense,* NMT $1000 and 2 - 5 yrs *2nd offense,* NMT $5000 and 5 - 10 yrs *Subsequent,* NMT $10,000 and 10 - 20 yrs				

NLT — Not Less Than   NMT — Not More Than   a/o — and or   ° — Uniform Narcotic Drug Act

SALE TO MINOR BY ADULT	OTHER OFFENSES	MITIGATION OF SENTENCE		
		SUSPENSION	PROBATION	PAROLE
Fines as prescribed in the general penalty and 10 - 30 yrs[80]	Filling oral prescription later reduced to writing: $100 fine	Prohibited in case of sale to minors		
NMT $50,000 and 20 - 40 yrs[83]	Maintaining or frequenting "opium joints" is a gross misdemeanor			
	Obtaining drugs by fraud: misdemeanors	Prohibited, except on first offenses, until minimum provided by statute has been served	Same	Same

GENERAL PENALTY PROVISIONS	ADDICTION	POSSESSION	POSSESSION FOR SALE	SALE AND SIMILAR TRANSACTIONS
WISCONSIN ° 85				
1st offense, 2 - 10 yrs *2nd offense,* 5 - 10 yrs *Subsequent,* 10 - 20 yrs	NMT 5 yrs, which may be served by commitment to a hospital for treatment	NMT 10 yrs		NMT 10 yrs
WYOMING ° 86				
1st offense, NMT $2000 and 2 - 5 yrs *2nd offense,* NMT $2000 and 5 - 10 yrs *3rd offense,* NMT $2000 and 10 - 20 yrs				

NLT – Not Less Than   NMT – Not More Than   a/o – and or   ° – Uniform Narcotic Drug Act

PENALTIES FOR VIOLATIONS *(Cont.)*

SALE TO MINOR BY ADULT	OTHER OFFENSES	MITIGATION OF SENTENCE		
		SUSPENSION	PROBATION	PAROLE
1st offense, 3 - 25 yrs *2nd offense,* 20 yrs - life in prison *3rd offense,* life imprisonment	Marijuana offenses: same penalties as narcotics offenses, except that there is no provision for hospitalization Penalty for use of marijuana: NMT 5 yrs Maintaining or frequenting a common nuisance: NMT $500 or NMT 1 yr	After first offense, prohibited until minimum sentence served		Same
1st offense, 10 - 20 yrs *2nd offense,* 20 - 50 yrs	Maintaining "opium den": $50 - $100 or 2 - 5 mos Frequenting "opium dens": $100 - $500 or 3 - 9 mos			

NOTES TO APPENDIX B

1. ALA. CODE tit. 22, §§ 232 through 258(20) (1940). Uniform Act was adopted in 1935. Before 1951, the general penalty applied to all offenses.
2. ALASKA COMP. LAWS ANN. §§ 17.10.010 through 17.10.240 (1962, Supp. 1965). Uniform Act was enacted in 1943. Before 1951 all offenses were punishable as follows: *1st offense:* not more than $5,000 or not more than 5 years or both; *subsequent offenses:* not more than $10,000 or not less than 2 years and not more than 10 years, or both. In 1951 the act was amended to read as at present, except for the doubling clause on sale offenses, separate penalties for sale to minors, and provisions denying suspension, probation, and parole to first offenders where sale was involved. These latter changes were made in 1953.
3. ARIZ. REV. STAT. ANN. §§ 36-1001 through 36-1024, 36-1061 through 36-1062 (1956, Supp. 1965).
4. ARK. STAT. ANN. §§ 82-1001 through 82-1026 (1960, Supp. 1965). Uniform Act was enacted in 1947. Before 1955 the penalty was as follows: *1st offense:* not more than $100 fine or not more than 6 months imprisonment, or both; *subsequent offenses:* not more than $500 fine or not more than 1 year imprisonment, or both.
5. CAL. HEALTH & SAFETY CODE §§ 11000 through 11797.
6. *Other offenses:* Writing nonconforming prescriptions, obtaining narcotics by fraud and deceit, inducing minor to violate prescription provisions — not more than 6 years (state prison) or not more than 1 year (county jail) (§ 11715.7); maintaining common nuisance: *first offense* — not more than 1 year (county jail) or not more than 10 years (state prison); *second offense* — 2-20 years (§ 11557); pretending to furnish narcotic — not more than 10 years; forging or altering prescription: *first offense* — 6 months to 1 year (county jail) or not more than 6 years (state prison); *subsequent offense* — not more than 10 years.
7. Probation by court or parole by county or state may be conditioned upon the administration of periodic anti-narcotics tests (§ 11722). Such tests may also be administered to persons arrested on narcotics charges at the time of arrest (§ 11723). The policy of the state favoring use of anti-narcotics tests and steps implementing policy appears in §§ 11390-11395.
8. COLO. REV. STAT. ANN. §§ 48-5-1 through 48-5-21 (1963, Perm. Supp. 1965). Uniform Act was enacted in 1935.

9. CONN. GEN. STAT. REV. §§ 19-244 through 19-268 (1958, Supp. 1965). The present form of the Uniform Act was derived from the 1949 revision with changes from time to time in definition and penalties.

10. §§ 19-265 and 19-265a read: "...shall be fined...*and* imprisoned...*or* be both fined and imprisoned...." (emphasis supplied). Until 1959 subsequent offenses were punished by life imprisonment.

11. DEL. CODE ANN. tit. 16, §§ 4701 through 4722 (1953, Supp. 1964). Uniform Act was enacted in 1935.

12. Until 1953 this was the only penalty, at which time tit. 16, § 4722 was amended, to provide heavier penalties for possession and transfer. Present penalties were established in 1955.

13. D.C. CODE ANN. §§ 33-401 through 33-425 (1961, Supp. 1966). Uniform Act was enacted in 1938 without significant change except for addition of Vagrant Narcotic Drug User provision.

14. FLA. STAT. §§ 398.01 through 398.24 (1960, Supp. 1965). Uniform Act was enacted in 1933.

15. GA. CODE ANN. §§ 42-801 through 42-822, 42-9917 through 42-9919 (1957, Supp. 1965). Uniform Act was enacted in 1935.

16. The statute does not distinguish between adult and minor seller.

17. HAWAII REV. LAWS §§ 52-1 through 52-61 (1955, Supp. 1965). Uniform Act was enacted in modified form in 1931.

18. Commitment procedures, §§ 52-50 and 52-61, state that a patient is not a criminal, nor is commitment a conviction, but it is intended that criminal laws shall be enforced against drug users and that treatment shall not be substituted for punishment.

19. IDAHO CODE ANN. §§ 37-2301 through 37-2323 (1961, Supp. 1965). Uniform Act was enacted in 1937.

20. Although § 37-2320 states the penalty for violation of "any provision of this act," § 37-2322 provides that "any violation of the provision of this act, the penalty for which is not herein specifically provided shall be deemed a misdemeanor and punishable as such."

21. ILL. REV. STAT. ch. 38, §§ 22-1 through 22-54 (1961, Supp. 1965). Uniform Act was enacted in 1935, repealed in 1957 and re-enacted in its present form. Ch. 38, § 602, habitual criminal law, provides that second offenders shall serve the full term provided for their offense. Subsequent offenders shall serve at least 15 years.

22. Addiction was made an offense by amendment of § 192.28-3 (now § 22-3) in 1959.

23. There was no provision governing mitigation of sentence until the 1959 amendment. § 192.28-38a (now § 22-41) provides that when any court grants parole and there is reason to believe that the defendant is an addict, such clemency shall be conditioned upon submission to periodic anti-narcotic tests. Such tests may also be conducted upon arrested persons suspected of using narcotics unlawfully, if the arrested person consents.

24. IND. ANN. STAT. §§ 10-3501 through 10-3552 (1956, Supp. 1961). Uniform Act was enacted in 1935 with subsequent changes, chiefly of definitions and penalties.

25. § 10-3538a added in 1957. The act makes it unlawful for an addict to appear in a public street or other public place unless he can prove that he is under care of a licensed physician for his addiction.

26. IOWA CODE §§ 204.1 through 204.23 (1965). Uniform Act was enacted in 1937.

27. KAN. GEN. STAT. ANN. §§ 65-2501 through 65-2522 (1963, Supp. 1965). Uniform Act was enacted in 1957.

28. The former provisions prohibited suspension, probation, and parole except for first offense.

29. KY. REV. STAT. ANN. §§ 218.010 through 218.250 (1955, Supp. 1966). Uniform Act was enacted in 1934.

30. The statute does not distinguish between an adult and a minor seller.

31. § 218.210(3) provides, however, that prior convictions as an addict under § 218.250 shall not be considered prior offenses for purposes of this subsection.

32. LA. REV. STAT. §§ 40:961 through 40:984 (1950, Supp. 1965). Uniform Act was enacted in 1934.

33. ME. REV. STAT. ANN. ch. 17 § 859, ch. 22 §§ 2361 through 2380 (1964, Supp. 1965). Uniform Act was enacted in 1941.

34. MD. ANN. CODE art. 27, §§ 276 through 306 (1957). Uniform Act was enacted in 1935.

35. MASS. ANN. LAWS ch. 94, §§ 197 through 217E, ch. 123, § 62 (1954, Supp. 1965). Uniform Act substantially was enacted in 1947 replacing prior statutes.

36. Ch. 94, § 213A provides a penalty for being in the company of a person, knowing him illegally to possess drugs; and for being present where drugs are kept without requiring scienter.

37. MICH. STAT. ANN. §§ 18.1071 through 18.1098, 18.1121 through 18.1127, 18.1131 through 18.1144.

38. § 18.1124 establishes this penalty and states that any person sent to any institution under this section shall receive psychiatric and medical treatment in an attempt to cure the addiction. §§ 18.1131 through 18.1144 deal with civil commitment of drug users. Such proceedings may not be instituted by state health officers when the subject is charged with or is under sentence for a criminal offense (§ 18.1133). Persons released after commitment shall report to the probation officer for two years (§ 18.1143). The patient is not deemed a criminal, nor his commitment a conviction (§ 18.1144). See also § 14.881.

39. § 18.1123 provides that suspension or probation on first offenses of possession may be granted by the judge. Statutes are silent as to suspension and probation for sale offenses and subsequent offenses of possession. Though narcotics offenses are not listed in § 28.1131 which denies probation to certain classes of crimes, the terms of the narcotics penalty provisions are construed to prohibit probation except for first offenses of possession.

40. MINN. STAT. §§ 609.155, 618.01 through 618.25 (1964, Supp. 1965). Uniform Act was enacted in 1947. The Minnesota habitual offender statute provides that commission of subsequent felonies within a 10-year period will subject the offender to a term of imprisonment the maximum of which may be for the maximum term authorized by law for the crime for which the defendant is being sentenced multiplied by the number of his prior felony convictions but not to exceed 40 years (§ 609.155).

41. MISS. CODE ANN. §§ 6844 through 6869 (1942, Supp. 1964). Uniform Act was enacted in 1936.

42. § 6866(b). There was no separate provision before 1960. This section applies to narcotics, amphetamine, or any compound having a similar action or effect on the human body.

43. MO. REV. STAT. §§ 195.010 through 195.210, 202.360, 560.161 (1959, Supp. 1965). Uniform Act was enacted in 1937.

44. Suspension, probation, and parole were denied by the 1957 legislation, but the provision was repealed in 1959.

45. MONT. REV. CODES ANN. §§ 54-101 through 54-128, 94-35-148 (1947, Supp. 1965). Uniform Act was enacted in 1937.

46. § 54-125(1) (Supp. 1959). Before 1959 the penalty for first offense was a fine of not more than $1,000 or not more than 6 months in county jail, or both. Subsequent offenses punished by fine of not more than $5,000 or prison, and for not more than 5 years, or both.

47. NEB. REV. STAT. §§ 28-451 through 28-472 (1964). Uniform Act was enacted in 1935.

48. NEV. REV. STAT. §§ 453.010 through 453.410. Uniform Act was enacted in 1937. The act includes barbiturates within "narcotic drugs."

49. § 453.210(1)(d) denies suspension, probation, and parole after first conviction for violations other than supply or sale. § 453.210(4) denies probation and parole to persons convicted of sale or supply. It does not mention suspension.

50. N.H. REV. STAT. ANN. §§ 318-A:1 through 318-A:26 (1966).

51. N.J. STAT. ANN. §§ 24:18-1 through 24:18-49 (1940, Supp. 1965). Uniform Act was enacted in 1933. The Narcotic Control Commission was created by §§ 24:20-1 through 24:20-5. Further criminal provisions: §§ 2A:98-1, 2A:108-9, 2A:170-77.3 through 2A:170-77.6.

52. Addiction to use of, or being under influence of narcotics is an offense under Disorderly Persons Act, N.J. STAT. ANN. § 2A:170-8 (Supp. 1960). Penalty is provided generally for disorderly persons in § 2A:169-4.

53. N.M. STAT. ANN. §§ 54-7-1 through 54-7-51 (1953, Supp. 1965). Uniform Act was enacted in 1935.

54. §§ 54-7-15 and 54-7-15.1 provide differing penalties for furnishing drugs to a minor. The latter section also includes conspiracy to do the prohibited acts and uses the term "knowingly."

55. N.Y. PUB. HEALTH LAW §§ 3300 through 3366, N.Y. PEN. LAW §§ 1751 through 1752. Uniform Act was enacted in 1933. Habitual offender law, N.Y. PEN. LAW § 1941(2), provides not less than 15 years and not more than life imprisonment for third narcotics felony; suspension and probation are not available, N.Y. PEN. LAW § 2188.

56. N.Y. PEN. LAW § 484c.

57. N.Y. PEN. LAW § 1533.

58. N.Y. PEN. LAW § 580a.

59. N.C. GEN. STAT. §§ 19-4, 90-86 through 90-113 (1953, Supp. 1965). Uniform Act was enacted in 1935.

60. N.D. CENT. CODE §§ 19-03-01 through 19-03-32 (1960, Supp. 1965). Uniform Act was enacted in 1917.

61. OHIO REV. CODE §§ 3719.01 through 3719.22, 3719.99 (1964, Supp. 1965). Uniform Act was enacted in 1935.

62. Penalty for possession only. Penalty for manufacture, see note 65 *infra*.

63. Penalties for other offenses:
    (1) Manufacturing and producing narcotic drugs, exceeding limits on possession of excepted drugs, evaporating drug preparations to increase concentration, illegally procuring drugs, issuing illegal prescriptions: *first offense:* fine, not more than $10,000, and not less than 2 years and not more than 5 years in prison; *second offense:* fine, not more than $10,000, and not less than 5 years and not more than 10 years in prison; *subsequent offense:*

fine, not more than $10,000, and not less than 10 years and not more than 20 years in prison.

(2) Possession for sale, sale, or dispensing on written order by unlicensed person, failure to keep required records, failure to label properly, maintaining a common nuisance, and unauthorized possession of hypodermics or other instruments for use with narcotics: *first offense:* fine of not more than $500 or not less than 1 year and not more than 5 years in prison; *subsequent offense:* fine, not less than $200 and not more than $1000, or not less than 1 year and not more than 5 years in prison.

(3) Knowingly permitting premises to be used for illegal keeping, dispensing, or administering of narcotic drugs; stealing drugs; obtaining drugs from more than one physician without disclosure; carnal knowledge of another; knowing the other to be under the influence of narcotic drugs: *first offense:* fine, not more than $10,000 and not less than 2 years and not more than 15 years in prison; *second offense:* fine, not more than $10,000 and not less than 5 years and not more than 20 years in prison; *subsequent offense:* fine, not more than $10,000 and not less than 10 years and not more than 30 years in prison.

(4) Conspiracy to violate certain provisions: *first offense:* not less than 10 years and not more than 20 years in prison; *second offense:* not less than 15 years and not more than 30 years in prison; *subsequent offense:* not less than 20 years and not more than 40 years in prison.

(5) Inducing unlawful use or administration of narcotics; using a minor in narcotics traffic; inducing a minor to violate any provision of the narcotics laws or to use a narcotic drug unlawfully: *first offense:* not less than 10 years and not more than 25 years in prison; *second offense:* not less than 25 years and not more than 50 years in prison.

(6) Violating pharmacists' or physicians' regulations, hindering enforcement of narcotics laws or violating regulations governing inspection of records: *first offense:* fine, not more than $500; *second offense:* fine, not more than $1000.

64. § 3719.99 denies probation to persons conspiring to violate certain provisions of the narcotics laws, and to second offenders convicted of inducing use, dispensing to minor, using minor in drug traffic, inducing minor to violate drug laws or to use narcotics.

65. OKLA. STAT. ANN. tit 63, § § 401 through 425, 451 through 457, 469, 470.11, 470.12 (1949, Supp. 1966). Uniform Act was enacted in 1935.

66. ORE. REV. STAT. § § 474.010 through 474.990, 475.010 through 475.990 (1965).

67. PA. STAT. ANN. tit. 18 § § 4608 through 4612 (Purdon 1963, Supp. 1965), tit. 35 § § 780-1 through 780-31 (Purdon 1964, Supp. 1965).

68. Penalties for violations of specific provisions relating to cocaine and eucaine are found in § § 824 and 825.

69. R.I. GEN. LAWS ANN. § § 21-28-1 through 21-28-67 (1956, Supp. 1965). Uniform Act was enacted in 1934.

70. S.C. CODE § § 32-1461 through 32-1495 (1962, Supp. 1965). Uniform Act was enacted in 1935.

71. S.D. CODE § § 22.1301 through 22.1324, 22.9920, 22.9920-1 (1939, Supp. 1960). Uniform Act was enacted in 1935.

72. TENN. CODE ANN. § § 52-1301 through 52-1323 (1955, Supp. 1965). Uniform Act was enacted in 1937.

73. § 52-1322 was amended to deny suspension to second and subsequent offenders in 1955. Before that time suspension was denied in all offenses.

74. Tex. Pen. Code art. 725b, 725c, 725d (Vernon 1961, Supp. 1965). Uniform Act was enacted in 1937.

75. Suspended sentence not available, but probation and parole are permitted under the Adult Probation Law, Tex. Code Crim. Proc. art. 781, even though addict may have prior felony.

76. Statutes provide that suspended sentence law shall not apply, but first offenders have the benefit of Adult Probation Law.

77. Utah Code Ann. § § 58-13a-1 through 58-13a-48, 76-42-9, 76-61-1 (1953, Supp. 1965). Uniform Act was enacted in 1953.

78. Vt. Stat. Ann. tit. 18, § § 4141 through 4163 (1959, Supp. 1965). Uniform Act was enacted in 1951. Certain other provisions relating to drugs, including narcotics, appear in § § 4101 through 4108.

79. Va. Code Ann. § § 54-487 through 54-519 (1950, Supp. 1966). Uniform Act was enacted in 1934.

80. The statute does not distinguish between an adult and a minor seller.

81. Wash. Rev. Code § § 69.32.010 through 69.32.960, 69.33.220 through 69.33.960, 9.91.030 (1962, Supp. 1965). Uniform Act was enacted in 1951.

82. In first offenses court may, in its discretion, impose a fine of not more than $1,000 or not more than 1 year in county jail, or both. (§ 69.33.410.)

83. The statute does not distinguish between an adult and a minor seller.

84. W. Va. Code Ann. § § 16-8A-1 through 16-8A-26 (1966). Uniform Act was enacted in 1935.

85. Wis. Stat. § § 161.01 through 161.28 (1959, Supp. 1966). Uniform Act was enacted in 1935.

86. Wyo. Stat. Ann. § § 35-348 through 35-371, 6-197 through 6-202 (1957, Supp. 1965). Uniform Act was enacted in 1937.

Appendix C

𝔗𝔯𝔢𝔞𝔰𝔲𝔯𝔶 𝔇𝔢𝔭𝔞𝔯𝔱𝔪𝔢𝔫𝔱
𝔅𝔲𝔯𝔢𝔞𝔲 𝔬𝔣 𝔑𝔞𝔯𝔠𝔬𝔱𝔦𝔠𝔰
𝔚𝔞𝔰𝔥𝔦𝔫𝔤𝔱𝔬𝔫, 𝔇.𝔠.

To:

The information requested below is utilized by the Federal Bureau of Narcotics in compiling statistical data on Narcotic and Marihuana arrests, convictions and seizures. Please complete this form and return by   , 19   , to District Supervisor, Bureau of Narcotics:

A Franked envelope is enclosed, for your convenience.

_____
District Supervisor

*Annual Report of Narcotic and Marihuana Arrests Convictions and Seizures, Calendar Year ____

Narcotics					Marihuana			
Arrests	Convictions	Arrests of Persons Under 21 Yrs. of Age	Convictions of Persons Under 21 Yrs. of Age		Arrests	Convictions	Arrests of Persons Under 21 Yrs. of Age	Convictions of Persons Under 21 Yrs. of Age

Seizures

Heroin	Morphine	Opium	Other Opium Alkaloids	Synthetics	Marihuana			
					Bulk	Cig.	Seed	Plant

*Except those in which Federal Officers participated.

_____   _____
Agency   Submitted By (Signature & Title)

SELECTED REFERENCES

ADAMS, SAMUEL HOPKINS. *The Great American Fraud.* Chicago: American Medical Association, 1912.

AMERICAN BAR ASSOCIATION AND AMERICAN MEDICAL ASSOCIATION JOINT COMMITTEE ON NARCOTIC DRUGS. *Drug Addiction: Crime or Disease?* Interim and Final Reports. Bloomington, Indiana: Indiana University Press, 1961.

AMERICAN MEDICAL ASSOCIATION, COUNCIL ON MENTAL HEALTH. "Report on Narcotic Addiction," *Journal of the American Medical Association,* CLXV (November 30, 1957), 1707-13; (December 7, 1957), 1834-41; (December 14, 1957), 1968-74.

ANSLINGER, HARRY J., and WILLIAM F. TOMPKINS. *The Traffic in Narcotics.* New York: Funk and Wagnalls Company, 1953.

BERGER, HERBERT. "The Richmond County Medical Society's Plan for the Control of Narcotic Addiction," *New York State Journal of Medicine,* LVI (March 15, 1956), 888-94.

BOBBITT, JOSEPH M. "The Drug Addiction Problem," *American Journal of Medicine,* XIV (May 1953), 538-39.

CALIFORNIA. CITIZENS' ADVISORY COMMITTEE TO THE ATTORNEY GENERAL ON CRIME PREVENTION. *Narcotic Addiction Report to Attorney General Edmund G. Brown.* Mimeographed, March 26, 1954.

CALIFORNIA REHABILITATION CENTER, CIVIL ADDICT PROGRAM. *Statistical Review, Narcotics Rehabilitation Advisory Council, Annual Report* (Cal. Youth and Adult Corrections Agency, 1966, 1967).

CALIFORNIA SPECIAL STUDY COMMISSION ON NARCOTICS. *Interim Report.* Los Angeles, California: Special Study Commission on Narcotics, December 9, 1960.

CALIFORNIA. STATE DEPARTMENT OF JUSTICE, DEVISION OF CRIMINAL LAW AND ENFORCEMENT, BUREAU OF CRIMINAL STATISTICS. *Narcotic Arrests in California: (July 1, 1959 — June 30, 1960).* Sacramento, California: State of California, Department of Justice, December 5, 1960.

————. *Summary Narcotic Statistics for California: 1954 — 1959.* Sacramento, California: State of California, Department of Justice, February 10, 1961.

CASRIEL, DANIEL. *So Fair a House: The Story of Synanon.* Newark, New Jersey: Prentice Hall, 1963.

CASRIEL, DANIEL, and C. DEITCH. "Permanent Cure of Narcotic Addicts," *Physicians Panorama* (October 1966).

CHAPMAN, KENNETH W. "Management and Treatment of Drug Addiction," *Journal of Chronic Diseases,* IX (March 1959), 315-26

CHICAGO POLICE DEPARTMENT, DETECTIVE DIVISION, NARCOTIC SECTION. *A Special Report in Summation of Narcotics Problem to be used with the Annual Report of the Narcotics Section for the Year 1959.* Unpublished memorandum to the Superintendent of Police, April 15, 1960.

CLAUSEN, JOHN A. "Social and Psychological Factors in Narcotics Addiction," *Law and Contemporary Problems,* XXII (Winter 1957), 34-51.

COLUMBIA UNIVERSITY, SCHOOL OF PUBLIC HEALTH AND ADMINISTRATIVE MEDICINE. *A Follow-Up Study of Treated Adolescent Narcotic Users.* Ray E. Trussell, Project Director. New York: Mimeographed, 1959.

COMMENT. "Narcotics Regulation," *Yale Law Journal,* LXII (April 1953), 751-87.

DAI, BINGHAM. *Opium Addiction in Chicago.* Shanghai, China: The Commercial Press, Limited, 1937.

DEQUINCEY, THOMAS. *Confessions of an English Opium Eater.* London: Oxford University Press, 1821.

DEROPP, ROBERT S. *Drugs and the Mind.* New York: Grove Press, Incorporated, 1960.

DEUTSCH, ALBERT. *What We Can Do about the Drug Menace.* ("Public Affairs Pamphlet," No. 186.) New York: Public Affairs Committee, Incorporated, September 1952.

DOLE, VINCENT, and MARIE NYSWANDER. Rehabilitation of Heroin Addicts after Blockade with Methadone," *New York Journal of Medicine,* LXVI (August 1, 1966), 2011.

DOLE, VINCENT, MARIE NYSWANDER, and MARY KREEK. "Narcotic Blockade," *Archives of Internal Medicine,* CXVIII (October 1966), 304.

EBERLE, E. G., and FREDERICK T. GORDON. "Report of the Committee on Acquirement of Drug Habits," *American Journal of Pharmacy,* LXXV (October 1903), 474-88.

FINESTONE, HAROLD. "Narcotics and Criminality," *Law and Contemporary Problems,* XXII (Winter 1957), 69-85.

FRANKEL, L. H. "Narcotic Addiction, Criminal Responsibility, and Civil Commitment," *Utah Law Review* (December 1966), 581.

FULTON, E. D. "Remarks in the House of Commons of Canada on Bill C-100, an Act to Provide for the Control of Narcotic Drugs, June 7, 1961," (24th Parliament, 4th sess.) *Canada House of Commons Debates,* CV (1961), 5982-88.

GEIS, GILBERT. *Narcotic Treatment Programs in California, Perspectives on Narcotic Addiction* (Chatham Conference, Mass. 1963).

"Harrison Narcotic Act," *American Law Reports,* Annotated, XIII (1920), 858-75.

Hearings, U.S. Congress. See UNITED STATES CONGRESS.

HOCH, PAUL H. and JOSEPH ZUBIN (eds.). *Problems of Addiction and Habituation.* New York: Grune and Stratton, 1958.

HONG KONG GOVERNMENT. *The Problem of Narcotic Drugs in Hong Kong.* Hong Kong: The Government Press, November 1959.

HOWE, HUBERT S. "A Physician's Blueprint for the Management and Prevention of Narcotic Addiction," *New York State Journal of Medicine,* LV (February 1, 1955), 341-49.

HYNSON, H. P. "Report of the Committee on Acquirement of the Drug Habit," *American Journal of Pharmacy,* LXXIV (November 1902), 547-54.

ILLINOIS INSTITUTE FOR JUVENILE RESEARCH AND THE CHICAGO AREA PROJECT. *Drug Addiction among Young Persons in Chicago.* Mimeographed, October 1953.

———. *Report of the Chicago Narcotics Survey (1953).* Mimeographed, 1953.

ILLINOIS NARCOTICS AND DANGEROUS DRUG INVESTIGATION COMMISSION. *A Report in the Interest of the Health and Safety of the People of the State of Illinois.* Danville, Illinois: State of Illinois, Second Report: 1959, Third Report: 1961.

INTERDEPARTMENTAL COMMITTEE ON NARCOTICS. *Report of the Interdepartmental Committee on Narcotics to the President of the United States.* Washington, D.C.: U.S. Government Printing Office, January 1961.

ISBELL, HARRIS. *What to Know about Drug Addiction.* ("Public Health Service Publication," No. 94.) Washington, D.C.: United States Government Printing Office, 1951 (Revised, May 1958).

KING, RUFUS. "Narcotic Drug Laws and Enforcement Policies," *Law and Contemporary Problems,* XXII (Winter 1957), 113-31.

———. "The Narcotics Bureau and the Harrison Act: Jailing the Healers and the Sick," *Yale Law Journal,* LXII (April 1953), 736-49.

KOLB, LAWRENCE. "Let's Stop This Narcotics Hysteria!" *Saturday Evening Post,* CCXXIX (July 28, 1956), 19, 50, 54, 55.

KOLB, LAWRENCE, and A. G. DUMEZ. *The Prevalence and Trend of Drug Addiction in the United States and Factors Influencing It.* ("Public Health Reports," Vol. 39, No. 21) Washington, D.C.: Government Printing Office (1924).

KUH, RICHARD H. "Dealing with Narcotics Addiction," *New York Law Journal,* CXLIII (June 8, 1960) 4; (June 9, 1960) 4; (June 10, 1960) 4.

LARIMORE, GRANVILLE W., and HENRY BRILL. *Report to Governor Nelson A. Rockefeller of an on the Site Study of the British*

Narcotic System. Unpublished mimeograph, March 3, 1959. A revised condensation appears in: *New York State Journal of Medicine,* LX (January 1, 1960), 107-15.

LINDESMITH, ALFRED R. *The Addict and the Law.* Bloomington, Indiana: Indiana University Press, 1965.

LINDESMITH, ALFRED R. *Opiate Addiction.* Bloomington, Indiana: Principia Press, Incorporated, 1947.

_____. "The British System of Narcotics Control," *Law and Contemporary Problems,* XXII (Winter 1957), 138-54.

_____. "Traffic in Dope: Medical Problem," *The Nation,* CLXXXII (April 21, 1956), 337-39.

LOWRY, JAMES V. "Hospital Treatment of the Narcotic Addict," *Federal Probation,* XX (December 1956), 42-51.

MACDONALD, R. ST. J. (ed.). *Current Law and Social Problems.* Toronto, Canada: University of Toronto Press, 1960.

MCGEE, RICHARD A. "The Administration of Justice: The Correctional Process," *National Probation and Parole Association Journal,* V (July 1959), 225-39.

MACHT, DAVID I. "The History of Opium and Some of Its Preparations and Alkaloids," *Journal of the American Medical Association,* LXIV (February 6, 1915), 477-81.

MAURER, DAVID W., and VICTOR H. VOGEL. *Narcotics and Narcotic Addiction.* Springfield, Illinois: Charles C. Thomas, 1954.

MEISLER, STANLEY. "Federal Narcotics Czar," *The Nation,* CXC (February 20, 1960), 159-62.

NATIONAL CONFERENCE ON PAROLE. *Parole in Principle and Practice. A Manual and Report.* New York: National Probation and Parole Association, 1957.

NATIONAL PROBATION AND PAROLE ASSOCIATION, ADVISORY COUNCIL OF JUDGES. *Guides for Sentencing.* New York: National Probation and Parole Association, 1957.

"New and Non-Official Remedies," *Journal of the American Medical Association,* XLVII (October 20, 1906), 1302-1303.

NEW JERSEY COMMISSION ON NARCOTIC CONTROL. *Report of Study and Recommendations.* Trenton, New Jersey: State of New Jersey, First Report: February 21, 1955; Second Report: March 1, 1956; Third Report: March 15, 1957; Fourth Report: March 15, 1958; Fifth Report: April 15, 1959; Sixth Report: April 15, 1960.

NEW YORK ACADEMY OF MEDICINE, COMMITTEE ON PUBLIC HEALTH, SUBCOMMITTEE ON DRUG ADDICTION. "Report on Drug Addiction," *The Bulletin of the New York Academy of Medicine,* XXXI (August 1955), 592-607.

NEW YORK CITY YOUTH BOARD, IN-SERVICE TRAINING DEPARTMENT. *Report of Three-Day Conference on Narcotic Addiction and the Teenager.* New York: New York City Youth Board, October 1959.

NEW YORK STATE DIVISION OF PAROLE. *An Experiment in the Supervision of Paroled Offenders Addicted to Narcotic Drugs: Final Report of the Special Narcotic Project.* Albany, New York: State of New York, 1959.

NEW YORK STATE JOINT LEGISLATIVE COMMITTEE. *Report on Narcotic Study.* Mimeographed, 1959.

NOTE. "Narcotics Regulation: A Study in Irresolution," *Temple Law Quarterly,* XXXIV (Spring 1961), 310-22.

NYSWANDER, MARIE. *The Drug Addict as a Patient.* New York and London: Grune and Stratton, 1956.

OHIO DEPARTMENT OF MENTAL HYGIENE AND CORRECTION, DIVISION OF BUSINESS ADMINISTRATION, BUREAU OF RESEARCH AND STATISTICS. *1959 Ohio Judicial Criminal Statistics.* Columbus, Ohio: Heer Printing Company, n.d.

PESCOR, MICHAEL J. *Follow-Up Study of Treated Narcotic Drug Addicts.* ("Public Health Report," Supp. No. 170) Washington, D.C.: U.S. Government Printing Office, 1943.

———. "The Problem of Narcotic Drug Addiction," *Journal of Criminal Law, Criminology and Police Science,* XLIII (November-December 1952), 471-81.

PROCEEDINGS OF THE WHITE HOUSE CONFERENCE ON NARCOTIC AND DRUG ABUSE. Washington, D.C.: U.S. Government Printing Office, 1962.

ROONEY, E. A., and D. C. GIFFONS. "Social Reactions to 'Crimes Without Victims'," *Social Problems*, XIII (Sprint 1966), 400-410.

SCHUR, EDWIN M. "British Narcotics Policies," *Journal of Criminal Law, Criminology and Police Science*, LI (March-April 1961), 619-29.

SHELLY, J. A., and A. BASSIN. "Daytop Lodge—A New Treatment Approach for Drug Addicts," *Corrective Psychiatry*, XI (July 1965), 186.

SHELLY, J. A., and A. BASSIN. "Daytop Lodge—Halfway House for Drug Addicts," *Federal Probation*, XXVIII (December 1964), 46.

STERNBERG, D. "Synanon House—A Consideration of Its Implications for American Correction," *Journal of Criminal Law, Criminology and Police Science*, LIV (December 1963), 447.

STEVENS, ALDEN. "Make Dope Legal," *Harper's Magazine*, CCV (November 1952), 40-47.

TERRY, CHARLES E., and MILDRED PELLENS. *The Opium Problem*. New York: The Bureau of Social Hygiene, Incorporated, 1928.

TERRY, J. G. *Santa Rita Rehabilitation Clinic Ten-Year Report, 1949-1959*. Alameda County, California: Alameda County Sheriff's Department, n.d.

TRUSSELL, RAY E. See Columbia University.

UNITED NATIONS, DEPARTMENT OF SOCIAL AFFAIRS. *Parole and Aftercare*. New York: United Nations, 1954.

UNITED STATES CONGRESS. HOUSE. COMMITTEE ON APPROPRIATIONS. *Hearings on Treasury and Post Office Departments Appropriations for 1961 before the Subcommittee of the Committee on Appropriations—January 26, 1960*. (86th Cong., 2nd sess.) Washington, D.C.: Government Printing Office, 1960.

UNITED STATES CONGRESS. SENATE. COMMITTEE ON THE JUDICIARY. *Hearings on the Scope of Soviet Activity in the United States before the Subcommittee to Investigate the Administration of the Internal Security Act and Other Internal Security Laws of the Committee on the Judiciary,*

February 28, 1957. (85th Cong., 1st sess.) Washington, D.C.: Government Printing Office, 1957.

———. *Narcotic Control Act of 1956.* ("Senate Report," No. 1997.) (84th Cong., 2nd sess.) Washington, D.C.: Government Printing Office, 1956.

UNITED STATES CONGRESS. SENATE. SPECIAL COMMITTEE TO INVESTIGATE ORGANIZED CRIME IN INTERSTATE COMMERCE. *Hearings before the Special Committee to Investigate Organized Crime in Interstate Commerce.* (82d Cong., 1st sess.) Washington, D.C.: Government Printing Office, 1951.

UNITED STATES DEPARTMENT OF JUSTICE, BUREAU OF PRISONS. *Federal Prisons — 1959.* El Reno, Oklahoma: United States Reformatory, 1960.

UNITED STATES PRESIDENT'S ADVISORY COMMISSION ON NARCOTIC AND DRUG ABUSE. *Final Report.* Washington, D.C.: U.S. Government Printing Office, 1963.

UNITED STATES PRESIDENT'S COMMISSION ON LAW ENFORCEMENT AND ADMINISTRATION OF JUSTICE. *The Challenge of Crime in a Free Society.* Washington, D.C.: U.S. Government Printing Office, 1967.

UNITED STATES TREASURY DEPARTMENT, BUREAU OF NARCOTICS (ed.). *Control and Rehabilitation of the Narcotic Addict: A Symposium.* Washington, D.C.: U.S. Government Printing Office, 1961.

UNITED STATES TREASURY DEPARTMENT, BUREAU OF NARCOTICS. *Graphic Results of Mandatory Penalties against Peddlers — Narcotic Control Act of 1956.* Washington, D.C.: no publisher given, December 31, 1958.

UNITED STATES TREASURY DEPARTMENT, BUREAU OF NARCOTICS. *Prescribing and Dispensing of Narcotics Under the Harrison Narcotic Law.* Washington, D.C.: U.S. Government Printing Office, 1946.

UNITED STATES TREASURY DEPARTMENT, BUREAU OF NARCOTICS. *Prevention and Control of Narcotic Addiction.* Washington, D.C.: U.S. Government Printing Office, 1960.

UNITED STATES TREASURY DEPARTMENT, BUREAU OF NARCOTICS. *Traffic in Opium and Other Dangerous Drugs — for the*

Year Ending December 31, 1959. Washington, D.C.: U.S. Government Printing Office, 1960.

UNITED STATES TREASURY DEPARTMENT, BUREAU OF NARCOTICS. *Traffic in Opium and Other Dangerous Drugs.* Washington, D.C.: U.S. Government Printing Office, 1961, 1966.

UNITED STATES TREASURY DEPARTMENT, BUREAU OF NARCOTICS. ADVISORY COMMITTEE. *Comments on Narcotics Drugs — Interim Report of the Joint Committee of the American Bar Association and the American Medical Association on Narcotic Drugs.* Washington, D.C.: U.S. Government Printing Office, 1959.

WIKLER, ABRAHAM. *Opiate Addiction.* Springfield, Illinois: Charles C. Thomas, 1953.

WIKLER, ABRAHAM, and ROBERT W. RASOR. "Psychiatric Aspects of Drug Addiction," *American Journal of Medicine,* XIV (May 1953), 566-70.

WINICK, CHARLES. "Narcotics Addiction and its Treatment," *Law and Contemporary Problems,* XXII (Winter 1957), 9-33.

WOOD, ROLAND. *The Civil Narcotics Program — A Five Year Progress Report,* (Cal. Rehabilitation Center, October 27, 1966), 28.

YABLONSKY, LEWIS. "The Anti-Criminal Society," *Federal Probation,* XXVI (September 1962), 50.

Index